The Life, Aftermath, and Legacy of Elmo Lewis

The Life, Aftermath, and Legacy of Elmo Lewis

A 21st Century Reexamination of the Story and Contemporary Impact of Brian Jones

By Thomas P. Athridge

Cover Art by Ever Billotte

Edited by Corey Parker

ISBN: 978-1-941771-33-4

Also by Thomas P. Athridge
American Presidents At War

Special Thanks

I would like to thank the following people who were instrumental and inspirational in assisting me through this book project, in no particular order:
Dr. Allan Hunter, Dr. Timothy Desmond, James Moran, Joanne Moran-Cruz, Setor Ayunyo-Akaba, Ken Sigmund, Alev Sezer-Jacobs, Janet Tropea, Reggie Braddy, Todd Harvey, Valda Morris-Slack, Mary, John, and Mary K. Athridge, Ethan Billote, Corey Parker, Keith F. Shovlin, Lia & Patrick Kerwin, Ted Westervelt, Al Tyas, Glenn Gardner, Jason Curry, Joanna Corwin, Andy Kader, Jim Ground, Rick Ground, Jim Desmond, Martin Andersen, Steve Negelski, Cheryl Livingston, Rosemary Brawner, Abbey Vasquez, Phil Sipkov, Joanne and the staff of the Brian Jones Friends and Fans Facebook page, the Brian Jones Preservation Society, Adam Rosenberg, James Wolf, Ebonye Flanagan, Al Ward, Ayanna Smoot, Chris Spehr, Sam Serafy, Juanita Betts, Shalin Ronald, the staff of the Little Falls Library in Bethesda, Maryland, the staff of the United States Serial and Government Documents Section at the Library of Congress, and the Copyright Office at the Library of Congress. And to the Rolling Stones themselves, especially Brian Jones, who have been such a huge inspiration to me personally since I was a little boy.

INSIDE

INTRODUCTION

This story is about Lewis Brian Hopkin Jones, who, as bass player
Bill Wyman writes about in his book *Rolling with the Stones*, is, in
fact, the creator of the band that would become the global rock &
roll phenomenon known as the Rolling Stones. According to
Wyman, a.k.a. William Perks, who is easily Brian's most vigorous
defender from within the band, "we were his brainchild and it was
Brian who named us. He was the driving force behind the band in
the early days. Brian was the original Rolling Stone." (pg 10, #1)
Though Brian Jones remains a controversial figure from within the

Rolling Stones organization and the music industry in general, according to Wyman, "as the years go by, I become even more convinced that he's entitled to that free pardon. Brian Jones is a legend and his legacy is there for all to hear. While the Rolling Stones damaged all of us in some way, Brian was the only one who died." (pg 330, #1)

But it is worth noting that when Brian started the band, they were not a rock & roll band at all—they were strictly a rhythm & blues band that played the songs of Jimmy Reed, Muddy Waters, Howlin' Wolf, Bo Diddley, Robert Johnson, and Little Walter. In fact, one night while playing in Hempstead, England, when Muddy Waters was performing on stage and learned of the presence of Wyman in the audience, he said, "I'm really glad someone from the Rolling Stones is here. I love them very much. If it wasn't for the Stones, none of the white kids in the States would have heard of Muddy Waters, B.B. King or any of them. Nobody knew my music in the States until they played it." (pg. 370, #1) In fact, according to Bill Janovitz in his book *Rocks Off: 50 Tracks That Tell the Story of the Rolling Stones*, of all the original members of the band, "Brian had, by far, the deepest musical knowledge and natural talent, and he taught Keith (Richards) much of the foundation of the blues. He was known for his all-around musicianship." (pg 8, #2) Brian earned praise from other musicians who noticed his talents, including Jimmy Page, who said, "Brian's slide playing was really clean and very authentic sounding." (pgs 42-43, #3) Wyman would echo Page's praises of Brian by saying, "he was a brilliant slide guitar player, and the first slide guitar player in England that ever was." (pg 24, #4)

It is interesting and most peculiar to me that someone of Jones's stature—the inventor and lead guitarist of the Rolling Stones—could be so casually written out of history, despite his role in and impact on the success of the band and modern culture. After all, Brian included among his best friends legendary figures such as Bob Dylan, Jimi Hendrix, and Robbie Robertson, who would also go on to reach the height of musical success in their own right. Why was Brian largely ignored and isolated from both history and music, despite his many accomplishments? He was even the only member of the Rolling Stones to ever play a musical instrument recorded on a Beatles song, when he played saxophone on "You Know My Name

(Look Up the Number)," which became a Beatles single. (pg 430, #5)

Brian's musical talents were extensive and complex: he was able to play approximately 36 musical instruments, including the guitar, slide guitar, harmonica, sitar, marimbas, dulcimer, piano, saxophone, and lute. (pg 15 #6) But as history records, there was also a very dark, self-destructive side to Brian that would ultimately cost him his dreams, his band, and his life. Brian is a member of the "27 club," which includes an all-star cast of legendary musicians whose influence is far-reaching and impactful. This club includes names such as Janis Joplin, Jimi Hendrix, Jim Morrison, Amy Winehouse, Kurt Cobain, Ron "Pigpen" McKernan, and legendary bluesman Robert Johnson.

Brian's short life was filled with controversy, violence, misogyny, and betrayal from a wide variety of sources. Brian had a profound dark side to him that hurt him on many different levels: business-wise in his band and relationship-wise with his family, girlfriends, and children. This would eventually lead to his expulsion from the band and his untimely death 3 weeks later. Brian himself knew that he wouldn't live very long, and it was his reckless obsession with music that catapulted him to the height of success with the Rolling Stones and to the bottomless pit of self-destruction that ultimately decided his fate.

The questions that I will explore in this book revolve around the following: why did Brian choose this destiny for himself? Did he envision the impact his band would have on the music industry he was trying to break into over 57 years ago, when he originally created it? What impact does Brian Jones have now, not only on the Rolling Stones, but also on modern/contemporary music? After all, according to Phillip Norman in his book about Mick Jagger, "since 1989, the Rolling Stones have earned an estimated 2 billion pounds from record song rights, merchandising, touring, and sponsorship." (pg 594, #6) Could Brian have foreseen, when he created the Rolling Stones, the magnitude of his creation's titanic impact and lasting legacy? Or was he just expecting it to be a rhythm & blues band, influenced by American R & B legends, under his direction? Also, why does Brian Jones seem to be mostly written out of history by both the Rolling Stones and by the music industry? What is Brian's legacy today? Was Brian murdered? If so, by whom?

I will investigate these questions and examine the life of Brian Jones, the aftermath of his death and creation that continued on without him, including the band's impact on music and culture, and the legacy of this often misunderstood yet deeply troubled young man, who remains an influential and controversial figure in the rock industry more than 50 years after his death in his swimming pool at Cotchford Farm on July 3, 1969 under tragic and possibly sinister circumstances. According to Bill Wyman, "Brian was an extraordinary mixture. He was the sincere true blues purist who wrote enthusiastic letters on behalf of the Stones to the music papers stating the case for our music. The other side of him craved the hedonistic world of the rich and famous pop star. In his short life, he achieved both ambitions, but his health couldn't keep pace." (pg 117, #5) It must also be remembered that, as Paul Trynka pointed out in his book about Brian, "Brian got many things wrong in life, but the most important thing he got right, for his music was world changing." (pg 3, #7) Apart from his career with the Rolling Stones, Brian wrote a film score for a movie called *Mord und Totschlag*, or *A Degree of Murder*, and produced an album of ethnic Moroccan music by the master musicians of Jajouka.

PART ONE
THE LIFE

CHAPTER 1

CHELTENHAM AND BRIAN'S EARLY DAYS

Brian's 27 years, 4 months, and 3 days of life began on February 28, 1942 at Park Nursing Home in a place called Cheltenham, Gloucestershire, South West England, which is about 75 miles east of the Wales border. Ironically enough, Cheltenham was known during Brian's youth as having the highest cases of illegitimate births in all of England, a fate that would involve Brian five different times (with five different women) in his life. Brian had an IQ of 135 and was described as an intelligent rebel at Pate's Primary School. Brian was 6 years old when his mother Louise sent him to piano lessons, and he became exceptional at the instrument (pg 6, #4). Brian's parents, Lewis Blount Jones and Louise Beatrice Simmonds, married in Wales in 1938. Brian had a sister named Pamela who died of leukemia at age 2 in 1943. Brian felt abandoned by his parents after the death of his sister, and Brian blamed his parents for pushing him away as a result of it. (pg 3, #8)

As a youth, Brian said of his musical influences, "Musically, I was guided by my parents. My mother was a piano teacher and my father played the organ. Later, there were several piano lessons in Cheltenham. I struggled to get the notes right at first, but eventually I found that I had a feel for the music from early on." (pg 322, #9). This was despite his father's wishes that Brian would become a dentist when he got older. (pg 4, #8) Lewis Jones was an aeronautical engineer with the Dowry Group who had studied at Leeds University. Brian's parents were both Welsh Methodists with strict rules of behavior. Brian's home life with his parents was very cold and distant. (pg 8, #7) Also compounding Brian's situation was the fact that he suffered from asthma, which set him apart from the other kids at school. Though Brian's parents discouraged his musical development throughout his academic career, Brian rebelled through his music, and it was a means of escape and therapy for him. (pg 20, #7)

Brian could read and write music and he could play the piano, clarinet, saxophone, and guitar at an early age. (pg 27, #10) Therefore, it can be successfully argued that Brian was vastly more interested in music than his family. (pg 60, #10) Brian was considered very educated in England, and by the age of 15 he achieved 9 O-level passes in the General Certificate of Education, which is the British National Subject Exam, and subsequently he entered the program for the optional and selective last two years of school in England. Brian would also be described as a brilliant guitar player by the age of 12. (pg 8, #4) Despite these talents that Brian displayed early on, both academically and musically, according to author and biographer Laura Jackson, "in those days, he was seen as a flat out trouble maker, who reveled in being insubordinate for the pure hell of it." (pg 9, #4) Brian was described in this time period as a rebel without a cause, by rebelling against " his parent's values, and against society's conventions. He gave himself a license to be selfish." (pg 28, #7)

Worth mentioning during this time in Brian's life was his hatred of authority. According to Alan Clayson's book on Brian Jones, bandmate Keith Richards said of Brian's attitude then, "Somewhere along the line, he decided that he was going to be a full-time professional rebel." (pg 21, #11) As a result of this, according to Pat Andrews, the mother of Brian's third child, Mark, "from when Brian was about 15, his mother and father felt that he was a bad influence on his sister Barbara, so he wasn't really allowed to have much to do with her." (pg 24, #11) Brian's parents were also against his pursuit of his professional musical ambitions. Regardless, Brian's determination to pursue this dream continued to gain momentum, causing much friction at home. (pg 6, #8) In fact, Brian would become obsessed with music, especially jazz. (pg 80, #5) The area where Brian grew up, called Cheltenham Spa, was described as "an old lady resting place, very pretty in its own way, but dullsville." (pg 77, #5)

Jones was characterized in his youth as a sexual athlete, and a prodigious woman chaser. (pg 77, #5) Ironically enough, it was original Stones bandmate Ian Stewart who said, "Brian's highly suspect character paved the way for international success." (pg 15, #8) But first would come some harsh realities that resulted from his reckless and chaotic behavior at this early age, consequences that would dominate the rest of his life. Despite his grades and intelligence, Brian impregnated a 14-year-old girl while he was 16 in 1958, a girl whose name was reported to be Valerie. Brian initially favored an abortion in this case, but Valerie refused this request and had the baby, a boy, who was then put up for adoption. (pg 7, #8) Brian was forbidden to see his baby or Valerie, so he left Cheltenham under a cloud of controversy.

Brian's second child was the result of a fling with a married woman named Angeline. The baby, a girl, suffered from epilepsy, and she claimed that Brian had suffered from this ailment also.

PART ONE: THE LIFE

CHAPTER 2

ELMO LEWIS IS BORN AND THE BLUES HE LIVED

After his expulsion from the Cheltenham community that had ostracized him, Brian went to Germany, where he played music in different bars for whatever money and experience he could gain. Upon Brian's return from exile to Cheltenham, he started playing in local bands, such as John Keen's band and Bill Nile's Delta Jazz Band. (pg 82, #5) Brian also played in skiffle bands, on washboard. Brian had an exceptional ability to play piano, clarinet, saxophone, and guitar at an early age, as well as harmonica and slide guitar in later years. (pg. 22, #10)

Brian would often travel from Cheltenham to London to pursue his education in music at the jazz and blues clubs of the city. Brian was heavily influenced by Alexis Korner, who himself was a great character of the contemporary music scene in Britain in the early 1960s. (pg 86, #5) Korner was a big blues influence on Brian, and the blues music of Robert Johnson, Howlin' Wolf, and Jimmy Reed consumed Brian in 1960. Korner was the leader of a band with Cyril Davies called Blues Incorporated, which occasionally employed the services of a drummer named Charlie Watts. Blues music provided Brian with an escape from his past and a pathway to pursue the professional musical ambitions that possessed his soul. (pg 92, #5) As Brian would years later tell his girlfriend Anna Wohlin, he always wanted to be a musician and play his own kind of music. Elmore James was a huge influence on Brian, who loved James's pure Delta blues from Mississippi. Brian said, "I discovered Elmo James and the earth seemed to shudder on its axis." (pg 336, #9) Charlie Parker was also a huge influence on Brian. Bill Wyman said, "Brian was an Elmore James devotee. His early stage name of Elmo Lewis and his bottleneck guitar work paid tribute to James." (pg 337, #9)

When Brian met Alexis Korner in London, an instant bond developed between the two over R & B music. Korner was impressed by Brian's enthusiasm and knowledge of the music. Brian met and befriended Korner's bandmate in Blues

Incorporated, Cyril Davies, who taught Brian how to play harmonica. (pg 105, #12) On Elmore James's gravestone, it says, "King of the Slide Guitar." The question that arises from this time period in his life is: Why did Brian gravitate towards the rhythm & blues style of music, especially the Delta blues of America? According to Bill Wyman, he said, "The blues isn't just a style of music, it's an attitude of mind. Blues is life and life is blues." A kid and young musical artist from Cheltenham couldn't have fully fathomed the depths of sorrow that these blues songs originated from in America within the African-American community. According to Wyman, "the roots of the blues lie in the slave trade, which is recognized today as one of the most brutal episodes in the history of the modern world (1619-1865). Inspired by suffering and despair, the blues are rooted in courage and the will to survive. The blues is the native language of black America, but it is recognized and loved in every corner of the globe." (pg 10, #9)

As history records, it took a brutal civil war between the northern Union Army and the southern Confederate Army from 1861 to 1865 for the slave practice to officially end in the United States. It took Congress to officially pass and ratify the 13th Amendment to the Constitution, which was done on December 6, 1865, to end slavery constitutionally. It states in section 1 that "neither slavery or involuntary servitude, except as punishment for a crime, where of the party shall have been duly convicted, shall exist within the United Sates or any place subject to their jurisdiction." Despite this victory, racism and suppression of African-Americans persisted, and newly released slaves were anything but equal. The struggle for equality and representation would continue well into the 21st century. Blues music produced songs that slaves would sing to each other to get through the most difficult times in their harsh circumstances. These songs were never written down, just sung and remembered by those who participated.

After the Civil War, African-Americans migrated to New Orleans, where, according to Wyman, "meanwhile the colorful story of the district of New Orleans was producing another highly rhythmic style of black music, which soon became known as jazz." (pg 12, #9) In other parts of the United States, blues from cities like Chicago and Memphis produced what was called urban blues, while the harsher reality of the deep- south for African-Americans formed the subgenre called Delta blues. This is where blues legend Blind Lemon Jefferson got his start. Also included in the southern Delta blues was Charley Patton and Eddie "Son" House. According to Wyman, "John Lee Hooker moved from Mississippi to Detroit while Muddy Waters (McKinley Morganfield) was one of the black musicians who left the plantations of the south and moved to Chicago, which soon became the epicenter of postwar blues. Muddy Waters switched from acoustic to electric guitar in 1944, becoming King of the Chicago Blues." (pg 14, #9)

But there can be no dispute whatsoever on the origins of the music that became rhythm & blues: it originated in the African-American community in post–Civil War America. According to Wyman, "the African tradition of passing on music orally, rather than through a recognizable series of annotated notes, was fundamental in the creation of the blues. When they arrived in their new homeland, the slaves were able to bring their music with them, keeping their traditions alive by the mere act of singing." (pg 56, #9) African-Americans found their voice in the churches, which were some of the earliest building blocks of the blues music that would be composed. According to Wyman, "In fact, it is absolutely certain that no one actually 'wrote' the earliest songs, as the blues emerged from the complex traditions of African-based music, developing rapidly during the last 40 years of the 19th century." (pg 55, #9) Wyman goes on to point out that, "even in despair, the blues is often filled with great and good humor. But given the situation that most black people found themselves in after the Civil War and during the early years of the 20th century, it is hardly surprising that the style contains an ample dose of the downbeat." (pg 71, #9)

Jazz traces its origins in New Orleans, going back to the 1930s. In fact, ragtime was a forerunner to jazz. The birthplace of the blues was considered to be the Mississippi Delta, located from Memphis, Tennessee to New Orleans, Louisiana. The great Muddy Waters himself grew up on Stovall's plantation in Mississippi, and would eventually move to Chicago, Illinois. In fact, by 1918, 110,000 African-Americans moved to Chicago from the south, which tripled the city's black population. (pg 104, #9) Muddy Waters' influences included Son House, Robert Johnson, Peetie Wheatstone, and Aaron Thibeaux Walker, also known as T-Bone Walker. It was when

Waters moved from Mississippi to Chicago that he began his career of singing the blues. Other hugely influential blues performers besides Muddy Waters include Chester Burnett (Howlin' Wolf), Otha Elias Bates McDaniel (Bo Diddley), Jimmy Reed, Mississippi John Hurt, and Riley B. King (B.B. King).

As Wyman points out, in an ironic twist of fate, "for the rest of the decade [1960s], the blues was one of the key ingredients of rock music, leaving its unmistakable mark on international superstars such as Jimi Hendrix, Led Zeppelin, Cream and Bob Dylan." (pg 15, #9) Charlie Patton (1899-1934) had a big impact on the blues music scene. The first blues song ever to be recorded was "Crazy Blues" on August 10, 1920, with Mamie Smith on vocals, which was written by Perry Bradford. (pg 76, #9) Bessie Smith became the Empress of the Blues during the 1920s. (pg 80, #9) Also, Ida Cox was a big influence, along with Lead Belly. Blues artists often sang about places that they could relate to or had traveled through. As Wyman says, "From the earliest days of the blues, songwriters regularly used place names in their lyrics, possibly instructed by the record companies to provide material that would appeal to people in particular areas. More likely is that performers used the songs in their acts, changing the city name to match the town wherever they were performing. Whatever the reason, it was the classic blues singers who pioneered the use of U.S. city and regional names in their songs, and this established a trend that has continued in rock, pop, and blues ever since." (pg 91, #9)

In the early 1960s, America was a more segregated and hostile nation, especially to African-Americans and their music. This just goes to show the high levels of racism and bigotry that existed in America at the time, especially in the pre–Civil Rights legislation world. However, in Britain, African-American blues players found a welcome home among the English youth, who wholeheartedly embraced these stars and their music. This is how Brian and other blues enthusiasts from England became so enchanted with this American rhythm & blues music, and took it to a new level. In fact, when British blues started, it began as something called skiffle. (pg 12, #9) Brian formerly played washboard in a skiffle group (pg 79, #5) Mick Jagger concurs with the assessment that English rock & roll music started with skiffle groups. John Lennon also had a skiffle group in Liverpool called the Quarrymen.

Skiffle had caught on with great success in England in 1955, which was greatly attributed to the success of Lonnie Donegan's song "Rock Island Line." Approximately 30,000 to 50,000 skiffle groups started in England as a result, including Lennon's group, which would eventually become the Beatles. Much to his parents' disapproval and leading to his eventual expulsion from his parents' house in 1960, Brian had no desire whatsoever to obtain a regular 9-to-5 job, but instead wanted to play music for a living. It was a man named Chris Barber who is credited with bringing the blues to England, and for bringing Muddy Waters over from America to play in England. (pg 3, #13) After working with Waters, Barber's band began playing electric blues with the help of Alexis Korner. Barber was also into jazz music. Barber then teamed up with Korner to play rhythm & blues music. After Brian met and befriended Alexis Korner, Korner invited Brian to stay with him and his wife at their London flat while he was in town. (pg 28, #4)

Back in Cheltenham, Brian had seen the Chris Barber band that featured American harmonica player Sonny Boy Williamson. By then, Brian had fallen deeply in love with the blues. (pg 27, #1) It is acknowledged that Barber brought the blues to England before John Mayall, whose later band the Bluesbreakers would, ironically enough, supply the Rolling Stones with Brian's replacement in the band, guitarist Mick Taylor, in 1969. Alexis Korner and harp player Cyril Davies left Chris Barber's band to form Blues Incorporated. Meanwhile, Brian had found a new girlfriend named Pat Andrews, who worked at a place called Boots the Chemist as a waitress. (pg 4, #11) Pat was 16 years old at the time of her relationship with Brian. While Pat describes Brian as intelligent and clever, she further states that he was not the easiest of men to understand. According to Andrews, "he was so up and down. Seventy-five percent of the time Brian was miserable because he was so thwarted musically at home. He felt deeply that he had no encouragement and it was so frustrating for him because music just ate away at him." (pg 17, #4)

During her relationship with Brian, Pat would spend her paycheck on Brian, on some store boots or guitar strings or records. (pg 13, #8) Pat would say of Brian, "he's got no feelings for anybody. He just uses people and throws them aside." (pg 113, #11) Andrews felt that Brian's estrangement from his family really hurt Brian psychologically. (pg 48, #7) She goes on to state that Brian victimizing others was directly related to Brian's parents victimizing him. (pg 16, #8) Brian's misogynistic violence reared its ugly head when he punched Andrews in the face during an argument, giving her a black eye. He would later apologize to her and they would be reunited. Brian eventually impregnated Pat, and despite the fact that Brian wanted her to have an abortion, Pat refused and delivered the baby in October 1961. (pg 22, #14) Brian's third child, Julian Mark Jones, was born on October 23, 1961. (pg 38, #1) Baby Julian was named after Julian "Cannonball" Adderley. However, Brian was cheating on Pat while she was pregnant with their son, and shortly after Julian was born, Brian left Pat and their baby and moved to London, where he could play music full-time. (pg 32, #4)

Meanwhile, Cyril Davies taught Brian how to flatten notes on a harmonica for a more bluesy sound, which Brian would later excel at. (pg. 38, #1) Although this would be Brian's first step away from the guitar professionally, he found success with it. Shortly thereafter, Brian had met his next girlfriend, and the mother of his fourth child, Linda Lawrence, at the Ricky-Tick Club in Windsor in 1962. Despite Brian's stated intentions to marry Pat Andrews, this was not meant to be. Brian was described as violent, insecure, and unpredictable due to his insecurities about other boys and Pat. (pg 20, #4) When Brian was introduced to Linda at the Ricky-Tick Club, she stated, "Brian offered to buy me a drink, we sat down and talked. After the show, he walked out onto the High Street of Windsor with me. We were just talking about music. I'd never heard rhythm & blues before. We linked straight away and had strong feelings for each other." (pg 200, #15) Linda was just 15 years old when she started dating Brian. (pg 46, #14)

Meanwhile, after Brian had left school officially, he found employment as a coal worker, then a factory worker, then a train conductor for three weeks, then a junior assistant in the architecture department of the Gloucestershire County Council. But Brian's obsession with Elmore James, Howlin' Wolf, Muddy Waters, Jimmy Reed, and Bo Diddley became all-encompassing. During this time, Korner and Davies' group Blues Incorporated was becoming quite popular on the London scene. Alexis Korner was born on April 19, 1928. (pg 26, #14) Korner was a great character of the contemporary music scene in Britain during the early 1960s, and was a big influence on Brian's pursuit of the blues. (pg 86, #5)

Brian was already a very talented guitar player, and he then called himself Elmo Lewis on stage, paying tribute to his favorite Chicago bluesman, Elmo James. (pg 27, #13) Brian's first band that he was in was called the Barn Owls. (pg 25, #7) Brian later joined a group called the Ramrods, playing saxophone, and then a band called the Cheltenham Six in 1960. (pg 15, #4)

Alexis Korner did the very first R & B LP, called "Live at the Marquee." By 1961, Brian had played in over 100 gigs. (pg 47, #7). Alexis and Cyril Davies founded the Ealing Jazz Club in a suburb of west London. (pg 35, #12) During this time, Brian became friends with Paul Pond, who would go on to form the group Manfred Mann. Brian and Paul considered forming a band together. Ginger Baker, the drummer who would later be in the bands Cream and Blind Faith, also knew and played music with Brian. Baker appreciated jazz, like Korner and Brian did. It was at the Ealing Jazz Club in March 1962, when Brian and Paul Pond were on stage together, that 3 guys named Michael Jagger, Keith Richards, and Dick Taylor walked in and sat in the audience to watch them play. Dick Taylor would go on to form the group The Pretty Things and went to Sidcup Art College. On stage, Brian had appeared nothing short of a musical messiah/genius with his bottleneck guitar skills. Keith said of Brian's performance that night, "He played 'Dust My Broom' and it was electrifying. He played it beautifully. We were very impressed." (pg 59, #10) They approached Jones after the show to talk.

PART ONE: THE LIFE

CHAPTER 3

BRIAN CREATES THE ROLLING STONES

Mick Jagger was born on July 26, 1943 at Livingstone Hospital in Dartford, Kent. Jagger grew up in Dartford and was approximately a year and a half younger than Brian. (pg 17, #6) Mick was the oldest child of Basil Fanshawe "Joe" Jagger and Eva Ensley Mary Jagger. Mick has a younger brother named Chris. Mick was born into a middle-class family, and he was considered to be a good student, as was Brian. Jagger's father Joe was a physical education/physics teacher. Jagger was a very well- educated young man, and had successfully passed 7 O-level classes and 3 A-level classes in his academic career. Before his career as a musician took off, Jagger had considered becoming a journalist or a politician. However, Jagger had discovered his passion for singing for his church choir as a youth, and this coincided with his discovery and passion for American R & B music around the age of 14.

Mick's friendship with Keith Richards began at age 4, when they both attended Wentworth Primary School in Dartford, but soon they had lost contact with each other, due to going to separate schools after Wentworth. Mick said of Keith, "We used to play together because we lived very close by. When he's about 5 years old, he used to dress in a cowboy outfit, Roy Rogers, with holsters and a hat. And he had these big ears that stuck out." (#16) Keith was born on December 18, 1943, approximately 5 months after Mick and almost 2 years after Brian. Keith was an only child born to Doris and Bert Richards. Bert was in the first wave on Normandy Beach on June 6, 1944, or D-Day. (pg 27, #13) After Wentworth, Keith attended Sidcup Art College along with original Rolling Stones bass player Dick Taylor. Keith's early musical inspiration was Elvis Presley. (pg. 97, #5) He was also influenced by Chuck Berry. (pg 43, #4) Keith also liked Jimmy Reed and Eddie Taylor. (pg 25, #13)

Years after their last encounter, on October 17, 1961, Mick and Keith randomly met again at the Dartford Train Station, taking the 8:28 train into London. According to Jagger, "I kind of lost track of him because we went to different schools, and then we saw each other at the train station." (#16) It was at that meeting at the train station that Keith saw what Mick had with him: an unusual amount of records from Chess Records in Chicago, including Muddy Waters, Little Walter, and Chuck Berry. Keith said of this encounter, "This cat's together, right? And he's got Best of Muddy Waters and Rockin' at the Hops by Chuck Berry under his arm. Hey man, nice to see you, but where'd you get the records?." (#16) From then on, Jagger and Richards collected many different records, which is how they got to know "the music, the labels, the business, learning the songs inside out." (pg 22, #13)

Mick had begun singing in a band with Dick Taylor and Phil May, where he was compared to a legitimate black bluesman. Taylor then recruited Richards into the band, as both Taylor and Richards attended Sidcup Art College. The first band with Mick, Keith, and Dick were called Little Boy Blue and the Blue Boys. (pg 26, #13) By the time Mick and Keith saw Brian play bottleneck guitar with Paul Pond onstage at the Ealing Jazz Club, they were all very impressed by his talents. Brian was an excellent slide guitar musician by then. At first, Mick idolized Brian. Keith Richards describes Brian: "when I first met Brian, he was like a little Welsh bull, he was broad and he seemed to be very tough." (pg 38, #13) According to Richards, the night they saw Brian play at the Ealing Jazz Club, "Alexis said 'we got a guest to play some guitar. He's come all the way down from Cheltenham just to play for you.' Suddenly it was Brian. He was sitting bent over, playing slide on his Hofner guitar and calling himself Elmo Lewis. He was the first person I ever heard playing electric slide guitar. Mick and I both thought he was incredible." (pg 33, #1) Shortly thereafter, Brian wanted to form his own band, and in the spring of 1962, he put up an advertisement in a periodical called *Jazz News*, seeking to do just that.

The first response to Brian's advertisement in *Jazz News* came from a boogie-woogie piano player named Ian Stewart, or Stu. Stewart was born on July 18, 1938 in Pittenweem, Fife in the United Kingdom. (pg 68, #7) Next to join the band were blues purists Geoff Bradford and Brian Knight. When Mick Jagger auditioned and was asked to join the band by Brian, he told him that Keith Richards had to be accepted with him, as they were part of a package deal. It is this part of history regarding the Rolling Stones—which lineup or lineups started the band that would become the legendary act known as the Rolling Stones—that, I believe, has been misinterpreted over time. Some would say that the hugely impactful meeting at the Dartford Rail Station between Mick Jagger and Keith Richards was the Big Bang moment that gave birth to the Rolling Stones. Although this was an important event in the band's creation, it was Brian Jones's ad in the *Jazz News* that truly created the band that still has an impact in the present. According to Bill Wyman, the story of the Rolling Stones starts with Brian, "because we were his brainchild, and it was Brian who named us." (pg. 10, #1)

After the show at the Ealing Jazz Club in March 1982, Mick spoke to Brian for the first time. Brian mentioned he'd be forming a band. Although Jagger had been hired to sing along in Blues Incorporated for scheduled shows, by June 1962, he had also begun rehearsing with Brian, Keith, Geoff Bradford, Brian Knight, and Ian Stewart on piano in Brian's new band. Bradford and Knight were described as blues purists, and more in line with the original description of the band based on the advertisement by Brian. However, Richards and Bradford clashed in the band immediately, because Keith liked Chuck Berry and Bradford only played strict blues. (pg 43, #4) This was coupled with the assumption that Bradford was a better musician than Keith, but Keith didn't respect Bradford. (pg 35, #14) Very shortly thereafter, both Bradford and Knight quit the band by simply refusing to play Chuck Berry. At this point, Dick Taylor was brought in as the bass player, with Brian and Keith on guitar, Ian Stewart on piano, Mick Jagger on vocals, and Tony Chapman on drums. It was Brian Jones himself who named the band the Rolling Stones, after the Muddy Waters song "Rollin' Stone."

Brian asked Paul Pond to join the band, but Pond said no to Brian in order to continue his university education, and he later joined the band Manfred Mann. Mick and Keith would audition for the Rolling Stones at Bricklayers Arms Pub in Soho's Lisle Street. (pg 35, #1) The Rolling Stones' first-ever gig was on July 12, 1962 at the Marquee on Oxford Street in London. For that show, the band consisted of Brian, Mick, Keith, Ian, Dick, and Mick Avory on drums, who would later go on to fame as the drummer for the group the Kinks. Brian was the best musician in the band then. As author Rich Cohen says, "Brian was the band's spirit. It was his vision. His dream." (pg 42, #13) Ginger Baker says that the star of the Stones in the early days was Brian. (pg 24, #8) Ray Davies of the Kinks concurs, saying, "Brian was probably the most conceited looking person I had ever met. But also one of the most compelling musicians ever on stage." (pg 32, #18) According to author Bill Janovitz, "Brian had by far the deepest musical knowledge and natural talent and taught Keith much of the foundation of the blues." (pg 8, #2) Even though Ian Stewart objected to the name Rolling Stones, the name became permanent anyway. The Stones were Brian's project, after all, because he ran the sessions, chose the songs, and set the schedule.

The Thursday night gig that the Rolling Stones regularly held at the Marquee gave them great exposure. Ginger Baker said, "Brian invited me and Jack Bruce to the first gig that the Stones played at the Cy Laurie Club on Windmill Street in Soho, and we went. Mick was just standing there stationary at the microphone singing, but Brian kept leaping all about the stage, playing lying on his back and even jumping into the audience while playing. It was Brian, not Mick, who was the showman of the band." (pgs 63-64, #4) Brian was the one who showed Mick Jagger how to play cross-harp, and he ran healthy and productive practices in those days. (pg 70, #7) Harold Pendleton, the former manager of the Marquee, said of Jones, "Brian was the genius of the Stones, it was his extremely brilliant idea that they should be the opposite of the Beatles. Brian was clearly the leader. It wasn't Mick. Brian called the tunes, Brian called the shots." (pg 79, #7) Despite this power within the band, Brian was an asthmatic, and it affected him greatly. Brian was scared to have an attack on stage. As the gigs continued, Keith said of Brian, "Singlehandedly we'd discovered we'd stabbed Dixieland to death. It really collapsed all because of us. Brian was so pleased to see the last jazz band disband, and us taking over the clubs. It was his happiest, proudest moment." (pg 69, #4)

It was Brian who merged all the influences and ideas into what would become the Rolling Stones. He envisioned that he and Keith would play double lead guitar when Brian wasn't playing the harmonica, which he might play on any given song in their set list. Brian, in those days, played all harmonica solos, and he and Mick were out in front on the stage together. (pg 67, #4) One night at the Marquee, after Keith Richards hit Harold Pendleton's head with his guitar after a rude comment, the Stones were banned from the Marquee. As a result, Dick Taylor quit the band. Tony Chapman, the drummer of the Stones before Charlie Watts, introduced the Stones to a new bass player named Bill Perks, formerly of the Cliftons. He was born on October 24, 1936 at Lewisham Hospital in southeast London. Bill changed his stage name to Bill Wyman. In 1962, when Bill met the Stones, he was more a rock & roller than a rhythm & blues fan. He was also 6 years older than Brian, and 7 years older than Mick and Keith. Unlike the rest of the band, Wyman was married—to a woman named Diane—and had a young son named Stephen. Wyman is the only member of the Stones to have served in the British military. Wyman served in the Royal Air Force in January 1955, going on to serve in West Germany. (pg. 20, #1)

When Bill Wyman went to his first audition at Weatherby Arms in Chelsea at the invitation of Tony Chapman, Bill said that only Ian Stewart and Mick Jagger talked to him and were friendly, while he describes Brian Jones and Keith Richards as mostly ignoring him at the bar—until they saw his bass AC-30 amplifier and his bass, which very much got their attention. Brian and Keith seemed much more impressed with Bill's equipment than with Bill himself. Mick asked him if he knew the music of black blues artists, to which Bill replied that he knew the work of Chuck Berry, Fats Domino, Eddie Cochran, Jerry Lee Lewis, Johnny Burnett, and Sam Cooke. Mick indicated that they favored more the music of Jimmy Reed and Muddy Waters. According to Wyman, "well when I first met them, the only people that would talk to me were Ian Stewart and Mick, because I met Ian Stewart the week before, so I went up there with a couple of amplifiers, I mean big ones, they only had funny little things and all the little speakers broken and all that, so when I arrived with all this stuff, their mouths dropped and their chins hit the floor. So I said you can use that one and you can use that one and they were like, wheee! Suddenly I was popular." (#16) Bill's first gig with the Stones was on December 14, 1962 at the Ricky-Tick Club in the Star and Garter Hotel in Windsor. (pg 41, #1) Bill immediately brought electricity and excitement to the Stones. (pg 40, #1)

Meanwhile, Charlie Watts was a graphic designer and an accomplished drummer playing with Blues Incorporated, which then consisted of Alexis Korner on guitar, Dick Heckstall-Smith on saxophone, Spike Heatley, Jack Bruce on bass guitar, and himself on drums. (pg 29, #19) Cyril Davies was in the band also. Although drummer Tony Chapman proved crucial in bringing Bill Wyman into the band, the Rolling Stones fired him at the end of 1962. After Ricky Fenson and Carlos Little played with the band, Charlie Watts's interest in playing with the Stones grew. Crucial was the fact that drummer Ginger Baker suggested to Brian to get Charlie Watts to be their drummer. Consequently, Charlie Watts's debut with the Rolling Stones took place on January 14, 1963 at the Flamingo Club, after finally being convinced by Alexis Korner to do so. Watts was born on June 2, 1941. (pg 90, #5) Ginger Baker replaced Charlie Watts as the drummer of Blues Incorporated. (pg 111, #1) At that point, the Rolling Stones consisted of Brian Jones, Keith Richards, Mick Jagger, Bill Wyman, Charlie Watts, and Ian Stewart. Having Bill Wyman on the bass guitar and Charlie Watts on the drums added great strength to the band. (pg 92, #6)

According to Bill Wyman, "the Rolling Stones that I joined was led by Brian Jones, there was no doubt whatsoever who led the group in every way. Brian called the shots partly because he had pulled the musicians together, but mainly what mattered most at that stage was music, and Brian was by far the most knowledgeable about what we were playing. He was the business manager too, he collected and controlled all the money." (pg 116, #5) Engineer Glyn Johns concurs with this assessment by saying, "Brian was pretty much the leader. He was certainly the spokesman for the group to me." (pg 44, #1) According to author Rich Cohen, Brian's life was "a sickness that he believed could only be cured by the blues." (pg 41, #13) Author Paul Trynka says, "Brian was responsible not just for the musical inspiration of the Rolling Stones, but their dark magic too. There were other aspects of his personality like his sexuality that also seemed portentous." (pg 84, #7) "It was Brian Jones alone who had a vision that raw electric blues could appeal to the youth of Britain rather than only to a narrow circle of bohemians." (pg 56, #7) Wyman concurs by saying, "Brian was the inventor and inspiration of the Rolling Stones, the band wouldn't have existed without him." (pg 76, #5) Ian Stewart, who would later claim to hate Brian, said of his stage presence in the beginning of the band, "when Brian was onstage playing, he was inciting every male in the room to hit him. At the start, Brian was the image of aggression in the Stones, much more than Mick." (pg 82, #13) Even Keith Richards said of the Rolling Stones, "Brian could have joined another group, but he wanted to form his own. The Rolling Stones were Brian's baby." (pg 34, #1)

In August 1962, Mick Jagger moved in with Brian in what would become the famous, if not notorious, flat in Chelsea at 102 Edith Grove, their dirty, filthy, and unsavory dwelling of a home. This is where the Stones legend and career began in the pit of bankruptcy, uncertainty, and uncleanliness. Brian's girlfriend at the time, Pat Andrews, had moved in also, along with their son Julian Mark, and she would cook for them and give Brian money for guitar strings/equipment. Soon Keith Richards moved into the Edith Grove flat, also. Brian initially had a job working at an electrical department at Bayswater, but he would soon be fired from this position. (pg 54, #4) Another friend of Brian's named Dick Hattrell, from Brian's youth, also moved into the Edith Grove flat. Brian's history with his friend Hattrell was quite cruel and unkind. Brian once tried to electrocute Hattrell in the apartment; other times he took Hattrell's money without asking, and locked him outside their Edith Grove flat during a snowstorm. Brian would make Hattrell walk behind the Stones on the street so as to not be seen in public with them. Keith Richards describes in his book, *Life*, Brian's treatment of Hattrell as "a cold-blooded vicious motherfucker, and cruel, cruel, cruel." (pg 102, #20) These cruel traits demonstrated the inner turmoil that turned Brian into an evil character to those around him, and his own karma would come back to haunt him in unimaginable ways in the years to come. Together with his misogyny, narcissism, and immaturity in relationships, these hedonistic practices would spell the ultimate fate that came to dictate the rest of Brian's short life.

PART ONE: THE LIFE

CHAPTER 4

THE STONES ASCEND IN POPULARITY IN THE LONDON BLUES SCENE

In August 1963, the Rolling Stones began their awesome ascent to eventual global musical dominance. This began with Brian Jones writing to the BBC to ask for an audition for his group to appear on the show "Jazz Club." In the letter, Jones wrote, "our musical policy is simply to produce an authentic Chicago R & B sound, using material of such R & B greats as Muddy Waters, Bo Diddley, and Jimmy Reed." (pg 25, #17) Yet the band continued to face problems outside the music world. Brian's reckless sexual behavior continued when he impregnated 16-year-old Linda Lawrence. To compound the problems they faced, the flat at Edith Grove had only one lightbulb dangling from the ceiling, a bathtub in the kitchen, and a bathroom two flights up. Wyman commented that "they lived like rats," in grotesque filth. (pg 44, #21) Wyman added, "it looked like it was bomb damaged." (pg 112, #5) They had no money for anything in Edith Grove, except what Mick was getting from his scholarship, and times were hard for Brian, Mick, and Keith. Brian said, "it was hard to concentrate on music when we were too hungry to think. We'd often go back to the apartment and think about silly things, like tearing up the blankets and making sandwiches of them." (pg 108, #5)

Charlie Watts, on the other hand, had a more stable life, living with his parents in Neasden and working as a graphic designer. Watts's work drumming in the band Blues Incorporated got him noticed by the Rolling Stones, who wanted him to join after Tony Chapman had been officially fired by the band. When Ian Stewart began his overtures to Charlie to join the Stones, Watts said, " 'Yeah, all right, but I don't know what my dad's going to say.' I thought they were mad. They were working a lot of dates without getting paid or worrying about it. I was earning a pretty comfortable living, which was obviously going to nosedive. But I got to thinking about it. I liked their spirit and I was getting very involved in R & B. So I said okay." (pg 45, #1) When Tony Chapman was fired from the

Rolling Stones, he told Bill to come with him so they could start a new band. However, Bill made it clear that he was staying with the Stones, so Chapman stormed out and left on his own. (pg 45, #1) Charlie Watts's first gig with the Stones was in Ealing on January 14, 1963. They were initially a six-piece band with Ian Stewart in the lineup. Brian desperately wanted his parents' approval during this time.

Meanwhile, a group from the northern English city of Liverpool was creating excitement throughout the music community: the Beatles. They were managed by the son of a well-to-do Jewish family who ran a very large store in Liverpool that his family owned, called NEMS, and his name was Brian Epstein. In the basement of Epstein's store was a record department, in which Brian took great interest, calling the records sold there "the finest record selection in the north." (pg 249, #22) Epstein's personal interests were more focused on theatre, opera, and ballet. But when a customer asked him if his store carried Tony Sheridan's record "My Bonnie" that featured a Liverpool group called the Beatles, Epstein went to a local venue, located a block away from his store, called the Cavern Club in October 1961 to see these Beatles live. Impressed with what he saw that day, Epstein offered the group his services as manager right away. In total, the Beatles played the Cavern Club on Matthew Street a total of 292 times. (pg 63, #23) With the addition of Richard Starkey on drums, also known as Ringo Starr, in place of their previous drummer Pete Best, and getting producer George Martin to work with them, the Beatles had become a well-oiled machine ready to take the world by storm. The Beatles released their first single written by the band, called "Love Me Do," on October 17th, 1962, and it made it to no. 17 on the charts.

Their next two singles, "Please, Please Me" and "From Me to You," both went to the top of the charts in England, and the Beatles' talent was gaining much attention in the singles market. Most important of all, these songs were written by John Lennon and Paul McCartney, showing all other musical acts, including the Rolling Stones, that you can write your own music with a successful songwriting formula. Certainly, the Rolling Stones and all other English groups took notice of this, and considered embarking on this practice established by the Beatles. As Mick Jagger said at the time, "I think everyone got turned on to the idea of writing songs by the Beatles. It was like, if the Beatles can write, we can write." (pg 54, #17) Although Brian's concept of the Rolling Stones when he formed the band was to cover songs by Jimmy Reed, Bo Diddley, Howlin' Wolf, Robert Johnson, Little Walter, and John Lee Hooker, it was clear that the standard of songwriting that was set by the Beatles affected any group who was set on challenging them for supremacy on the charts.

For all of Brian Jones's gifts as a musician, songwriting was not among them. However, Brian himself was particularly blown away by the success of the Beatles, and he wanted the same fame and fortune for himself. This included wanting to be totally mobbed in public, as the Beatles were. (pg 58, #24) Meanwhile, by the start of 1963, the Rolling Stones had played all of the outer London boroughs of Richmond, Putney, Twickenham, Eel Pie, and Windsor. (pg 56, #25) Brian, who was then the undisputed leader of the Rolling Stones, befriended experimental filmmaker Giorgio Gomelsky, who was a big R & B enthusiast. Gomelsky had previously lived in Chicago, where R & B had a big impact, and he ran his own club, the Station Hotel, in Richmond. Brian convinced Gomelsky to book the Rolling Stones there at a crucial time, when their act was improving and growing in popularity. Gomelsky booked the Rolling Stones to play the Station Hotel in Richmond on February 24, 1963.

Gomelsky remembered Brian's enthusiasm by saying, "I opened a rhythm & blues club as far as possible from the west end. This was the Station Hotel in Richmond. Having overheard my ranting and ravings to journalists in pubs, Brian Jones knew of my dedication to the cause and, in turn, bent my ears about his band, 'the best band in the land' as he used to lisp to me on every possible occasion. This ended up in the residency booking at the Richmond Club." (pg 209, #15) Gomelsky also said of Jones, "Brian was determined to be a star at any price." (pg 74, #13) The club was re- named the Crawdaddy. A young Eric Clapton saw the Stones at the Crawdaddy during this time (pg. 67, #4), a venue about 30 minutes outside of central London (pg 45, #21). The Stones were also gaining in popularity at the Red Lion in Sutton on Wednesday nights, and their natural talent was starting to garner them attention from throughout the London musical community. The Stones also played the Flamingo Club on Wardour Street to great success. (pg 113,

#20) Gomelsky also got the Stones booked at Ken Colyer's club in Soho called Studio 51, another success for the Stones.

After these successful gigs in early 1963, the Stones were approached by engineer Glyn Johns about recording their material to tape. Ian Stewart was friends with Johns, (pg 88, #7) who was very impressed with Stewart's collection of jazz and blues records. (pg 32, #26) According to Johns in his description of Brian Jones in March 1963, "Brian was very much concerned about the sounds that I would produce on tape. He wanted the Jimmy Reed type sound, which was virtually unheard of in England." (pg 49, #1) The Stones' recording session with Johns at IBC Studios was on March 11, 1963, where they recorded 5 numbers: 2 Bo Diddley songs ("Road Runner" and "Diddley Daddy"), 2 Jimmy Reed songs ("Honey What's Wrong?" and "Bright Lights, Big City"), and the Muddy Waters song "I Just Wanna Be Loved." Although these songs didn't initially interest record companies, the Stones' drive and ambition, led by Jones, set them on a course to global superstardom in a very short amount of time.

Meanwhile, the Beatles had released their first album on Capitol Records on March 25, 1963, called *Please Please Me*, and it took the world by storm. What was astounding at the time was the number of original compositions written by Lennon and McCartney on that album: 8 out of 14 songs. The album skyrocketed to no. 1 in England and would remain there for 30 weeks. (#33) On April 14, 1963, after the Beatles had taped a performance on the television show "Thank Your Lucky Stars," they were convinced to go see the Rolling Stones that night at the Crawdaddy Club in Richmond. The Stones described seeing the Beatles in the audience, in their matching suits, as the "four-headed monster" in the room, and the Stones were awed by their presence. Bill Wyman remembers thinking, "Shit, that's the Beatles! And I got all nervous." (pg 31, #17) The Beatles were very impressed with the Stones' performance that night, especially by Brian's multi-instrument-playing talent. John Lennon thought that Brian was a better harmonica player than him, and he said to Brian, "You really play that thing, don't you?." Brian had asked Lennon about his harmonica playing on the track "Love Me Do." George Harrison said of the Rolling Stones' performance that night, "It was a real rave, the audience shouted and screamed and danced on tables. They were doing a dance that no one had seen until then, but we all know of as the shake. The beat the Stones laid down was so solid, it shook the walls and seemed to move right inside your head. A great sound." (pg 54, #1)

The Beatles were invited back with the Stones to the infamous Edith Grove apartment, and they accepted. There, Brian, Keith, and Mick talked about music with the Beatles until 4 a.m. They listened to the IBC demos that the Stones had recently done, and to the blues albums that were among their favorites. During this meeting with the Beatles and Stones at Edith Grove, John Lennon voiced his opinion of Jimmy Reed's music as "crap," as it was not the type of music influencing the Beatles at the time. Yet the Beatles were very impressed by the Rolling Stones and their act, and they invited the band that night to their performance at the Royal Albert Hall as their guests the following Thursday. It seemed that the mutual respect the two groups had for each other would guide the course of music history for the remainder of the decade. They parted company late that night unaware of the pandemonium and mania that both groups would soon experience on a global scale. But by now, both groups' rockets were launching into space.

When the Stones attended the Royal Albert Hall show on April 18, 1963, Jagger said, "They invited us to one of their gigs at the Albert Hall. It was incredible for us to watch. I'd never seen hysteria on that level before. We were so turned on by those riots." (pg 55, #1) Brian and Giorgio even helped the Beatles carry their musical equipment into the venue, and fans swarmed and mobbed them, thinking incorrectly that they were the Beatles. Brian was exceptionally impressed by the Beatles' success, and he desperately wanted to be a star, with all the attention that went along with it. (pg 68, #12) Brian said, "This is what we like, being mobbed by people. This is what we want." (pg 55, #1)

It became clear that Brian was obsessed with the idea of pop stardom, despite the fact that Jones originally created the Rolling Stones as a R & B cover band. (pg. 12, #2) However, Jones was described as emotionally fragile, hypersensitive, and ill-suited to the demands of fame. (pg 11, #18) Also, Brian suffered from asthma, and was terrified about having an attack on stage. Yet Brian knew that he wanted the same fame and fortune that the Beatles were now getting, and he wanted to be regularly mobbed by fans, just like they were. (pg 59, #24) It was Brian who played all harmonica solos for the Rolling Stones then, and it was he and Mick who were out front together for the band. (pg 67, #4) It is said that Mick Jagger hated the attention that Brian got from the audience, and wanted to take him on for leadership of the group. (pg 26, #8)

It was at this time that Gomelsky was introduced to Peter Jones, who was the editor of a popular publication called *Record Mirror*. He connected the Stones with the business duo of Andrew Loog Oldham and Eric Easton while Gomelsky was out of town attending his father's funeral. Oldham and Easton officially met the Rolling Stones on April 28, 1963. Andrew asked Charlie Watts who the leader of the Stones was, and Watts pointed to Brian. (pg 194, #15) Jones acted on behalf of the Rolling Stones in meeting with the Oldham-Easton duo, and would cut a deal with them to acquire their services as managers of the band. At the time, Oldham worked at NEMS, the company owned by Beatles manager Brian Epstein. (pg 194, #15) During these initial discussions, Easton suggested that Jagger should be replaced by someone who sounded "less black." Brian Jones immediately agreed with this suggestion, lobbying for his friend Paul Pond as a suitable replacement. However, Oldham overruled them both and called both Jones and Easton "completely insane" for these suggestions.

Nevertheless, on May 1, 1963, Brian Jones, as leader of the band that he formed, signed the management deal with both Oldham and Easton that included Jones receiving an extra 5 pounds a week above the pay rate of the rest of the band. (pg 51, #14) Brian had considered himself the star of the band, and thought he could take on Mick as an on-stage personality. (pg 67, #24) However, this arrangement that Brian made with the Easton-Oldham duo would have consequences for Brian's relationship with his bandmates. Keith Richards says, "He had this arrangement with Easton that as the leader of the band, that he was entitled to this extra payment. Everybody freaked out. That was the beginning of the decline of Brian. We said 'fuck you' ." (pg 158, #5) Keith goes on to say, "It started with little things like that, which exacerbated the friction between us as it went on and he became more and more outrageous. In the early negotiations it was Brian who would go to the meeting as our leader, we were not permitted [to attend] by Brian." (pg 189, #20)

When the decision was made by management to remove Ian

Stewart from the stage lineup of the Rolling Stones, thankfully he agreed to the job of road manager. Stewart, or "Stu," hated Brian, whom he really blamed for his demotion from within the band, despite the decision having been made by Andrew Oldham. According to Stu, "there were quite a few things wrong [about] Brian. He was allergic to a lot of things, he used to suffer very badly from asthma, and had great breathing problems and always carried an inhaler and pills." (pg 143, #5) Stu's bitterness towards Brian would continue for the remainder of Brian's time in the Rolling Stones. The differences between Brian and the rest of the band became exacerbated, according to Stu, by the fact that "When we started playing outside of London, Brian said that 'I'm the leader of this group, and I think I'll stay at the best hotel. All the rest of you can stay in a cheaper hotel.' Of course, the rest of the band just laughed at him and that was it. From then on, it was all over for him as the leader. He started to isolate himself because of his attitude." (pg 158, #5) These were the seeds of self-destruction that Brian had planted for himself, and the harvest was his downfall from grace.

Like Brian Epstein, Andrew Loog Oldham was Jewish and known for always being very sharply and neatly dressed. Although Oldham was only 19 years old at the time, he learned at an early age the value of shocking people, and that the first thing you had to do was get their attention. (pg 45, #15) Bill Wyman agrees by saying of Oldham, "Andrew Loog Oldham was a vital ingredient in our success. He was young enough to understand and share our outlook and he had a talent for exploiting the unexploitable." (pg 56, #1) It is said that the new manager of the Rolling Stones wanted them to be more pop stars than R & B stars, and his influence on this concept would have profound implications for the direction of the band and for the power of the Rolling Stones being taken away from Brian Jones. Andrew was mentored and heavily influenced in the beginning of his managerial career by producer Phil Spector. (pg 85, #27)

It was at this time that Decca Records company executive Dick Rowe came into the picture. Rowe was infamous for his decision to turn down the Beatles the previous year, letting them sign and become hugely successful with their rival company, EMI. Rowe instead signed the less successful Brian Poole and his band. (pg 45, #17) Rowe ran into Beatle George Harrison at a talent show that

Harrison was judging back in Liverpool, and Rowe bitterly complained to Harrison about losing talent of the Beatles' caliber to another company. It was there that Harrison recommended that Rowe sign the Rolling Stones, which he had the wisdom of doing on May 14, 1963. (pg 63, #24) Rowe and Easton made the deal instead of Oldham. (pg 100, #7) Before Brian signed the contract with Oldham and Easton's company, Impact Sound, and the Decca Records contract, there was still a small legal matter that needed sorting out. Brian wanted to sign the offer for a three-year deal, but the Stones were still technically under contract with IBC. So Brian fooled IBC Studios into thinking that the Stones were breaking up and requested to buy back the tapes recorded as souvenirs, which they successfully did for 90 pounds. (pg 67, #25) This left a bitter taste in the mouth of engineer Glyn Johns. (pg. 59, #1)

Once the Decca deal was complete, the Rolling Stones were in the studio, recording Chuck Berry's "Come On" and Muddy Waters song "I Just Wanna Be Loved" as the B-side (written by Willie Dixon). By this time, Brian had softened his stance on pure R & B for more commercially successful pop songs, although Oldham and Jones didn't agree on trading R & B completely for pop songs. (pg 65, #24) Consequently, the Rolling Stones would record more pop songs but played mostly R & B live. In the deal that Jones signed with Impact regarding royalties on record sales, the Stones received a 6% royalty. (pg 61, #1) Unknown to the band, Impact was getting 14% from Decca, plus 25% of the Stones' 6% payment. (pg. 61, #1)

Meanwhile, Gomelsky's club the Crawdaddy would close in June 1963. Gomelsky was devastated to lose the Stones to Oldham and Easton, but was supportive in their efforts to climb the national charts. The song "Come On" was dominated by Brian's harmonica playing, and made it onto the British charts, reaching as high as no. 21, but the Stones themselves were not big fans of the song. (pg 101, #7) Interestingly enough, the Stones didn't use Decca's studios to record, but independently recorded and retained ownership of the copyright of the songs that were recorded. (pg 68, #25) The Rolling Stones would play a total of 18 gigs in May 1963, and by July, the band was asked to play on the popular UK television show "Thank Your Lucky Stars."

The Stones would also record versions of Benny Spellman's song "Fortune Teller" and the Coasters' song "Poison Ivy." (pg 65,

#1) During this time, Andrew had the Stones wearing suits, like the Beatles had done, but with the Stones this idea didn't last long. After a while, the Stones complained that they had few clothes to choose from because of their lack of money. Another problem was that Brian was dating Pat Andrews and Linda Lawrence at the same time. Pat would say of Linda, "Linda was dazzled by Brian then, of course, the pivot of a popular band and one obviously on the rise. And there's nothing more ruthless than a young girl out to get her clutches into someone's boyfriend." (pg 70, #25) Brian would eventually leave Pat and their son Julian Mark for Linda, who, as already mentioned, would become impregnated by Brian later that year. Lawrence was just 16 years old at the time. To make matters worse, by mid-August 1963, Eric Easton had completely taken over Brian's responsibilities of overseeing the band's finances. Right away, the other members of the Stones started receiving better payments than under Brian's leadership. In August 1963, the Stones played the popular television show "Ready, Steady, Go," gaining them new fans and exposure throughout England. That August, the Stones recorded Chuck Berry's "Bye Johnny," Barrett Strong's "Money," and Arthur Alexander's "You Better Move On." (pg 40, #17) But Brian was certainly not happy with the spotlight being taken away from him by Andrew, who was much more in favor of giving this to Mick Jagger.

As the gigs throughout Britain increased from July through September 1963, Oldham was despondent over the fact that the Stones needed a new song to stay in the charts. As fate had it, on September 10, 1963, Oldham decided to go out for a stroll while contemplating a new song for the Stones to record. All of the sudden, he ran into both John Lennon and Paul McCartney coming out of a taxi after they had just left a Variety Club luncheon at the Savoy Hotel. The Beatles had just received an award there for being Top Vocal Group of the Year. Despite the fact that both Lennon and McCartney had consumed several drinks at this event, they listened to Oldham's problem about needing a song, so they offered the Stones a song they were still working on for their next album, called "I Wanna Be Your Man." This song was set aside for drummer Ringo Starr to sing on their next album, called *With the Beatles*, due for release that November. Lennon and McCartney promptly went down to Olympic Studios to finish the song literally in front of the

Rolling Stones, to the Stones' utter amazement. John Lennon would say, "I remember teaching it to them. We played it roughly, so Paul and I went off to the corner of the room and finished the song while they were still talking, right in front of their eyes we did it." (pg 72, #24) Although the Stones were excited to be given this song by the Beatles and took the song to no. 1 on the British charts, Lennon insisted that the song was just a throwaway for the group, saying, "We weren't going to give them anything great, right?." (pg 72, #24) The Stones' version of the song has Brian playing brilliant slide guitar, differentiating the Stones' more R & B version from the Beatles' version. Bo Diddley praised Brian's slide guitar on "I Wanna Be Your Man." (pg 156, #5) Keith Richards also praised Brian's performance on the slide guitar, saying, "I dig that steel solo, Brian made that record with that bottleneck." (pg. 53, #17)

The subsequent Beatles album *With the Beatles* was released on November 22, 1963 and was no. 1 in the album charts for 21 weeks. (#33) This Beatles album had 8 Lennon/McCartney songs with 6 cover songs, and had George Harrison's first original composition, "Don't Bother Me." This release showed that the Beatles had staying power, with their blockbuster singles "I Want to Hold Your Hand" and "She Loves You" soon to follow. The former track finally broke the Beatles into the American market by giving them their first no. 1 single in the United States. But the important point is that Lennon and McCartney showed Andrew Oldham and the rest of the Rolling Stones the importance of writing original material. It was clear that it was going to be a challenge going forward for the Rolling Stones to keep finding interesting cover songs to remake and market to the public when the Beatles were making more money, specifically John Lennon and Paul McCartney. As Keith Richards said, "it had never crossed my mind to be a song writer until Andrew comes to me and Mick and said, 'how many good records are you going to keep making if you can't get new material? You can only cover as many songs as there are, and I think you're capable of more' ." (pg 250, #15) Oldham criticizes both his partner Eric Easton and Brian Jones by saying, "Putting further distance between group leader Jones and his merry men was Easton's foolish decision to cave in to Brian's unjustifiable demand for an extra 5 pounds a week as payment for his now-imagined management liaison duties. He would also distinguish himself as a team player by staying alone in hotels that were somewhat nicer then the dumps the other Stones were being booked into, and arranging his own transportation to avoid Stu's overcrowded bus." (pg 244, #15) There was real heat between Oldham and Jones for control of the group, and, as previously stated, Jones vehemently disagreed with Oldham on trading R & B for pop. (pg 67, #24)

For the remainder of 1963, the Stones criss-crossed England, playing gigs into January 1964. They would visit Gloucester, Somerset, Yorkshire, Hampshire, and London. The Stones gained valuable exposure in their first national tour in England, touring with the Everly Brothers and Bo Diddley. As their spokesman in 1963, Brian says of the Rolling Stones' progress, "So far, we've raved only in clubs and dance halls, but now we're looking forward to raving on our first theatre tour with the Everly Brothers. For us, the big thrill is that Bo Diddley will be on the bill! ." (pg 51, #17) The Rolling Stones also scored some valuable appearances on British national television shows like "Thank Your Lucky Stars," "Ready, Steady, Go," and "Saturday Club." (pg 23, #17) But by the beginning of 1964, thanks to Oldham's influence, Mick and Keith wrote their first songs together, called "It Should Be You" and "Will You Be My Lover Tonight?" which George Bean recorded in January 1964. They also wrote "That Girl Belongs to Yesterday." Engineer Glyn Johns said, "Andrew's pushing Mick and Keith to write songs is what really caused Brian to be left behind." (pg 98, #1) Also around this time, Andrew moved in with Mick and Keith and Mick's girlfriend Chrissie Shrimpton at 33 Mapesbury Road, having finally left the infamous Edith Grove apartment. Brian moved in with girlfriend Linda Lawrence at her parents' house. (pg 76, #1)

PART ONE: THE LIFE

CHAPTER 5

BRIAN LOSES POWER AND BEGINS TO CRUMBLE

Andrew Oldham's vision of the band's image and musical progression had a huge impact on their newfound success. Oldham's plan of making Jagger and Richards the composers/songwriters of the band permanently shifted the ultimate power from Brian Jones to Mick Jagger and Keith Richards. It was clear that Brian Jones couldn't write songs. (pg 75, #24) Oldham's experiment of locking Mick and Keith in his kitchen to write songs paid off handsomely and altered the course of music that the Stones played, from R & B towards a more pop/rock & roll sound. Engineer Glyn Johns says, "Brian was loath to pay attention to anyone but himself. He didn't respect the pop song structure, and thought it involved little more than rhyming moon with June. Mick and Keith knew there was more to it than that and appreciated how hard it was to 'keep things simple' ." (pg 96, #27) In fact, an argument can be made that once Andrew Oldham had taken control of the Rolling Stones as their manager, Brian's influence as a leader rapidly vanished, and Brian's decreasing influence on the Rolling Stones was evident once they started getting famous. (pg 126, #6)

To cope with this shift in power within the band, Jones became a heavy drinker. (pg 100, #12) During this time, Brian was physically abusive to Linda Lawrence and experienced wild mood swings that led to violence against her at the drop of a dime. (pg 88, #12) These outbursts were fueled by jealous rages that Brian would direct towards Linda, before and after the birth of their son, Brian's fourth child, Julian Brian, in July 1964. They were similar to the jealous rages that he directed against Pat Andrews. (pg 20, #25) Brian began showing signs of weakness and unreliability as early as August 1963, by not turning up for gigs and being hospitalized for exhaustion. Stu always filled in for Brian on stage when this would happen (pg 147, #5), and it happened in part because Brian didn't like the spotlight being taken away from him once Andrew and Mick took control of the Rolling Stones. (pg 98, #4) Bill Wyman said that Brian suffered from a mild form of epilepsy and also greatly from asthma. As a result of these conditions, Brian began to succumb to self-loathing and become reckless in his actions. (pg 107, #7) Still, despite his asthma, Brian smoked two packs of cigarettes a day. (pg 110, #4)

Yet the first Rolling Stones album, released in April 1964 as *England's Newest Hitmakers*, was heavily influenced by Brian. (pg 115, #7). This album from this rebellious group of musicians showed the strength of the band and brought a fresh breath of air into the musical landscape. Although the songs on the album have some rhythm & blues feel to them, such as "I Just Wanna Make Love to You" by Willie Dixon, the album has a more rock & roll feel to it than Brian's original concept of what the Rolling Stones would be. For example, the Rolling Stones version of "I Just Wanna Make Love to You" has a more rock & roll sound than the Muddy Waters version. The album also included covers of Buddy Holly's song "Not Fade Away" and Chuck Berry's "Carol," which definitely give the album a more rock & roll vibe, comparable to the Beatles recordings at the time. The album included a Jagger-Richards composition called "Tell Me" and a cover version of Bobby Troup's song "Route 66." This solid album showed the world what the Rolling Stones could do, and now it was up to the band to show what they could do *live*: it was time for their first American tour in June 1964.

Meanwhile, Brian's downfall, both in the band and in his life, had tightened its grip over him, and his fate would take a dark turn in the years ahead. In Paul Trynka's book on Brian Jones, he says, "Brian's life up until the spring of 1964 had been a quest for vindication. There after it was a tragedy, for vindication brought no happiness, only sorrow." (pg 120, #7) "Brian's conduct and presence in the band was described as powerful, yet vulnerable. Resourceful yet unreliable." (pg 116, #7)

Yet Brian's dominance on harmonica and influence on that first Rolling Stones album cannot be denied. The power shift that Andrew Oldham initiated, towards Mick Jagger and Keith Richards as the newly appointed song makers, had a more lasting impact on the future of the band. According to Keith Richards, "It was Andrew that really forced Mick and I to sit down and try it, and get through that initial period when you write absolute rubbish things you've heard and rewriting other people's songs until you start coming up with songs of your own. Andrew made us persevere." (pg 98, #17) Although their first tour of the United States was described as unsuccessful, compared to the crowds and publicity that the Beatles had generated on their first visit to America, the Rolling Stones still made an impact on the American youth, soon achieving fame comparable to that of Beatlemania. Linda Lawrence was still pregnant with Brian's fourth child, Julian Brian, when Brian went on tour to the United States. On June 20, 1964, the Rolling Stones landed in New York City to a crowd of about 500 fans—not bad for starters, but still pale in comparison to the Beatles' first visit, which drew thousands of fans waiting to meet them and a no. 1 U.S. hit at the same time.

The Rolling Stones' first concert in the United States took place at the Swing Auditorium in San Bernardino, California, followed by two shows in San Antonio, Texas. It was at these San Antonio shows that the Stones met saxophonist Bobby Keys, who would later play often with the Stones, both live and in the studio. (pg 135, #1) Ironically enough, Bobby Keys was born on the same day as Keith Richards in Buddy Holly's hometown of Lubbock, Texas. Keys thought that Keith Richards and Charlie Watts were the heart and soul of the band when they first met in 1964.

The Rolling Stones went on to play shows to smaller audiences in Minneapolis, Minnesota; Omaha, Nebraska; Detroit, Michigan; Pittsburgh, Pennsylvania; and Harrisburg, West Virginia, and a sold-out show at Carnegie Hall. The Stones show in Nebraska sold a fraction of the 15,000 available seats. Keith Richards describes in his book *Life* that the most hostile people towards the Stones during their first U.S. tour were white people, mostly at their rural performances. (pg 164, #20) Keith describes the first half of their first U.S. tour as a "semi-disaster." (pg 157, #20) During their first television appearance, on the "Hollywood Palace Show" hosted by notorious legendary "Rat Pack" member Dean Martin, he mercilessly mocked the Stones while introducing them to the American audience. This was despite the fact that Martin's kids asked the Rolling Stones for autographs. (pg 124, #1) Additionally, according to Wyman, "In truth, we had the last laugh. On a later U.S. tour, Brian had an affair with one of Dean Martin's daughters." (pg 134, #1)

Most importantly during this tour of the United States, the

Rolling Stones made their way to the legendary Chess Studios in Chicago, Illinois, where they cut 13 tracks. This included a song given to them by Bobby Womack called "It's All Over Now," which would later become a no. 1 song for them. (pg 33, #2), It was at this visit to Chess Studios where the Stones met legendary bluesman McKinley Morganfield, also known by the name Muddy Waters, who was there helping to paint the ceiling and to assist in transporting the Stones amplifiers from the car into the studio. Blues writer and performer Willie Dixon was also there. Brian himself was dissatisfied with the Stones' recording of "It's All Over Now," thinking that it sounded too country/western. (pg 235, #5) The Stones also recorded an original composition called "Stewed and Keefed." (pg 228, #5) In his description of Brian's guitar skills, blues legend Muddy Waters said, "that guitar player ain't bad." (pg 129, #1) Chuck Berry, who visited the studio while the Stones were there, though partially ignoring them, would go on to say, "Swing on gentlemen, you are sounding most well, if I may say so." (pg 129, #1) The Rolling Stones returned to London on June 22, 1964 after a U.S. tour that was described as premature and ill conceived, with no big hit to capitalize on, but it certainly made an impact on the British-music scene in the American market.

However, Brian's personal struggles were ever present, and his relationship with Linda Lawrence would often turn violent and hostile. Brian started engaging in heavy drinking and drug use during this time, and became more of an outcast from the band. At the same time, Brian began a relationship in the summer of 1964 with a girl named Dawn Molloy, whom he would also impregnate in a short amount of time—they only dated for three months. In fact, on the same night as the birth of Brian's son Julian Brian (July 23, 1964), the Rolling Stones appeared on the popular British TV show "Top Gear." Dawn Molloy delivered Brian's fifth child in March 1965, but gave the child up for adoption. In fact, by May 1965, both Linda Lawrence and Dawn Molloy had sued Brian over paternal rights and child support money.

Brian consequently paid off both Linda and his son Julian in one lump sum, and that ended Brian's legal and financial responsibilities to them. (pg 125, #4) Mick Jagger and Andrew Oldham would aid in paying Dawn Molloy $2000 to relinquish any claims on Brian's earnings, (pg 65, #21) and this sum was deducted from his pay. (pg 259, #5) In a July 1969 article in the *Sunday People*, Dawn Molloy officially commented about her and Brian's baby. "I've had our baby adopted. I've realized that the love that Brian claimed to have for me didn't exist. I'm not really sure if mine did either. It was all a foolish mistake." (pg 151, #1)

In contrast, manager Andrew Oldham married his girlfriend Sheila Klein on September 16, 1964 in Scotland, and Charlie Watts married his girlfriend Shirley on October 14, 1964. (pg 148, #17) Upon their return from the United States, the Stones resumed touring England and Holland. A typical set list, from their show at the Leeds Queen Hall, was "Walking the Dog," "High-Heeled Sneakers," "You Can make It if You Try," "Not Fade Away," "Can I Get a Witness?" "I Just Wanna Make Love to You," and "It's All Over Now." (pg 249, #5) By now, fans had taken screaming to a frightening new level, and it grew more intense with the band's growing popularity. Brian expressed his concern over the increasing pandemonium at shows by saying, "When fans really start raving they seem almost like enemies. You know in your heart that all they're trying to do is make contact, to touch you or talk to you. But what it seems is that thousands of kids are trying to tear you apart, to throw things at you, knock you over. That drives us into ourselves, so that the only people we talk to properly are the other people in the group." (pg 241, #5)

CHAPTER 6

THE ANTI-BEATLES

While the Stones were becoming enormously famous, their competition, the Beatles, had an extraordinarily successful 1964. After playing to an estimated 73 million people on the "Ed Sullivan Show" on February 9, 1964, and being the only group in history to hold all five top songs on the Top 100 countdown in April 1964, the Beatles' third album, *A Hard Day's Night*, was released on July 10, 1964 with an accompanying film of the same name. The album spent 21 weeks at no. 1. (#33) When the album and film were released, the Beatles played 25 shows in 30 days. At the Beatles' Vancouver, Canada show, 7,000 kids had rushed past security to the stage, which resulted in 240 kids going to the hospital for injuries. The Beatles played their famous Hollywood Bowl concerts in August 1964. Similar to what the Stones had experienced in June 1964, the Beatles ran into the same bigotry from a heavily segregated situation in Jacksonville, Florida. For their scheduled September show, the promoters of the Gator Bowl, where the Beatles were scheduled to play, had listed the concert as a segregated show. When the Beatles learned of this, they refused to play the show unless the audience was desegregated. This was no idle threat coming from a group as big as the Beatles, still cresting high on their wave of American popularity. So, in the end, the promoters backed down and the audience was desegregated. This act ensured that members of all races could simultaneously enjoy the Beatles' live show as a combined unit, as the Beatles intended them to do. Ironically enough, the date of this Beatles concert in Jacksonville, Florida was September 11, 1964.

At the time, the Rolling Stones were marketed to the general public as the anti- Beatles, whose lovable mop-top image had captured teenage hearts throughout the world. The Stones were billed as more dangerous, more violent, and less sympathetic. The question asked by their manager to the general public was, "Would you let your daughter marry a Rolling Stone?." The Stones had every intention of proclaiming themselves the new bad boys of the

"British Invasion," with a much harder edge than other groups, including the Beatles. The Rolling Stones began their second U.S. tour in October 1964, which included their much-anticipated first appearance on the "Ed Sullivan Show." They performed on that show on October 25, 1964, playing the songs "Time Is on My Side" and "Around and Around." This coincided with the release of a new album in the States, called *12 × 5*. Though the album mostly consisted of cover songs, there were several Jagger-Richards original compositions on it, including "Good Times, Bad Times," "Congratulations," and "Grown Up Wrong," while a couple of others ("2120 Michigan Avenue" and "Empty Heart") were credited to Nanker Phelge. Nanker Phelge was a group pseudonym paying homage to the grossness of former Edith Grove roommate Jimmy Phelge, who would put soiled underwear on his head and walk around completely nude, spitting at his roommates. (pg 44, #1) All in all, with "Around and Around," "Time Is on My Side," and their surprisingly poppy version of "Under the Boardwalk," *12 × 5* is a fine album. Additionally, it showed that the Stones could compete with the Beatles and other British and American groups, as they were clearly getting better and better as the tour went on.

The next single, which epitomized the direction Brian wanted the Rolling Stones to take, was Willie Dixon's "Little Red Rooster," which rocketed to no. 1 on the UK charts in November 1964. This song features Brian playing a brilliant slide guitar, which epitomizes Brian's vision of the Rolling Stones as a rhythm & blues band. They also recorded "I Just Can't Be Satisfied" by Muddy Waters to stay true to their blues roots. Brian himself said, " 'I Can't Be Satisfied' is my favorite track. I played bottleneck guitar on it and it has one of the best guitar solos I've ever managed." (pg 164, #1)

Brian's enthusiasm was tempered by his prophetic vision of eternal rebellion by the youth: Brian said, "Every generation brings a fresh wave of ideas, and if this is stifled, society and culture would be doomed. Our children will be rebelling against us in 20 years time." (pg 184, #17) Despite his excitement, Brian's asthma problems caused him to miss several shows on the second U.S. tour, and he was replaced with Ian Stewart. Wyman blames bronchitis and extreme exhaustion for Brian's absences, combined with drinking too much and smoking marijuana. By the time the Stones landed in Chicago on November 11, 1964, Brian collapsed and was hospitalized. He missed four shows. Stu blamed Brian's drug use and his self-indulgence. When Brian responded with songs of his own that he would bring into the recording studio, they were immediately dismissed by the trifecta that was Oldham-Jagger-Richards. This fundamental power shift in the band had its consequences for both Mick and Keith, and for the rest of the band—particularly Brian. Oldham said, "Now that I looked to Mick and Keith to provide material for recording, the other Stones, particularly Brian Jones, often felt redundant and unappreciated. Both Charlie Watts and Eric Easton told me that Brian had song writing ambitions, but he was too scared to put his songs forward. Jones didn't have the firm foundation I required to build a Brill building hit machine. On the one hand, he was obsessed with duplicating the stardom of the Beatles, while on the other hand, he remained a blues purist and distrusted our efforts to reach the widest possible audience." (pg 287, #1) To further exacerbate the situation, Brian didn't want to play Jagger-Richards compositions, instead preferring the strictly rhythm & blues material the band used to play. Jones hated playing Jagger-Richards songs, but was forced to do so once the power shift took place. (pg 129, #12) Although Jones craved to be treated like a star, he hated his situation inside the Rolling Stones. (pg 129, #12)

Brian's inability to write songs would cripple his standing in the band. As a result, Brian became a very heavy drinker to cope, causing further problems for himself and the band. (pg 110, #12) The Rolling Stones were gaining in popularity, and their touring schedule became ever more taxing, yet the Stones had little to show for it financially. It was around this time that the Stones met two key figures who would become very influential, particularly for Mick, Keith, and Brian. Their names were Prince Stanislas Klossowski de Rola, or his "Stash," and art dealer Robert Fraser. The Stones ended 1964 with 2 no. 1 singles in the United Kingdom and a no. 1 album, and a no. 11 album in the United States. This certainly enhanced their status in the music world. Brian had two more kids in 1964, although he was never really involved in any of their lives. In fact, all five of Brian's children had little or nothing to do with Brian from this point forward.

Meanwhile, the Beatles' fourth album, *Beatles for Sale*, was released in December 1964 and spent 11 weeks at no. 1. But by then the Beatles and Rolling Stones were influencing other emerging London bands, including a band from Shepherd's Bush, London, originally called the Detours, then the Who, then the High Numbers, then back to the Who. The Who considered themselves to be an R & B band, similar to the Rolling Stones. Also, a band formed in southwest London in May 1963 that was managed by Giorgio Gomelsky—the Yardbirds—that took over at the Crawdaddy Club when the Stones left and made quite a splash in the London blues scene. The original Yardbirds line-up of Keith Relf on vocals, Anthony "Top" Topham on lead guitar, Paul Samwell-Smith on bass guitar, Jim McCarty on drums, and Chris Dreja on rhythm guitar had the same influences as the Stones: Jimmy Reed, Howlin' Wolf, Muddy Waters, and Bo Diddley. But when Topham left in May 1963, shortly after the band formed, to be replaced by a young and quite talented guitarist named Eric Clapton, this changed the trajectory of the Yardbirds into a legit contender in the London music scene. Drummer Jim McCarty and Clapton would butt heads in the band, and when the Yardbirds released their single "For Your Love," which Clapton thought was too poppy a song for an R & B band, Clapton quit the band. He would be replaced by guitarist Jeff Beck, who himself would eventually be replaced by guitarist Jimmy Page. And a young American soldier from the 101st Airborne Division, who got out of the army in 1964 and would soon tour with Solomon Burke, Otis Redding, the Isley Brothers, Curtis Mayfield, and Little Richard before eventually exploding into rock superstardom, became a close friend of Brian Jones: his name was Johnny Allen Hendrix, better known as Jimi Hendrix.

The year 1965 began with the Rolling Stones touring Australia to rave reviews, followed by a show in Singapore. It was at this point that Mick and Keith walked into the studio in January 1965 to record a song, releasing their work to the public on February 26, 1965. The name of the song they wrote that changed the trajectory of the band was called "The Last Time." This song was considered more commercial than their previous no. 1 hit "Little Red Rooster," which is more of a blues-oriented song. "The Last Time" shot up to no. 1 on the U.K. charts. Now, Brian would have to play this song live at every performance, further rubbing in the fact that he had lost control over the band and only adding to the tension between Brian and the trifecta of Mick, Keith, and Andrew. As Keith

Richards described it, "It was the period where everything: songwriting, recording, performing, stepped into a new league. At this time, Brian was going off the rails." (pg 173, #20) In Rich Cohen's book *The Sun & the Moon & the Rolling Stones*, he says, "Paranoid and increasingly jealous of Mick and Keith's partnership, Jones spent his rage on women. The keener the paranoia, the more violent the outburst." (pg 128, #13) Brian had a terrible habit of beating up girls he'd met on the road. Even Charlie Watts, normally mild mannered, said of Brian, "He was a little prick." (pg 128, #13) Richards echoes Watts' assessment of Brian by saying, "He was not a good man." (pg 128, #13) Brian was sadistic, as well as narcissistic and manic depressive. (pg 135, #7). By this point, Brian actually considered leaving the Rolling Stones.

In the film *Charlie Is My Darling* (#34), which is a documentary of Rolling Stones shows in Ireland in early 1965, Brian himself says, "Let's face it, the future as a Rolling Stone is very uncertain. My ultimate aim in life was never to be a pop star. I enjoy it, with reservations, but I'm not really sort of satisfied either artistically or personally." On the question of how marriage had eluded him, Brian said, "Very simple answer to that question. I haven't really found the girl I want to marry. In any case, the whole prospect of marriage rather frightens me. It's like signing a contract: whenever I sign a contract for anything, I want to read it carefully, because you know you're signing a part of you away, and you get married. I feel you're signing your whole life away, and if I could get married for a year, just a year's contract, I'd be much happier." Brian could be considered the king of hypocrisy for this outlandish statement, considering that he already had five children with five different women, none of whom he took care of or paid any attention to. Brian adds during the film, "Our sort of success is a first-class ticket to a lot of other things. On the other hand, there's not much physical freedom, we have to choose very carefully where we go on holidays because of our sort of peculiar success." Brian concluded his comments with, "Yes, I've never really thought very far ahead at all, I've always been a little apprehensive about the future."

The Stones released an album in the United Kingdom called *Number 3*, followed by the release of their American album *Rolling Stones Now* on February 13, 1965. Although there were cover songs on the album, including Solomon Burke's "Everybody Needs Somebody to Love," Chuck Berry's "You Can't Catch Me," and Willie Dixon's "Little Red Rooster," the album included the Jagger-Richards compositions "Surprise, Surprise," "Off the Hook," "What a Shame," and "Heart of Stone." The Rolling Stones began their third North American tour in April 1965, and concluded on May 29, 1965. (pg 182, #1) But by now, Brian was very upset by Mick/Keith/Andrew's dominance over what Brian still felt was his band. Brian had missed many concert dates by April 1965, adding to the increasing tension within the band. To make matters worse, on March 18, 1965, Mick, Brian, and Bill were busted for urinating on a gas station wall after being prohibited from using the restroom by the attendant. Although their eventual fine was miniscule, it was a symbolic beginning to the legal trouble that would haunt Mick, Keith, and Brian for years to come. As a result of this, because the Stones couldn't just stop at any rest area, the more public ones they went to brought many insults, especially toward Brian. Brian was prone to violence when he got drunk. (pg 129, #4) In 1965, the Stones' relations with the police were never good in any country. (pg 128, #4)

In Clearwater, Florida, Brian had spent the night with a teenage girl, whom he had violently beaten up. When she left the Gulf Motel needing immediate medical attention, road manager Mike Dorsey went into Brian's room to have a word with him, an encounter that also turned violent. This time, it was Brian who got beaten up, and he suffered a couple of cracked ribs, with no sympathy from any member of the entourage. It is rumored that Brian committed this unacceptable act of violence in the Florida motel room because of sexual impotence resulting from his drug use. (pg 87, #10) Author Laura Jackson blames Brian's clashes with Mick and Keith, his heavy drinking, smoking two packs a day despite his asthma, and his violence against women on his feelings of hurt, confusion, and frustration stemming from his unhappiness from his loss of control of his band and his dreams. Jackson said these factors played a large part for claiming Brian's short life. (pg 111, #4) Jackson also says that this fueled the belligerence and anger that Jones frequently succumbed to. Engineer Glyn Johns directly blames Brian for his alienation from the band he created, and Brian's friend Phil May describes his personality as his own worst enemy. Ian

Stewart blamed Brian's drug use and his self- indulgence for his downfall. (pg 135, #7) I think that those opinions are all correct, and they heighten the argument that Brian should have in fact left the Rolling Stones then, instead of trying to continue with them. But, as history records, he stayed in the band, which led to his downfall. He could have had some success with another band had he left the Stones, but we'll never know the answer to that question.

PART ONE: THE LIFE

CHAPTER 7

ANITA ENTERS THE PICTURE

Everything changed for the Rolling Stones when, on the road in Tampa, Florida on that spring tour of America, Keith Richards and Mick Jagger wrote the song that would be their first no. 1 hit in the States, called "(I Can't Get No) Satisfaction," recorded in Los Angeles, California at RCA Studios on May 12, 1965. (pg 318, #5) According to author Rich Cohen, Brian knew that the song "was a gun pointed at his head. It estranged Brian from Mick and Keith. When the song hit number one, it was over and out for Brian. And he hated it. And he rebelled." (pg 132, #13) Photographer Gered Mankowitz said Brian had a cruel streak in him and was addicted to amphetamines. (pg 69, #21) It is said that Brian was showing signs of depression on the third American tour, and he was already looking for a way out of the band altogether.

Brian had moved into Elm Park Lane in Chelsea during the spring of 1965. This was after his official breakup with Linda Lawrence and being officially thrown out of her parents' house. Linda Lawrence claims that Oldham tried to get her to sign an agreement to stay away from Brian and not cause any more trouble, which she did. Linda wound up in a relationship with the singer Donovan Leitch, whose popular song "Sunshine Superman" was a well-known acknowledgment to LSD. (pg 208, #7) Brian's demons would haunt him and hurt him through the remainder of his musical career. Brian always wanted the spotlight, and would become jealous when he didn't get it. (pg 316, #5) Bill Wyman said of Brian, regarding this phase in his career as a Rolling Stone, "As fame and pressure of life on the road hit us, Brian's behavior became a liability." (pg 315, #5) Brian felt the alienation from Mick, Keith, and Andrew. Yet the Rolling Stones juggernaut was in full ascension mode as the band played the "Ed Sullivan Show" for a second time, despite Sullivan saying he would never book the Rolling Stones again after their first appearance. (pg 312, #5)

Despite the success of the Jagger-Richards original composition "(I Can't Get No) Satisfaction," hitting no. 1 in both England and

America, the Stones were still not financially stable. (pg 322, #5) As stated earlier, it was reported that Brian was thinking of leaving the Rolling Stones. In fact, Brian was rumored to have talked to Eric Clapton, Paul Jones, Jet Harris, and Viv Prince about starting a new band in 1965. (pg 126, #7) According to Mick Jagger, their initial record deal with Decca Records was a bad one, earning merely cents on every album sale. Looking to solve this problem, Andrew flew to Miami, Florida to attend a Columbia Records convention on July 26, 1965. It was there that Oldham met American manager Allen Klein, an accountant from New York with a no-nonsense attitude who had been successful in recovering his clients' full royalties from the record companies they had signed with. Klein's specialty was channeling money from record companies to his artists through audits and contract restructuring. Klein, however, only worked with established stars, and not unknown up- and-comers. (pg. 57, #27) Klein's list of stars that he managed included Sam Cooke, Bobby Vinton, the Dave Clark Five, the Animals, Herman's Hermits, Donovan, Lulu, and the Kinks. The Rolling Stones and the Beatles would eventually join this impressive stable.

Klein was born in December 1931, and his mother died when he was 9 months old. (pg 4, #27) Klein had a bitter streak in him from this early loss, an important similarity to what John Lennon felt when he, too, lost his mother in a car accident when he was a teenager, which helped Klein land the Beatles in 1969. Andrew's meeting in July 1965 at a Miami hotel brought in Klein to help manage the Rolling Stones, first as co-manager with the team of Oldham and Easton. Bringing Klein into the business picture would ease Eric Easton completely out of management of the Rolling Stones, much to Brian Jones' disagreement. Jones thought that the Stones getting rid of Eric Easton also meant getting rid of him. Jones thought Oldham was the one behind this coup within the band.

That month, July 1965, the Rolling Stones album *Out of Our Heads* went no. 1. This album not only had the no. 1 Jagger-Richards songs "The Last Time" and "(I Can't Get No) Satisfaction," but other original Jagger-Richards compositions as well, including "Mercy, Mercy" and "Play With Fire." They also had strong cover versions of "The Spider and the Fly," "That's How Strong My Love Is," and "I'm All Right."

Meanwhile, the Beatles released their fifth album, *Help!* along with a color film of the same name that was directed by Dick Lester. On June 12 of the same year, the Beatles were awarded with MBEs, which made them official members of the British Empire, by the English monarchy and government. The album *Help!* stayed at no. 1 for 9 weeks. The Beatles had a similarly bad record deal to that of the Stones (before Klein became their manager), and made most of their money by playing live. Because of the enormous crush of fans wanting to see the Beatles live, they had to switch performances to big stadiums to accommodate the masses of fans willing to buy tickets to see them. On August 15, 1965, the Beatles were introduced by Ed Sullivan at Shea Stadium in New York, to an estimated 56,000 people who roared their approval. Mick, Keith, and Brian were also there, as guests of the Beatles in the dugout. By then, the Beatles had considered stopping playing live altogether, due to the madness and danger that Beatlemania presented. They played in England for the last time at the end of 1965. But things were happening for the Rolling Stones at around this time, also.

The Rolling Stones did a tour of England in July 1965. Oldham formed the company Immediate Records with business partner Tony Calder. Once Allen Klein became the Stones' co-manager, he renegotiated the Rolling Stones' contract with Decca Records with Sir Edward Locke himself. This was done entirely by Klein, with the Stones standing behind him as he spoke, and Klein got them a better contract than the Beatles had with EMI/Capitol Records. Keith Richards said of Klein, "I still think it was the best move Oldham made to put us together with him. Whatever happened later with Allen Klein, he was brilliant at generating cash. And he was also spectacular, at first, in blasting through the record companies and tour managers who had been overpaying themselves, and being very attentive to business." (pg 178, #20) Richards continues, "With us, Klein was very much Colonel Tom Parker with Elvis." (pg 179, #20) Bill Wyman never liked or trusted Klein and tried to stop his advances in the beginning by voting no, but Wyman was outvoted by the other four Stones. (pg 329, #5)

The Stones continued playing concerts in Germany and in England through September 1965. Brian moved to 13 Chester St. in Belgravia after he broke up with Linda and moved out of her house. (pg 107, #4) Brian can also lay claim to being the first member of the Rolling Stones to try LSD, the same year John Lennon, George Harrison, and their wives were given LSD unknowingly by a dentist friend of Lennon's named John Riley at a party Riley was hosting. (pg 422, #22) LSD, at the time, was legal until 1966. According to author Rich Cohen, "Brian began to deteriorate soon after his first acid trip." (pg 147, #13) Jones soon struck up friendships with Bob Dylan and Robbie Robertson and spent lots of time in New York with both artists. Interestingly, the Dylan songs "Ballad of a Thin Man" and "Like a Rolling Stone" were written about Brian Jones. (pg 82, #2)

After his official break-up with Linda Lawrence, Brian dated model Danièle Ciarlet, a French actress calling herself Zouzou. (pg 84, #10) But Brian's life in the Rolling Stones was forever altered when, on September 14, 1965, he met Anita Pallenberg in Munich, Germany while on tour. This beautiful blonde actress/model was born in Italy on April 6, 1942. Anita came from an artistic family based in Rome, and she had family contacts in Spain, France, and Germany. Anita was educated in Germany and was fluent in four languages. (pg 341, #5) Bill Wyman said, "This was a romance which would drastically affect his [Brian] and our future." (pg 341, #5) It is said that Anita had to comfort a crying and upset Brian Jones on that first night they met, because Brian had gotten into an argument with Mick and Keith. This is how they began their relationship. Mick Jagger's former girlfriend Marianne Faithfull said of Anita Pallenberg, "How Anita came to be with Brian is really the story of how the Stones came to be the Stones. She almost single handedly engineered a cultural revolution in London by bringing together the Stones with the jeunesse dorée [the young and the wealthy]." (pg 80, #2) When asked about Pallenberg's relationship with Brian, Faithfull said, "I think Anita loved Brian very much, but he was very difficult to love. There were strange things going on with them, and there were bruises on her arm and we knew it was Brian." (pg 86, #2)

Brian and Anita were together for 15 months. Anita Pallenberg said of Brian, "He was a tortured personality. Insecure as hell and totally paranoiac. He had a volatile temper and he would react to frustration with physical violence. In his tantrum, he would throw things at me. Whatever he could pick up, lamps, clocks, chairs, plates of food. Then when the storm inside him died down, he'd feel guilty and beg me to forgive him." (pg 142, #11) During his relationship with Anita, Brian re-ascended to a relevant leader of the band, and the music scene in general. When the album *Out of Our Heads* went to no. 1 in 1965, Brian was voted the most handsome man in pop by a *Record Mirror* survey. (pg 137, #4) Meanwhile, Mick Jagger and Chrissie Shrimpton became engaged in 1965. (pg 176, #6) However, it was Brian and Anita's relationship that gave the two a unique platform in the rock and pop world. Brian and Anita were alike in their extreme personalities. (pg 170, #7)

According to author Paul Trynka, "Anita's arrival on the scene seemed to give him [Brian] even more license to act in a willful fashion." (pg 173, #7) Photographer Gered Mankovitz describes Anita as "manipulative, wicked, and evil." He describes Brian and Anita together as "very manipulative, dangerous people." (pg. 55, #8)

Further problems developed when Brian's relationship with Anita began to strain his relationship with the other Stones. Brian started missing concerts altogether. (pg 142, #4) As Keith Richards said in his book *Life*, when Brian had been hospitalized in Chicago, Keith had to play both his part of the song and Brian's. But when pictures surfaced of Brian out partying and having fun, Keith was understandably angry at Brian. Brian also never thanked Keith for covering for his absence on stage, but just made the excuse of "I was out of it." Keith said, "That's when I had it in for Brian." (pg 190, #20) Brian would continue his cruel banter with Keith Richards with statements such as, "I saw Bob Dylan yesterday and he doesn't like you." This was the love-hate relationship that Brian had with Keith, but Keith also describes Brian as funny sometimes. Yet Brian is also described in the studio as difficult, insulting, and obnoxious. (pg 73, #21) Mick and Keith responded to this by constantly teasing Brian about his looks. According to Andrew Oldham, "The Rolling Stones and I may have been childishly cruel to Brian on occasion, but he asked for it." (#15). Part of the reason for Brian being so difficult in the studio was because it was hard for him to start playing Jagger-Richards songs when that was not what he had envisioned when he first created the band. According to Keith when speaking of Brian, "Having to come into a studio and learn a song that Mick and I had written would bring him down. It was like an open wound." (pg 73, #21) In contrast, his new girlfriend Anita was described as fearless and confident. (pg 121, #12)

The Rolling Stones album *December's Children (and Everybody's)* was released on October 27, 1965. In my opinion, this was a solid piece of work by the band. Although there are some great cover songs on the album, including "You Better Move On," and "Route 66," it also has some great Jagger-Richards original compositions, including "Get Off of My Cloud," "As Tears Go By," "Blue Turns to Grey," and "I'm Free." At the end of 1965, Tom Keylock replaced Mike Dorsey as the Stones' road manager. The Stones finished 1965 with their fourth American tour, from October to December 1965, where Pallenberg joined Brian for a week. (pg 211, #1) The Stones' next single, "19th Nervous Breakdown," was written by Mick Jagger about his fiancée Chrissie Shrimpton. Keith Richards was with girlfriend Linda Keith at the time.

Brian moved into 1 Courtfield Road in South Kensington, England (pg 9, #18) and he also visited Greenwich Village in New York to see Bob Dylan. (pg 353, #5) The Stones recorded the songs "Mother's Little Helper" and "19th Nervous Breakdown" between December 3 and 10, 1965. (pg 234, #17) By then, Mick and Keith were the ones doing the television interviews instead of Mick and Brian. "19th Nervous Breakdown" made it to no. 2 in England in February 1966. (pg 243, #17)

Brian Jones' life at this time was described as hedonistic. (pg 24, #18) Brian's friendship with art dealer Christopher Gibbs influenced Brian to buy expensive antiques. (pg 24, #18) Brian was taking large quantities of LSD at his Courtfield Road house with Anita, which made him extra paranoid. (pg 24, #18) As Keith Richards puts it, "I never saw a guy so affected by fame. It went to his head over the next few years of very difficult road work in the mid-1960's and we could not count on Brian at all. He became a pain in the neck, a kind of rotting attachment. When you're schlepping 350 days a year on the road, and you've got to drag dead weight, it becomes pretty vicious." (pg 189, #20) Meanwhile, the Beatles ended 1965 with the release of their album *Rubber Soul* in December, which featured only Lennon/McCartney compositions and two George Harrison originals. The album spent 8 weeks at no. 1. Also, the Shepherd's Bush, London group the Who played 236 shows in 1965 and scored their first no. 1 hit with the song "I Can't

Explain," written by guitarist Pete Townshend. The Stones were considered Mods (for "modern jazz" or "modernists"), just like the Who. The Mods in London liked black American music, similar to that produced by Motown Records. (pg 91, #17)

As the year 1966 began, Brian gave an interview to the *Record Mirror*, released on February 12, 1966, which summed up his state of mind within the band: "I'm not personally insecure, just unsure. I would like to write, but I lack confidence." (pg 218, #1) Brian goes on to say, "I enjoy being with the Stones. It gives me satisfaction. I take music seriously and it allows me to express myself. I made a mess of my life earlier. I chucked away a career at university because I didn't like the school rules. The uniform bit wasn't me. My life has been all escapism." (pg 217, #1)

The Rolling Stones toured Australia from mid-February to early March 1966. On April 6, Keith bought the infamous residence that he still calls home in West Wittering, Sussex, an estate called Redlands. This house would play a pivotal role in the Stones' legacy the following year. Also in April 1966, the Rolling Stones released their album *Aftermath*. This was the first Rolling Stones album with all Jagger-Richards compositions. *Aftermath* went to no. 1 for 11 weeks. (pg 374, #5) The quality songs on this album include "Under My Thumb," "Out of Time," and "Stupid Girl," referring to Mick's relationship with Chrissie Shrimpton. (pg 112, #24) Other gems include "Lady Jane," "Mother's Little Helper," and "What to Do," which would all prove to be among their most solid original creations from their long list of unforgettable albums. However, it was Brian who stepped up, above and beyond the call of duty, on *Aftermath*, playing marimbas (African xylophone) on "Under My Thumb," dulcimer on "Lady Jane," and sitar on "Paint It Black." Jones's friend Phil May describes Brian during the making of the *Aftermath* album, "He was amazing. He could literally play any musical instrument you put in his hands, regardless if he'd ever seen it before. He must be remembered for that." (pg 148, #4) Brian also played lead guitar, rhythm guitar, bells, piano, organ, a baroque-sounding harpsichord, as well as the instruments mentioned above. (pg 148, #4) In fact, Bill Wyman says that Brian wrote the song "Paint it Black," but he is not credited with this on the album. (pg 173, #7) A later track, "Ruby Tuesday," was credited to Jagger and Richards, even though Jones and Richards actually wrote the song. (pg 202, #7) "Ruby Tuesday" was about Keith's girlfriend at the time, Linda Keith. Some attribute this as retaliation for the deal that Brian had cut with Eric Easton and Andrew Oldham in the beginning, which gave Jones an extra five pounds above the pay for the rest of the group.

However, there is no doubt whatsoever that Brian's impact on this album is immense and dominant. According to engineer Glyn Johns, "In the early days, Brian's ability to get a tune out of almost any instrument that was lying around the studio contributed enormously to the variety of sound of the band, playing recorder on Ruby Tuesday, finding marimbas left by a session percussionist and coming up with the part for Under My Thumb that relentlessly drove the song." (pgs 80-81, #26) Even Andrew Oldham, who hated Brian by this point, admitted Brian's contributions on every track of the album. According to Oldham, "It is Brian's marimbas that make Under My Thumb so singular. Brian could pick up any instrument and master it. But with a fragile and volatile personality damaged further by drugs and increasingly triangulated out of power in his own group, his insecurity became acute and he grew deathly paranoid." (pg 90, #2) Oldham adds, "Brian's contributions can be found on every track. You can hear his colour all over the record like Lady Jane, or Paint it Black. In some instances, it was more than a decorative effect. Sometimes Brian pulled the whole thing together." (pg 246, ##17)

Author Richard Havers said, "With Mick and Keith writing the band's material, Brian's role was as a decorator, decorating their records with his innate musical sense, but no longer was he at the heart of the band." (pg 254, #17) On the 1966 tour of America and England, Keith said of Brian's ability, "Mick and I were being merciless on him. The harder the work got, the more awkward Brian got, and the more awkward Brian got, the more fucked up he would get himself when he didn't get his way, until we'd be working three weeks in the [Midwest] with one guitar player, namely me. That was when I learned what the Rolling Stones were all about. You can't cover what you want from the Stones with one guitar." (pg 156, #4) Keith also said, "He barely ever played guitar in the last few years with us. Our whole thing was two guitars and everything else wove around that. And when the other guitarist isn't there half the time, or has lost interest in it, you start getting overdubbing. A lot of those records is me four times." (pg 191, #20) Richards says that he did both guitar parts (rhythm and lead) on both the *December's Children* album and the *Aftermath* album. (pg 192, #20). Yet when Keith's relationship with model Linda Keith had ended, he drifted towards Brian and Anita, eventually moving in with them.

Around the time that Les Perrin, who would later be an influential figure for the band, took over as head of the Stones' public relations. (pg 136, #25) The Stones were supposed to make a film in 1966 called *Only Lovers Left Alive*, but it never happened), which shows that, although the Stones were catching up to the Beatles in popularity, they still couldn't quite match the Beatles' success. (pg 253, #17), In May 1966, Brian and Anita moved in together. (pg 377, #5) This was at the Courtfield Road apartment. Meanwhile, Bill and Diane Wyman had split up in early 1966 (#5), and Bill's next girlfriend was named Astrid Lundström. On June 1, 1966, at Abbey Road Studios, Brian Jones visited the Beatles and helped with their recording of the song "Yellow Submarine," which was to appear on their upcoming album *Revolver*, released in August. Brian clinked glasses for sound effects and sang backing vocals for the chorus. Marianne Faithfull was also at the session, although she wasn't yet Mick Jagger's girlfriend.

In June 1966, the Rolling Stones met Jimi Hendrix in New York City, where he was playing at the time, which began the friendship between Brian and Jimi. Ironically, Jimi was having an affair with Linda Keith, who was still Keith Richards' girlfriend at the time. Jimi tried LSD for the first time in 1966 while in New York, forming a common bond with Brian. The same year, the bass player for the group The Animals, Chas Chandler, became Hendrix's manager and took him to England. Brian Jones said of Jimi, when he played to rock royalty at the Bag O'Nails in London, "It's all wet down in the front. It's wet from all the guitar players crying." (pg 178, #28) Jimi and Brian did, in fact, become good friends, with Brian offering to produce Jimi in the future and introducing him at the Monterey Pop Festival the following year.

Brian's final tour in America came in June and July 1966. (pg 236, #1) There were noticeable changes in Brian after the 1966 American tour, in that he was more reclusive and sullen. Apparently, Mick and Keith weren't even talking to Brian during their 1966 Stones tour with Ike and Tina Turner. (pg 146, #11) Brian immersed himself in self-examination, including escapism.

Brian said of his role in the Rolling Stones, "I can identify myself with the group, but I'm not sure about the image. I'm so contradictory, I have this need for expression, but I'm not sure what it is I want to do." (pg 364, #5) As Brian's intake of LSD grew larger, bandmate Keith Richards said, "Acid to Brian was something different than to your average drug taker. Acid made Brian feel he was one of an elite. Brian saw it as a sort of Congressional Medal of Honor." (pg 192, #20) Richards continued, "Brian on acid was a loose cannon. Either he'd be incredibly funny or he'd be one of those cats that would lead you down the bad road when the good road closes." (pg 205, #20) Brian, Keith, and Anita went to Morocco on holiday with antique dealer Christopher Gibbs on August 28, 1966. There were stories of fighting between Brian and Anita. Brian injured his hand while trying to punch Anita but instead hitting a metal frame. (pg 385, #5) Due to this, Brian was unable to play guitar during the Rolling Stones' appearance on the "Ed Sullivan Show" on September 11, 1966. (pg 254, #17) But Brian was already playing guitar less and less with the Stones, both live and in the studio.

CHAPTER 8

FINALLY, BRIAN WRITES MUSIC OF HIS OWN

Meanwhile, the Beatles took the first three months of 1966 off. George Harrison had developed a keen interest in Indian music, and by then Harrison was becoming a much better songwriter/composer. In fact, on the next Beatles album, released on August 8, 1966 and called *Revolver*, Harrison had three songs that made the final cut. This would be one of, if not *the*, strongest and best of Beatles albums in their catalog. *Revolver* remained at no. 1 on the album charts for 8 weeks (#33). The Beatles played in Hamburg, Germany for the last time in June 1966, then they went to Tokyo, Japan for two shows on June 30. But then disaster struck.

In the Philippines, the Beatles unintentionally snubbed the country's first lady, Imelda Marcos, by not attending a reception at the palace. The Beatles were harassed all the way out of the Philippines, and all the money they had earned from their concert there was taken away from them. It was a very ugly situation. John Lennon received widespread criticism when a newspaper article cited an earlier article by Maureen Cleave, in which Lennon was quoted (despite being taken out of context) as saying he thought the Beatles were bigger than Jesus Christ. Lennon's statement and the backlash from it followed the Beatles on what would be their last-ever tour. So, on August 11, 1966, Lennon went on camera to apologize and try to explain what he actually meant in the context of the conversation.

Then, the Memphis, Tennessee, show was threatened by the Ku Klux Klan, which promised terrorist acts during the Beatles' performance. Thankfully, the Klan only made it as far as the parking lot, and the threatened violence never materialized. The Beatles were scared but still performed the dates that were scheduled. Also in August 1966, the Texas sniper incident took place at the University of Texas, in which 49 people were killed or injured by a crazed killer. By the time the Beatles played the August 29, 1966 show at Candlestick Park in San Francisco, California, they had unanimously decided that they would stop touring altogether and focus solely on making albums.

Meanwhile, the Rolling Stones toured England, Scotland, and Wales in September through October 1966. (pg 244, #1) Ike and Tina Turner would be their opening act, along with the Yardbirds. Brian and Anita were regularly fighting during this time, and Brian had a brief affair with Marianne Faithfull before she became Mick Jagger's permanent girlfriend, following his break-up with Chrissie Shrimpton on December 17, 1966. Keith Richards also had an affair with Faithfull during this time. Jimi Hendrix, too, had an affair with Faithfull, but she would eventually choose Mick Jagger because he had the most money. (pg 76, #21) Shrimpton attempted suicide the day of the break-up.

Ironically, December 17, 1966 was the day of the death of their dear friend and Guinness heir Tara Browne in a car crash, which devastated Brian especially. Browne's girlfriend (and later Brian Jones's girlfriend) Suki Potier survived the car accident. The Beatles would reference Browne's death on their song "A Day in the Life" on their next album, *Sgt. Pepper's Lonely Hearts Club Band.* (pg 77, #21)

At the end of 1966, Brian did write the film music score to the work entitled *Mord und Totshlag*, which is German for "A Degree of Murder." To assist with composing the film music, Brian hired Jimmy Page of the Yardbirds on guitar, later of Led Zeppelin fame, Nicky Hopkins on piano, Peter Gosling on background vocals, and Kenney Jones, later of the group The Faces and Keith Moon's temporary replacement in the Who after Moon's death in 1978, on drums. All the music from the soundtrack to this film was written, produced, and arranged by Brian, with Glyn Johns as the engineer. Here is clear evidence of Brian's ability to write music that had quality. During this recording, Brian played the sitar, organ, recorder, clarinet, dulcimer, harpsichord, autoharp, and harmonica brilliantly and with command over the rest of the music. The film itself starred Anita Pallenberg, who was then Brian's girlfriend, Hans Peter Hallwachs, Manfred Fischbeck, Werner Enke, and Angela Hillebrecht. In this film, Pallenberg's character is violently attacked by her boyfriend, whom she eventually shoots and kills during this struggle. The rest of the film is Pallenberg's character recruiting willing participants at the local pub to help her properly dispose of the body, which they would eventually do after

Pallenberg's character has affairs with two of them. They finally choose a dump site, where the boyfriend's body is buried in a gravel pit by a construction site. The film ends with a forklift discovering the body and transporting it, upside down, to a different location in the construction area, just like another piece of equipment. The film was directed by Volker Schlöndorff. It had similarities, in a surreal avant garde kind of way, to the atmosphere the Beatles created in their film *Magical Mystery Tour* a year later (a film that was misunderstood by critics, who didn't realize that it was intended to be an artful music video, not a proper film as they had done with *A Hard Day's Night* and *Help!*). Although Brian's work was praised for this project, he proved to be unreliable at showing up to the studio or committing to ideas, similar to the criticism of Brian leveled by the Rolling Stones, which would ultimately be his undoing in the very band that he created. (pg 210, #7)

The Stones were having tax problems then, with Klein not properly paying the taxes owed to the UK Internal Revenue Service, and also not paying the band members all they were owed. Instead, Klein paid them in small increments, at a time when repeated calls for help from the band members went mostly ignored by Klein. Furthermore, Jones did the infamous Nazi uniform photo for the West German magazine *Stern* in November 1966. This received widespread criticism from the public, despite Pallenberg encouraging Brian to do this, and he received backlash for it. (pg 54, #8)

Back in the studio, by November 1966, the Stones were cutting tracks that would become their album *Between the Buttons*, which included the songs "Let's Spend the Night Together," "Miss Amanda Jones," "Yesterday's Papers," and "She Smiled Sweetly." 1967 would turn out to be a pivotal year for the Rolling Stones, and the beginning of the end of Brian's role in it. The *Between the Buttons* album was released in January 1967, and the Stones were booked on the "Ed Sullivan Show" to promote it. However, Sullivan put his foot down against the lyrics of the song "Let's Spend the Night Together," instead insisting that the band change the title and their lyrics for the show to "Let's Spend Some Time Together," which they did. Knowing the size of the audience they would be playing to (an estimated 9.25 million people), they wisely went along with the adjustment to promote the song on the wildly popular show. (pg

256, #1) Yet, at a show at the London Palladium later that month, they refused to go out for a final wave with all the other acts, causing a huge fight between the band and Andrew Oldham.

Once Mick Jagger left Chrissie Shrimpton for Marianne Faithfull, Keith started hanging around Brian and Anita more (pg 162, #4), even moving in with them in their Courtfield Road apartment. (pg 404, #5) As far as Brian and Anita's relationship went, "Brian wanted to be the star of the relationship and for Anita to be his chick with a star. It was getting on her." (pg 142, #12)

CHAPTER 9

BUSTED AND THE BREAK-UP
OF BRIAN AND ANITA

On February 5, 1967, an article in the British publication *News of the World*, called "The Secrets of Pop Star Hideaways," wrongly reported Mick Jagger admitting to taking LSD and other drugs, when it was actually Brian Jones they had talked to. Mick Jagger then filed a lawsuit against the newspaper. One week later, on February 12, 1967, a day that would live in infamy in the history of the Rolling Stones, Keith Richards' house at Redlands was raided by the police after a tip from the newspaper *News of the World*. (pg 59, #8) It was thought that David Schneidermann, who was also known as "the Acid King" to those in the Rolling Stones' circle, was the informant to the police from within Keith's house.

Schneidermann himself would disappear from the country to an undisclosed location shortly after the bust. However, according to Keith in his book *Life*, "it was Patrick, my Belgian chauffeur, who sold us out to the *News of the World*, who in turn tipped off the cops who used Schneidermann." (pg 210, #20) Brian and Anita were not there at the moment of the bust, but were planning on going to Keith's house at Redlands later that day. In what can't be a coincidence, Beatle guitarist George Harrison and his then-wife Pattie Boyd had attended the party that day at Redlands, but had just left shortly before the raid, showing that Scotland Yard was after the Rolling Stones and not the Fab Four. The bust was spearheaded by the controversial Detective Sergeant Norman Pilcher, who, in time, would also bust Beatle John Lennon. (pg 407, #5) Also busted in the raid was art dealer Robert Fraser, who was taken into custody for possession of white tablets that turned out to be heroin. Both Mick and Marianne Faithfull, by then Mick's girlfriend, were present in the house during the bust, with Faithfull dressed only in a rug. Jagger was charged for possession of tablets that he claimed help him fight fatigue and that were legally prescribed to him in Italy.

With Jagger, Richards, and Fraser awaiting trial for their

arrests, scheduled for June, Brian, Anita, and Keith decided to get out of town and drive to Morocco in Keith's Bentley, with Tom Keylock at the wheel. Keylock worked for the Rolling Stones full-time at this point, and was a former paratrooper skilled in combat. (pg 146, #25) Along the way, Brian became ill while traveling to Spain on their way to Tangier, and he was hospitalized as a result. (pg 410, #5) The mountain air at the location they were in was very thin, which exacerbated Brian's asthma problems. (pg 146, #25) According to Anita Pallenberg, "It was Brian who suggested that we drive on without him to Tangier, where we should wait for him at the Hotel Minzah. That meant that Keith and I could be alone. By the time we reached Valencia, we could no longer resist each other, and Keith spent the night in my room. In the morning, I realized, as Keith did, that we creating an unmanageable situation, so we pulled back as best we could during the rest of the journey." (pg 172, #4) This began the relationship between Keith and Anita, which would last until 1981. This episode occurred around Brian's 25th birthday on February 28, 1967. Anita's defection to Keith Richards had a cataclysmic effect on Brian and, as a consequence, on the band's future. (pg 427, #5)

According to Keith Richards in his book *Life*, "Brian's relationship with Anita had reached a jealous stalemate when she refused to give up whatever acting works she was doing to fulfill domestic duties as his full-time geisha flatterer and punching bag. Whatever he imagined, including orgies, which Anita always resolutely refused to do." (pg 212, #20) Meanwhile, Brian was sending telegrams to Anita ordering her to come back to the hospital in France and collect him. In an ironic twist of fate, the trip to Morocco with Keith and Anita was Brian's idea. (pg 165, #13) Anita would return to Toulouse to take Brian to London for more medical attention. (pg 216, #20) From there, they flew back to Marrakesh to meet up with the others, including Mick and Marianne.

But Brian returned to his openly misogynistic ways and violently beat up Anita again. This beating was partially due to Anita's refusal to participate in group sex with hookers (pg 411, #5), and occurred before Brian had learned of Keith and Anita's affair. (pg 173, #4) Finally having enough of Brian and his abusive ways, the Stones entourage decided to abandon Brian and return to

London without him, in effect also enabling Anita to break up with Brian—for her new boyfriend Keith Richards—for good. Stones friend Brion Gysin took Brian into the central square, called Djemaa el Fna, in order to distract him with Moroccan music, tea, and souvenir shopping. (pg 265, #1) While Brian was caught off-guard by this calculated maneuver, the others left him by taking a ferry to Málaga, then flying from Madrid to London. They were assisted by Tom Keylock every step of the way. No note, no phone call—just simple and total abandonment by the band and his girlfriend. Brian was apparently suicidal after hearing the news. (pg 149, #4)

Keith and Anita then returned to Keith's flat at St. John's Wood. (pg 220, #20) Brian was quoted to have said after Anita's defection, "They took my music, they took my band, now they've taken my love." (pg 63, #8) According to Marianne Faithfull, "the fact that a member of Brian's own group took Anita away poisoned any real possibility of the Stones ever functioning the way it had before. There was really no chance for Brian to survive in the group after that." (pg 155, #11)

PART ONE: THE LIFE

CHAPTER 10

BRIAN AT MONTERREY

Brian was a broken man, and his drinking habits became much worse. (pg 150, #25) Brian checked himself into the Priory Clinic in Roehampton on March 9, 1967 for depression. (pg 177, #4) From Keith Richards' point of view regarding Anita, he said, "It's been said that I stole her, but my take on it is that I rescued her. Actually, in a way, I rescued him. Both of them, they were on a very destructive course." (pg 221, #20) Keith said of his personal relationship with Brian after that, "He never forgave me. I don't blame him." (pg 221, #20) Anita told Brian, no matter how many times he tried to get her to come back to him, that she would never come back and that their relationship was permanently over. In fact, by the end of 1968, Keith had impregnated Anita. (pg 264, #20) By the time Keith and Anita became a couple, Bill Wyman said, "the band would never be the same again." (pg 266, #1)

But after Brian's stay at the Priory Clinic in Roehampton, the Rolling Stones went back on tour to West Germany, Austria, Italy, Poland, Switzerland, Holland, and Athens, Greece, on April 17, 1967, the band's last stop. This would be Brian's last tour as a member of the Rolling Stones. On this tour, the Stones were subjected to invasive body searches in all nine countries that they performed in, including strip searches. (pg 151, #25) To make matters worse, following Mick and Keith's bust in February, Brian was also arrested, on May 10, 1967 at Brian's Courtfield Road flat, along with his friend Prince Stanislauus Klossowski De Rola, also known as Stash. They were charged with possession of marijuana, cocaine, and methedrine, also known as speed. (pg 164, #24) Stash claims that the police had planted the evidence. (pg 91, #10) Thus, Brian and Stash were charged under the Dangerous Drugs Act of 1965 by the infamous and previously mentioned Detective Sergeant Norman Pilcher. (pg 427, #5) Now Brian, Mick, and Keith were all in serious legal trouble and facing jail time for their infractions of the law, and they were convenient scapegoats for the authorities to punish and make an example of for all of society to witness.

Meanwhile, on June 1, 1967, the Beatles released the album that would widely be regarded as their masterpiece, called *Sgt. Pepper's Lonely Hearts Club Band.* This phenomenal piece of work, from a band who had turned their attention strictly towards studio recording after giving up touring after their 1966 American tour, would remain at no. 1 for an astounding 23 weeks and in the charts for the next three years. (pg 263, #17) Mick Jagger wanted to respond with the Stones' own psychedelic album, which Brian fought hard against behind the scenes, arguing that the Beatles had done something unique and original and that the Stones should instead respond with an R & B album. However, Brian was out voted by the others.

With Brian in so much trouble and in isolation from the Stones, ironically enough, on June 8, 1967, he made history by appearing at the EMI recording studios on Abbey Road and playing an instrument on a Beatles track, the song "You Know My Name (Look Up the Number)." Brian played a saxophone solo on the track that fit perfectly with the arrangement of the melody, and he would claim the prestige of being the only member of the Rolling Stones ever to play an instrument on a Beatles track. Paul McCartney, who invited Brian to the Beatles' session, said of him, "he had a good old sense of humor, I remember laughing and giggling a lot with him." (pg. 244, #7) Towards the end of the month, Brian, Mick, and Keith were in the studio, along with a host of other guests, for the recording of the Beatles song "All You Need Is Love," as they sang along while the band played the song.

While the Beatles were enjoying the fruits of their golden summer, Mick and Keith's trial was set for June 27, 1967, and they were facing serious consequences from their arrests the previous February.

Attorney Michael Havers represented Jagger, Richards, and Fraser. When the trial concluded, Jagger, Richards, and Fraser were found guilty of the crimes being levied against them. Judge Leslie Block sentenced Richards to 12 months' imprisonment at Wormwood Scrubs penitentiary and a 500-pound fine, followed by Fraser's sentence of six months' imprisonment, and concluding with Jagger's sentence of three months' imprisonment and a 100-pound fine. (pg 441, #5) After spending one night in prison, Mick and Keith were freed on bail, but they were not allowed to leave the country. The rock & roll world loudly protested this seemingly harsh and unfair punishment, including their friends in the band the Who, who recorded the Stones songs "Under My Thumb" and "The Last Time" in tribute to the band, with all royalties from the recording being donated to charity. As fate had it, influential newspaper columnist William Rees-Mogg wrote a famous editorial called "Who Breaks a Butterfly on a Wheel?," pointing out that Jagger's and Richards' sentences were unduly harsh for the crimes they were accused of. These protests from the public impacted the prosecutors from the courts, and in July 1967, their sentences were overturned on appeal—except for Fraser's, which was sustained. (pg 454, #5)

In the previous month, Brian had flown to California to attend the Monterey Pop Festival, held June 16-18, 1967. This festival included performances from Otis Redding, the Mamas and the Papas, Jefferson Airplane, the Who, and The Jimi Hendrix Experience. Brian was treated like rock royalty backstage, and he was happy to be there soaking in the California vibe. Brian would go on to introduce his friend Jimi Hendrix to the audience, whom he said was "the most exciting guitar player I've ever heard." Hendrix gave a memorable performance to the crowd at Monterey that night. Ironically, though, Brian's life was falling apart as Hendrix's star was ascending. (pg 91, #10) Yet it was Paul McCartney who helped Hendrix get booked at the festival, and not Brian. During this time, Brian discovered the drug Mandrax, also known as Quaalude. This helped him to blot out reality and sleep. (pg 256, #7) After briefly dating Keith Richards' ex-girlfriend Linda Keith, Brian eventually hooked up with Suki Potier, the girlfriend of his friend Tara Browne, the Guinness heir who died in the car accident in December 1966. Looming in his mind was that now Brian too was in legal peril, like Mick, Keith and Robert Fraser, from when he and Prince Stanislaus Klossowski were arrested by the police at Brian's Courtfield Road flat for marijuana possession on May 10, 1967. (pg 436, #5) According to Stash, "the drug bust that he and I went through was the beginning of the end. Brian went through a catastrophic change during the aftermath of that bust." (pg 91, #10) Brian's trial was scheduled for October 30, 1967.

In August 1967, the Stones went on a brief holiday with their individual families. Towards the end of the month, as Mick Jagger accompanied the Beatles to their meeting with the Maharishi Mahesh Yogi in Wales to focus on exploring meditation practices and new philosophies of living, the horrible news came in on August 27, 1967. The Beatles' manager, Brian Epstein, who was scheduled to join the Beatles in their retreat in Wales, was found dead in his apartment of an accidental drug overdose. He was 32 years old. This event forever changed the course of the Beatles, who would only survive another 2 years and 9 months before breaking up in May 1970. Meanwhile, Andrew Loog Oldham lost his power as the manager of the Rolling Stones. In less than two years, Klein would have both the Rolling Stones and the Beatles as his clients. When Klein convinced John Lennon to permit him to become his manager in March 1969, Ringo Starr and George Harrison followed suit, causing a huge rift between these three Beatles and Paul McCartney, who fought hard against Klein becoming their manager.

When Epstein died, the Rolling Stones were recording the album that would become *Their Satanic Majesties Request*. Earlier in the month of August, the Rolling Stones recorded the song "We Love You" to thank the fans for sticking with them throughout their turbulent legal problems and jail threats, even though Brian still had to face his day in court in October. John Lennon and Paul McCartney helped sing backing vocals on the "We Love You" track.

In court on October 30, Stash's charges were dropped. Brian was charged with possessing marijuana and allowing marijuana to be smoked in his home, along with possession of methedrine and cocaine. Brian pleaded guilty to the marijuana charges, but not guilty to all of the other charges. James Comyn was Brian's attorney. Judge Reginald Ethelbert Seaton sentenced Brian to nine months in jail at Wormwood Scrubs, and he was granted bail the next day, pending his appeal. After 24 hours behind bars, Brian was released from prison.

On December 12, 1967, in the appellate court, Lord Chief Justice Parker and two other law lords granted Brian a lighter sentence of three years' probation, with regular medical treatment and a 1,000-pound fine. (pg 299, #1) Brian was warned by Judge Seaton that he would be sent to prison if he failed probation. (pg 167, #25) Brian was relieved, after being suicidal at the thought of going to prison for almost a year, but was also still alienated from Mick and Keith during this time, due to their legal troubles and his being advised by his attorney to stay away from the two.

Yet from May to October, the Stones were well at work on *Their Satanic Majesties Request*, which was seemingly heavily influenced by the Beatles' *Sgt. Pepper* album, released earlier in June 1967. I have read many books and articles in researching this project, and the majority of them are rather harsh and critical of this particular Stones album. In direct comparison to *Sgt. Pepper* or the Beatles' previous or subsequent albums (*Revolver* and *Magical Mystery Tour*), the album *Their Satanic Majesties Request* is not as good. However, it does have some strong tracks on it, including "Citadel," "She's a Rainbow," "2000 Man," Bill Wyman's composition "In Another Land," with Wyman on vocals, and the legendary psychedelic track "2000 Light Years From Home," with Brian Jones playing the Mellotron. These tracks, along with the flow of the album in general, give it life and meaning, but also show the tolls that law enforcement harassment and the subsequent busts of Mick, Keith, and Brian had taken on the band. While the Beatles had been left alone (for the time being) by law enforcement, the Rolling Stones had suffered a tough year in which they were dealing with serious legal issues that threatened both the existence of the band and the very freedom of Mick, Keith, and Brian. Some of their critics harshly reviewed the new album, but it did reflect the strain of the individual turmoil of the band's members.

The Beatles would soon face similar criticism with the release of their *Magical Mystery Tour* film on the BBC the day after Christmas in 1967, also known as Boxing Day in England. This was a film they made and directed themselves shortly after the death of their manager, Brian Epstein. This film was universally criticized by the press as too weird and not well written, but the Beatles were attempting to make a more artsy, abstract film as opposed to a "proper" or straightforward film, as they had done before. The Beatles would face more struggles in the coming year with the creation of their own company, Apple Corps, and the challenges that came without an official manager to represent them. But the album *Magical Mystery Tour* was a solid effort and a memorable album that included "I Am the Walrus," "The Fool on the Hill," and four no. 1 singles, plus a fifth song on the second side of the album, which gave it great strength compared to the Rolling Stones album *Their Satanic Majesties Request*. In fairness to *Their Satanic*

Majesties Request, it did make it to no. 2 on the Billboard charts and went gold. (pg 476, #5) According to Nicholas Fitzgerald, in his book *Brian Jones: The Inside Story of the Original Rolling Stone*, Brian held the slimmest of hopes that the failure of *Their Satanic Majesties Request* would convince Mick to change direction and listen to him. (pg 221, #31)

CHAPTER 11

BRIAN PRODUCES MOROCCAN MUSIC, AND HIS FINAL STONES PERFORMANCE

In 1968, the Rolling Stones partnered with producer Jimmy Miller to create what would become one of their best albums, *Beggars Banquet*. This was released late in 1968 and featured a return to a more rock & roll/R & B sound. The song "Jumpin' Jack Flash" was written and recorded during the months of March and April 1968, and it was about Keith's gardener. It was a huge success for the Stones and went to no. 1. They played it live at the *NME* Poll Winner's concert in Wembley to great success.

But trouble was once again brewing for Brian Jones when, on May 20, 1968, he was again busted by the police when they raided his flat with a search warrant. Initially, Brian didn't answer the door when the police knocked, but they still found their way inside. When asked by the police why he didn't answer the door, after approximately 10 minutes of knocking, Brian responded, "You know the scene man, why do I always get busted?." (pg 304, #1) During the search, police found a ball of blue wool that contained 44 grams of hashish resin. (pg 175, #25) This arrest put Brian in serious legal jeopardy of failing the probation imposed on him by Judge Seaton the previous year. Even Mick and Keith were sympathetic to Brian's situation, with Keith giving Brian a place to stay at Redlands. (pg 305, #1) In fact, it has been documented that Brian was in a state of perpetual breakdown from the years 1967 to 1968. (pg 170, #18)

In early 1968, Brian and engineer Glyn Johns returned to Marrakesh, Morocco to record the G'Naouva with the Master Musicians of Jajouka. (pg 168, #25) The G'Naouva people were a religious fraternity from Sudan. Brian's idea was to record these musicians and have African-American soul musicians overdub them. Brian loved Jajoukan music, and he is credited by the Jajoukan people for bringing their music to the general public with the eventual release of the *Pipes of Pan at Jajouka* album in 1971, two years after Brian's death. Glyn Johns said of Brian, "For me,

Brian, as a person, was an asshole but I really respected him as a musician. I went off to Morocco with him and taped the G'Naouva. Brian's idea was to take the tapes back to New York and use black musicians along with it. It was a clever idea, but in the end, nothing came of it." (pg 209, #4) Brian discovered the G'Naouva musicians in the market square in Marrakesh during his initial visit in 1966. Despite Glyn Johns' cooperation and interest in Brian's foray into Jajoukan music, newly installed producer Jimmy Miller was not enthusiastic about it, despite Brian wanting to make the Jajoukan music more mainstream. (pg 209, #4) Even Glyn Johns claims that his relationship with Brian was strained, and says that Brian only had himself to blame for his problems. (pg 86, #26)

Meanwhile, the Rolling Stones were back to work, at Olympic Studios, on their next album, which was a back-to-the-roots album of R & B. (pg 275, #7) Jimmy Miller was firmly in control of the recording studio, having been recruited by Mick and Keith. The album that became *Beggars Banquet* was created without any input from Brian. However, Brian did play brilliantly on the track "No Expectations" on his slide guitar.

Jimmy Miller had once been a writing partner of Parliament-Funkadelic creator George Clinton, who said of Miller at the time, "I was happy to see that Jimmy was working with them, but it also changed my perception of the Stones. It proved to me, as much as anything else, that they were serious about rooting their music in American sounds." (pg 49, #29) According to Miller, by this point, Brian only showed up to practice when he felt like it. (pg 157, #11) According to Mick Jagger, Brian rarely showed up to practice during the *Beggars Banquet* sessions. "Brian wasn't really involved on *Beggars Banquet*, apart from some slide guitar on 'No Expectations.' That was the only thing he played on the whole record. He wasn't turning up to the sessions and he wasn't very well. In fact, we didn't want him to turn up, I don't think." (pg. 131, #10) It was clear to everyone that Mick Jagger and Keith Richards had taken full artistic control of the band at this point, and Brian's days as a member of the band he created were truly numbered. However, Brian did contribute to the song "Street Fighting Man" by playing sitar and a tamboura, which is a Turkish instrument for making a drone sound that's similar to a lute. (pg 141, #2) Nicky Hopkins played piano on that song. However, it was Mick and Keith who were in firm control of the songs being created for the album. For example, the song "Sympathy for the Devil" was based on the Russian novel *The Master and Margarita*, written by Mikhail Bulgakov, a book Marianne had left for Mick to read. (pgs 290-291, #7)

Pat Andrews, former girlfriend and mother of Brian's child Julian Mark, said of Brian by mid-1968, "by now he was surrounded by people who were with him for all of the wrong reasons. They wanted something from him, to bask in his limelight. He was aware of the falseness, I'm sure, and that would've hurt, I knew him. He'd have seen through them instantly. But what could he do? That was his life by then." (pg 183, #25) Meanwhile, his relationship with his then-girlfriend Suki Potier was becoming violent and destructive. According to Potier, "Brian was the only woman that he ever really loved." (pg 9, #18) It is said that Brian was most attracted to women who looked like him. In August 1968, when Brian was on the balcony of his Marrakesh hotel, he collapsed and blacked out. Potier stated that this was a common occurrence with Brian. (pg 308, #1) While on this trip, Brian beat Potier very badly, to the point that she required hospitalization. (pg 107, #14)

Brian would have his day in court, again, on September 25, 1968, where he faced his second marijuana possession charge, again facing Judge Reginald Seaton. Brian was convicted of possession of marijuana in his flat, but was only fined 50 pounds, with 150 pounds in court costs, and was spared jail time by the court. His probation, however, was extended past the point of his original sentence. Brian said after the trial, "It's great not to be in jail. I was sure that I was going to jail for at least a year. I never expected that I'd be going home, it was such a wonderful relief. This summer has been one long worry for me. I knew I was innocent, but everything seems to happen to me." (pg 83, #30) The problem now was that this second conviction prevented him from touring the United States with the Rolling Stones, which would be one of the major reasons for his departure from the band during the following year. Mick, Keith, and Suki Potier were with Brian in court that day, showing support and band solidarity.

Now that Brian was spared jail, the Rolling Stones had an album to promote: *Beggars Banquet* was released to the public on December 5, 1968. Meanwhile, Mick was working on his acting skills, starring in the film *Performance*, also starring Keith's girlfriend (and formerly Brian's girlfriend) Anita Pallenberg. By this point, according to author Bill Janovitz, "It tore Brian up to watch his role as band leader and, in his mind, leader diminish as Mick and Keith's star rose, with their bank accounts rising along with them. His insecurities about his role in the group and easy access to drugs proved to be a lethal combination. The Stones were past the point of fighting with Brian, who could be found more often than not lying on the floor in a stupor." (pgs 110-111, #2) Tony King says of Brian, "Brian was a cunt, very difficult for anybody to get on with. A fallen angel, with a golden halo surrounding an angelic face, but the soul of a devil." (pg 249, #15)

To escape the pressures and the hassle of city life, from both fans and police in London, Brian decided to buy a house in the country for more privacy and peace of mind. On November 21, 1968, Brian bought Cotchford Farm in East Sussex, which happened to be the former house of author A.A. Milne, who wrote the book *Winnie-the- Pooh*. The family that lived at Cotchford Farm before Brian was the Taylors, who succeeded the Milne family (pg 192, #25). In fact, William the Conqueror himself once lived at Cotchford Farm. (pg 309, #1) Brian purchased the property for 35,000 pounds. (pg 113, #14) This house came equipped with many references to Winnie the Pooh, including a statue of Milne's son Christopher Robin. However, the house was badly in need of repairs. Therefore, to help with renovations of Cotchford Farm, Brian hired Frank Thorogood, via Tom Keylock, for this job. Thorogood had previously worked on Keith Richards' house at Redlands and photographer David Bailey's house. It is interesting to note that both Richards and Bailey complained of Thorogood's work and exorbitant pricing, just as Brian would soon do. (pg 93, #8) Thorogood was technically an employee of Rolling Stones Inc., and therefore could not be fired by Brian, but only by the company. (pg 229, #4) Thorogood was said to be very much in control of Brian's life during his last year. (pg 108, #8) Thorogood was reported to have hired three people to assist him with the renovations at Cotchford Farm, whose names are only known as Mo, Johnny, and David. (pg 114, #14) Mary Hallett was the lady who stayed at Cotchford Farm to assist the owner with chores and such. She was born at Cotchford Farm in 1911, and also worked for the Taylor family and A.A. Milne's family before Brian moved in, so Brian continued to employ her at the property. (pg. 199, #25) Ironically, it was Brian who was the last Rolling Stones member to buy a house. (pg 113, #14)

The Stones' bodyguards and chauffeurs were considered thugs from London's East End. This was to give the Rolling Stones a harder edge. Keith Richards had good relations with them, but Brian didn't. These thugs earned the infamous title of being the "Stones Mafia." (pg 114, #8) During this time, Brian was described as unhappy, and he always thought that people were following him and out to get him, which are signs of the mental trauma and strain Brian endured from his drug busts and convictions. When the launch party for the album *Beggars Banquet* took place, on December 5, 1968, it seemed that Brian was only there for his promotional duties as an official member of the band; in reality, he had little to do with the creation of this album. The Stones themselves were still having problems obtaining any money from their manager Allen Klein, who, in truth, was spending their fortune on himself. Also around this time, Mick Jagger and his girlfriend Marianne Faithfull experienced the tragedy of a miscarriage while Faithfull was 7 months' pregnant. At the launch party, Mick Jagger threw a meringue pie in Brian's face, which started a food fight between all guests in attendance.

Still, the album had been very well received, and the Rolling Stones were ready to go out and promote it. They decided on having a variety show in which they would be the headliners, called "The Rolling Stones Rock and Roll Circus," to promote the material from the new album. The show included guest performances from Jethro Tull, the Who, Taj Mahal, Marianne Faithfull, and John Lennon and Yoko Ono (with their newly formed band called The Dirty Mac, featuring Eric Clapton, Mitch Mitchell, Keith Richards, and Ivry Gitlis). The show was filmed on December 11 and 12, 1968 in London, and ended up including 14 hours of filming that would eventually be condensed to a show of a little over an hour. According to author Howard Sounes, Brian had telephoned the director of the show, Michael Lindsay-Hogg, crying the night before the recording, saying that the Stones were being horrid to him and that he didn't want to appear in the film. Jones appeared overweight, strung out, and very much in decline to Lindsay-Hogg, who was concerned for Jones' well-being at the time.

According to Lindsay-Hogg, "He changed. I first met him on 'Ready, Steady, Go' in April of 1965, when he was still himself. But he had become a very different person in only three years. His looks were shot. And he just seemed to be fading as a person, unlike Mick and Keith, who were coming into their own at the time. They'd all become very famous, and they were still very young, but they had had life experiences at that point which often people in their 50's and 60's had never had. Mick and Keith were talented and tough, with great will power, and Brian had none of those things to the degree the other two had." (pgs 131-132, #10)

Nonetheless, Brian appeared in the Rolling Stones portion of the show in what would prove to be his last concert appearance with the band. The show begins with all of the circus performers coming out first, followed by the Rolling Stones, followed by John and Yoko, the Who, Eric Clapton, and Marianne Faithfull. Mick Jagger introduces the show, and is one of only three Rolling Stone members with a speaking role in this performance. Brian is not one of them.

The show proceeds with Jethro Tull performing "A Song for Jeffrey," with Tony Iommi (of later Black Sabbath and Heaven & Hell fame) on guitar. Next came the Who, delivering a masterful performance of their song and self- described mini-opera, "A Quick One, While He's Away," which may have been the most standout performance of the entire show. They would be followed by the group Taj Mahal, with their version of "Ain't That a Lot of Love," followed by Marianne Faithfull's performance of the song "Something Better." Following Faithfull's performance was John Lennon's band for the evening, the Dirty Mac, which gave a spectacular performance of the Beatles song "Yer Blues," and marked Lennon's first performance on a stage before an audience since the Beatles' last live performance, at Candlestick Park in San Francisco on August 29, 1966. Ironically, Lennon performed this song with his band the Dirty Mac less than three weeks after the Beatles had released their self-titled double album, also known as the *White Album*, which he had refused to play live with the Beatles after a very tense recording session. Next, the Dirty Mac played the song "A Whole Lotta Yoko" with Ono on lead vocals and with violinist Ivry Gitlis. Finally, the hosts came out, playing songs from their newly released album and other new material, including "Jumpin' Jack Flash," "Parachute Woman," "No Expectations," "You Can't Always Get What You Want," "Sympathy for the Devil," and "Salt of the Earth." Although the Stones performance is masterful, it is clear that Brian was falling behind the others, reduced to shaking maracas during the song "Sympathy for the Devil" when a second guitarist would have been more preferable, due to the complexity of the song.

It was clear by this point that Brian's star was fading in the band, and the other band members were fed up with his situation by then. While the band wanted to tour America to support their new album, Brian could not get a visa to do so because of his two previous drug convictions in 1967 and 1968. (pg 191, #25) Mick Jagger very much wanted to tour America, but he knew the sad reality was that Brian needed to be officially removed from the Rolling Stones because of "his drunkenness, drugginess, and terrible vulnerability to police raids." (pg 303, #6) Brian, by now, was heavily abusing the drug Mandrax, or Quaalude, and feared that he would be thrown out of the Rolling Stones and be replaced by Eric Clapton of the recently defunct band Cream. The Stones felt they had to tour, due to the financial crisis facing each member of the band thanks to the mismanagement of Klein, who was not properly paying them, their tax accountants, and their unpaid bills. In an ironic twist of fate, John Lennon met Klein during his performance on the "Rock and Roll Circus," and would eventually convince three of the Beatles to sign with Klein in 1969, with only Paul McCartney refusing. Just as Klein himself had predicted, he would manage the two supergroups, the Beatles and the Rolling Stones, at the same time, albeit briefly. The Rolling Stones were not happy that Klein had also become the Beatles manager.

When the Rolling Stones got together in February 1969 for the recording sessions of what was to become the *Let it Bleed* album, Brian was still turning up for practice, but his contributions were few. Jones did play percussion on the song "Midnight Rambler," and autoharp on the song "You Got the Silver," but that would be it for Brian's role on that album. It was time for the Rolling Stones to actively seek out Brian's replacement in the band. In a huge twist of irony, Mick Jagger actually reached out to the person who would eventually become the other permanent guitarist of the band,

Ronnie Wood, who was then the guitarist of the band the Small Faces, after his work in the bands the Birds and the Jeff Beck Group.

However, in the days before texting, e-mails, or answering machines, Jagger's call was answered by Ronnie Lane, who informed Jagger that Ronnie Wood would not be interested in this offer, as he was already committed to the Small Faces, without Wood ever receiving the offer from Jagger. (pg 84, #19) Wood would officially join the Rolling Stones in 1975. Therefore Jagger approached 20-year-old Mick Taylor, who was the guitarist in John Mayall's Bluesbreakers, to see if he would be interested in taking the spot, to which he agreed. It was Ian Stewart, who was never a fan of Brian, who suggested Taylor should replace Jones so that they could tour America. (pg 291, #17) By then, Brian was described as dead weight, a nuisance, and an albatross within his own band. By May 31, 1969, Mick Taylor was officially recording tracks at Olympic Studios, including his first tracks with the band, "Honky Tonk Woman" and "Live With Me." At this point, it appeared clear that the band had to inform Brian that he was being removed from the Rolling Stones.

CHAPTER 12

BRIAN'S STAR FADES AWAY AT COTCHFORD FARM

On June 8, 1969, Mick, Keith, and Charlie Watts drove to Cotchford Farm to meet with Brian to tell him the news that he was fired from the band. He was offered 100,000 pounds outright, with yearly annuities of 20,000 pounds for as long as he lived. By this time, Brian had stopped dating Suki Potier and begun dating Swedish model/student Anna Wohlin, who was 22 years old. Though he was dismissed from the band, Jones put out a statement saying that he was leaving the Rolling Stones, partly because they became a rock & roll band and not the rhythm & blues band that Brian had conceived them to be.

Brian said, "I no longer see eye to eye with the others over the disks we are cutting. We no longer communicate musically. The Stones music is not to my taste anymore. I have a desire to play my own brand of music rather than that of the others. No matter how much I appreciate their musical concepts, the only solution is to go our separate ways, but we shall remain friends. I love those fellows." (pg 326, #1) Ex- girlfriend Linda Lawrence was glad that Brian had left the Stones and was hoping that they could spend more time together with their son, Julian. Sadly, this was not meant to be. For the last 3 1/2 weeks of Brian 's life, he spent time at Cotchford Farm with his live- in girlfriend Anna Wohlin and builder Frank Thorogood, who also lived in a separate apartment on Brian's property with his girlfriend, nurse Janet Lawson. (pg 198, #12) Brian lacked the ability to be close to anyone, and he was in social isolation. According to author Jeremy Reed, "one could say that Brian journeyed home to childhood in order to die." (pg 73, #18)

Brian had reunited with his former mentor, Alexis Korner, in hopes of getting another band together, with the likes of possibly John Lennon and Jimi Hendrix being involved. Meanwhile, the first show the Stones played with Mick Taylor on television was "The David Frost Show" on June 16, 1969. (pg 291, #17) It was reported that John Lennon avoided Brian's phone calls by then because he knew that meant trouble. (pg 9, #31) Jones had become a big fan of the American group Creedence Clearwater Revival, and wanted to make music similar to theirs. Brian was also interested in creating a new type of music with the Master Musicians of Jajouka from Morocco. (pg 49, #32) Brian seemed happier since his departure from the Rolling Stones, and was speaking optimistically about his future.

Although Jones and Korner had not spoken during the height of the Rolling Stones' years on top of the music charts, Alexis and Brian were very happy to have found each other in Brian's final weeks on Earth. Brian had expressed a desire to reunite with his sons Julian and (Julian) Mark in the years ahead to make up for his absence in their lives. (pg 60, #32) Brian also wanted to repair the relationship with his dad.

Brian had expressed his desire to marry Anna and have children with her. (pg. 164, #32) According to Anna, "Brian was a complex personality. He was irresistibly charming, kind-hearted, cheerful, amusing, funny, curious, energetic, and moral, but also cynical, wicked, annoying, lazy, weak, nervous, restless, aggressive, and menacing. He was a dreamer and a seeker." (pg 11, #32) Also according to Anna, "he was impulsive and unpredictable. That was one of the reasons why I didn't take Brian's talk about marriage and children too seriously." (pg 164, #32) Apparently, Brian wanted to name their daughter Johanna, which may have been inspired by the Bob Dylan song "Visions of Johanna" on his brilliant 1966 album *Blonde on Blonde*.

Brian once said that he wanted to be in the greatest rock & roll band in the world, but he hadn't considered what the consequences would be. (pg 115, #32) Brian still complained of Anita Pallenberg's betrayal when she left him for Keith. Even so, Brian and Anna were actually planning on going to the free Rolling Stones concert scheduled for July 5, 1969 in Hyde Park. As far as Frank Thorogood's work on Brian's Cotchford Farm house, Brian was very unhappy with it, or the lack of it, and it seemed that Thorogood and his men were more interested in partying with Brian's liquor and with girls they were having affairs with than doing the actual work that they were paid to do. Brian wanted to fire Frank for his sloppy and time-consuming work. Jones kept in touch with Keith Richards after he left the band about this problem, and Keith told Brian that he didn't like Thorogood, either. (pg 181, #32)

By July 1, 1969, the pollen count at Cotchford Farm was listed at 335, which was very high for asthma sufferers. Although Brian was talking optimistically about new groups he'd like to be in, he knew they would not have the same success as the Stones. At this particularly vulnerable point in Brian's life, "it should be remembered that Brian had been living dangerously for years, flirting with death on a daily basis through reckless use of drink and drugs." (pg 167, #10)

On the morning of July 2, 1969, Brian was feeling the effects of the very high pollen count, and had his inhalers stationed at spots around his house and pool should he need them. According to Mary Hallett, who last saw Brian alive that morning, "I didn't see much of Brian that morning, just really the once when he did his best to tell me that he had people arriving who would be staying the night. It was hard to understand what he was saying. That was the last time I saw Brian. I left around 1 pm, but I never dreamt that last time we spoke that anything like that would happen." (pg 207, #25) There were reports that Brian had been drinking all day as well as using the drugs Tuinal and Mandrax. (pg 205, #13) This is contradicted by Anna Wohlin's report that Brian had been sober that day, and was in bed when Thorogood and Lawson showed up to the home around 10:00 pm. Despite Brian vehemently telling his girlfriend Anna that he was going to fire Thorogood for his shoddy and incomplete work, Brian decided to have some drinks with Thorogood and Lawson that night, which eventually turned into an invitation to go for a swim in the pool. It was claimed that Jones had consumed approximately 6 or 7 brandies that night with Thorogood and Lawson, yet the toxicology report from the autopsy would mildly contradict those numbers. Lawson and Thorogood noticed Brian walking unsteadily on his feet while on the diving board, and Lawson claims that she told both Thorogood and Jones that they shouldn't be swimming under those circumstances—but her protests were disregarded by both Jones and Thorogood. Brian's inhaler was found by the side of the pool that evening. According to Wohlin, she claims that Brian and Frank were in the pool together, teasing and dunking each other under the water in a hostile way. Wohlin left the pool to receive a phone call in the house from Sweden, according to Janet Lawson, who had also left to go inside, leaving Brian and Frank alone in the pool. These are the moments when things become murky that evening.

A couple of days prior, a beam from the ceiling that Thorogood and his men installed in the kitchen collapsed, nearly killing Anna, who was standing nearby. (pg 178, #32) Brian angrily fired Frank for this on the phone, but still hadn't completely gotten rid of him by the evening of July 2.

Meanwhile, Anna's phone call that she went in to answer was a dead line. Minutes later, the phone rang again and it was Anna's friend Terry from London. (pg 193, #32) After approximately 10 minutes, Wohlin says that Janet Lawson called her from downstairs, saying something was wrong with Brian. According to Wohlin, Thorogood was in the kitchen smoking a cigarette. Wohlin claims that she discovered Brian lying spread eagle at the bottom of the pool. Wohlin says that she dove into the pool to pull Brian out of the water, and said that she had to ask Thorogood several times for help in getting Brian out of the pool. (pg 194, #32) Janet Lawson claimed to be in the music room when Brian drowned.

When the ambulance arrived shortly after midnight at Cotchford Farm on the morning of July 3, 1969, Brian Jones, aka Elmo Lewis, was pronounced dead. He was 27 years old.

BIBLIOGRAPHY

1. *Rolling with the Stones*, by Bill Wyman (with Richard Haver). New York, NY: DK Publishing, 2002.

2. *Rocks Off: 50 Tracks That Tell the Story of the Rolling Stones*, by BIll Janovitz. New York, NY: St. Martin's Press, 2014.

3. *No Quarter: The Three Lives of Jimmy Page*, by Martin Power. New York, NY: Overlook Omnibus Books, 2016.

4. *Brian Jones: The Untold Life and Mysterious Death of a Rock Legend*, by Laura Jackson. London, UK: Little, Brown, 1992, 2009.

5. *Stone Alone*, by Bill Wyman (with Ray Coleman). New York, NY: Viking Penguin, 1990.

6. *Mick Jagger*, by Phillip Norman. New York, NY: HarperCollins/Jessica Productions, 2012.

7. *Brian Jones: The Making of the Rolling Stones*, by Paul Trynka. New York, NY: Penguin/Random House, 2014.

8. *Paint It Black: The Murder of Brian Jones*, by Geoffrey Giuliano. London, UK: Virgin Books, 1994.

9. *Bill Wyman's Blues Odyssey: A Journey to Music's Heart and Soul*, by Bill Wyman (with Rich Havers). New York, NY: DK Publishing, 2001.

10. *27: A History of the 27 Club Through the Lives of Brian Jones, Jimi Hendrix, Janis Joplin, Jim Morrison, Kurt Cobain and Amy Winehouse*, by Howard Sounes. Boston, MA: De Capo Press, 2013.

11. *Brian Jones*, by Alan Clayson. London, UK: Sanctuary Publishing, 2003.

12. *Death of a Rolling Stone: The Brian Jones Story*, by Mandy Afeto. London, UK: Sidgwick & Jackson, 1982.

13. *The Sun & the Moon & the Rolling Stones*, by Rich Cohen. (New York, NY: Spiegel + Grau, 2016.

14. *Who Killed Christopher Robin? The Murder of a Rolling Stone*, by Terry Rawlings. London, UK: Helter Skelter Publications, 1994, 2005.

15. *Stoned: A Memoir of London in the 1960s*, by Andrew Loog Oldham; interviews and research by Simon Dudfield; edited by Ron Ross. New York, NY: St. Martin's Press, 2000.

16. *25 x 5: The Continuing Adventures of the Rolling Stones* (VHS tape, 130 minutes). New York, NY: CBS Music Video Enterprises, 1989.

17. *The Rolling Stones: On Air in the Sixties, TV, and Radio History as It Happened*, by Richard Havers. New York, NY: HarperCollins, 2017.

18. *Brian Jones: The Last Decadent*, by Jeremy Reed. London, UK: Creation Books, 1999.

19. *Ronnie*, by Ronnie Wood. (London, UK: Macmillan, 2007.

20. *Life*, by Keith Richards (with James Fox). New York, NY: Little, Brown, 2010.

21. *Mick: The Wild Life and Mad Genius of Jagger*, by Christopher Andersen. New York, NY: Gallery Books, 2012.

22. *John Lennon*, by Phillip Norman. New York, NY: HarperCollins, 2008.

23. *John*, by Cynthia Lennon. New York, NY: Crown Publishing, 2005.

24. *Beatles vs. Stones*, by John McMillian. New York, NY: Simon & Schuster, 2013.

25. *Golden Stone: The Untold Life and Tragic Death of Brian Jones*, by Laura Jackson. New York, NY: St. Martin's Press, 1992.

26. *Sound Man: A Life Recording Hits with the Rolling Stones, The Who, Led Zeppelin, The Eagles, Eric Clapton, the Faces ...*, by Glyn Johns. New York, NY: Blue Rider Press, 2014.

27. *Allen Klein: The Man Who Bailed Out the Beatles, Made the Stones, and Transformed Rock & Roll*, by Fred Goodman. New York, NY: Houghton Mifflin Harcourt, 2015.

28. *Room Full of Mirrors: A Biography of Jimi Hendrix*, by Charles R. Cross. New York, NY: Hyperion Press, 2005.

29. *Brothers Be, Yo Like George, Ain't That Funkin' Kinda Hard on You? A Memoir*, by George Clinton (with Ben Greenman). New York, NY: Atria Books, 2014.

30. *The Rolling Stones Chronicle: The First Thirty Years*, by Massimo Bonanno. New York, NY: Henry Holt, 1990.

31. *Brian Jones: The Inside Story of the Original Rolling Stone*, by Nicholas Fitzgerald. New York, NY: Putnam, 1985.

32. *The Murder of Brian Jones: The Secret Story of My Love Affair with the Murdered Rolling Stone*, by Anna Wohlin and Christine Lindsjoo. London, UK: Blake Publishing, 1999.

33. *Eight Days a Week: The Touring Years* (97 minutes). London, UK: Apple Corps; 2016.

34. *Charlie Is My Darling* (64 minutes). Mannheim and Heidelberg, Germany: International Filmfestival Mannheim-Heidelberg; 1966.

PART ONE: THE LIFE

PART TWO
THE AFTERMATH

PART TWO: THE AFTERMATH

CHAPTER 13

THE AFTERMATH OF BRIAN'S DEATH

WAS BRIAN MURDERED?

Shortly after midnight on the morning of July 3, 1969, Brian Jones's 27-year, 4- month, and 3-day life had officially come to an end. The band that he was responsible for creating was informed that night, at Olympic Studios, of Brian's death, and its members were shocked and deeply saddened by the news. The decision was made by the band to proceed with performing the concert at Hyde Park in London that was already scheduled for July 5, in order to introduce Jones's replacement in the Rolling Stones, Mick Taylor. Initially, both bass player Bill Wyman and drummer Charlie Watts had suggested canceling the show, but both Mick Jagger and Keith Richards disagreed with that notion. It was agreed by all members of the band that the concert at Hyde Park was to be dedicated to Brian Jones, and so it was. It is tragically ironic that Brian was initially scheduled to be at the show, with girlfriend Anna Wohlin in the audience, in an effort to show solidarity with his former bandmates. Sadly, fate would deny Jones that opportunity. The free Hyde Park show attracted approximately 250,000 to 500,000 attendees.

When the police arrived at Cotchford Farm the night Brian died, police constable Albert Evans reported finding a small bottle of brandy that was four fifths consumed, a bottle of vodka two thirds consumed, and a small bottle of whisky half consumed. (pg 160, #1) During Brian's autopsy, which was conducted by Dr. Albert Sachs, it was discovered that Brian had been suffering from severe liver dysfunction: his liver was twice the size and mass of what it should have been for someone of his age and weight. Brian's inhaler was found by the side of the pool at Cotchford Farm the night Brian died.

In her book *The Murder of Brian Jones: The Secret Story of My Love Affair with the Murdered Rolling Stone,* (#2) Brian's then-girlfriend Anna Wohlin blamed herself for deciding to leave the pool area that night to go inside the house to answer a phone call. Brian died mere minutes later. Despite Wohlin's initial testimony shortly after the incident, in which she stated that Brian's drowning in his pool was accidental due to his asthma and drinking/drug-related activities that night, she now says that she is convinced that Frank Thorogood—whom Brian had just fired based on his expensive and shoddy work at Cotchford Farm—finally snapped and killed Brian when the chance arose. It happened when both Wohlin and Janet Lawson left the pool to enter the house, leaving Thorogood and Jones alone in the pool, with no witnesses.

Lawson later testified in the inquiry regarding Brian's death that she felt that both men were too intoxicated to be swimming, and she told them so, but her concerns were ignored by both men. When Lawson left the pool to go in the house, only Jones and Thorogood remained in the pool, and they then reportedly engaged in a "dunking contest" with each other.

According to Wohlin, "there was no doubt in my mind, Frank had killed Brian. He finally lost his self-control." (pg 203, #2) Wohlin continues, "I was convinced that Brian's death was due to foul play. There is no way that my beloved Brian, who was like a fish in the water, could have drowned, and in my confused state, I was scared of being the next victim." (pg 197, #2) Wohlin said that Thorogood was shaking and nervous when he entered the house and lit a cigarette in the kitchen, leaving Brian by himself in the pool. When Brian's body was discovered by Lawson and Wohlin at the bottom of the swimming pool, Thorogood was reportedly reluctant to help them pull Brian's body from the pool. (pg 203, #2)

However, because Wohlin didn't actually see Frank Thorogood killing Brian Jones in his pool, and Thorogood emphatically denied such an act (instead claiming that Brian had drowned on his own after Thorogood left the pool to have a cigarette), ultimately, no one was charged with murder that night. At the formal hearing on July 7, 1969 in East Grimstead, U.K., it was ruled that Brian Jones's death was caused by a combination of an asthma attack and an overdose of alcohol and drugs. It is interesting to note that the police did discuss arresting and charging Thorogood with manslaughter in the death of Brian Jones, but it was never pursued by law enforcement.

When Rolling Stones tour managers Tom Keylock and Les

Parrin arrived at Cotchford Farm after Brian had died, it was agreed that Anna Wohlin should be relocated immediately. Keylock recruited the assistance of Rolling Stones Inc. assistant Joan Fitzsimmons to transport Wohlin to Rolling Stones bass guitarist Bill Wyman's house, where he lived with his then-girlfriend Astrid Lundström, for a couple of days while the arrangements for Brian's funeral were being made. It is reported by Wohlin that though Bill Wyman, Astrid Lundström, and Charlie Watts showed kindness and sympathy to her during her time of grief immediately following Brian's death, the other members of the Stones didn't. (pg 318, #2) Tom Keylock blamed Brian's death on drugs and alcohol abuse and further believed that Keith Richards was a tougher man than Brian, which explains why he survived his bouts with drugs and Jones didn't. (pg 165, #1)

In a book written by Nicholas Fitzgerald, who was a close friend of Brian's and heir to the Guinness beer fortune, called *Brian Jones: The Inside Story of the Original Rolling Stone,* (#3) he claims that he drove that night to Cotchford Farm to check on Brian with his friend Richard Cadbury. Fitzgerald was concerned after he claims to have called Brian earlier that night. The person who answered failed to put Brian on the phone, and Fitzgerald could hear what sounded like a party or a smaller gathering. Fitzgerald also claims that Brian's ex-girlfriend, Suki Potier, advised him to check on Brian. Fitzgerald states in his book that when he and Cadbury arrived at Cotchford Farm at around 11:15 pm and got out of the car, he saw three people apparently holding someone— resembling Jones—down under the water, while a man and a woman were out of the pool looking on at a short distance. Fitzgerald goes on to say that he was grabbed from behind while witnessing this supposed murder and was angrily told by this unknown person, "Get out of here, Fitzgerald, or you'll be next!" and then was pushed from behind in a silent command to leave the premises. Cadbury and Fitzgerald ran towards the car, got in, and fled the scene. Fitzgerald later claimed that the individual who attacked and threatened him from behind at Cotchford Farm that night was Tom Keylock, despite Keylock's statement to police saying that he wasn't at Cotchford Farm at the time of Brian's death.

There has been credible skepticism of Fitzgerald's account of

Brian's death, including from author Howard Sounes, who says in his book *27: A History of the 27 Club* that Fitzgerald's account of Brian's death is false. (#4) Fitzgerald's absurd claims in his book include his accounts that Brian was paid 250,000 pounds to leave the Rolling Stones in June 1969, when more accurate statistics estimate the figure to be more in the range of 100,000 pounds.

Fitzgerald further claims in his book that Keith Richards and Anita Pallenberg attended Brian's funeral in Cheltenham, U.K. on July 10, 1969, when, in fact, neither was present. Also in dispute is Fitzgerald's account of Brian's murder, which he supposedly witnessed with Richard Cadbury; this story has been widely discredited as false. Fitzgerald's only other witness to his claim, Richard Cadbury, disappeared forever the next day after Fitzgerald and Cadbury returned to London. Former Rolling Stones bass guitarist Bill Wyman stated his opinion of Brian's death: "I am not going to play amateur psychologist and nor do I want to reopen the debate about Brian's death. There have been too many conspiracy theories, often started by people with a vested or mercenary interest. Others were deluded. I think now, as I did then, that it was a dreadful accident." (pg 330, #5) Wyman was always Brian's most ardent and adamant defender from within the band, and he considers Jones a "legend, and his legacy is there for all to hear."

In an interview conducted for *Rolling Stone* magazine by Robert Greenfield in the August 19, 1971 issue (https://www.rollingstone.com/music/music-news/keith-richard-the-rolling-stone-interview-238909/), for which both Keith Richards and Anita Pallenberg were interviewed, when asked about Brian's death being an accident, Richards stated, "Well, I don't want to say. Some very weird things happened that night, that's all I can say. It could have well been an accident. There were people there that suddenly disappeared.... None of us were trying to hush it up. We wanted to know what was going on. We were at a session that night, and we weren't expecting Brian to come along. He'd officially left the band. And someone called us up at midnight and said, 'Brian's dead.' Well, what the fuck is going on? We had these chauffeurs working for us and we tried to find out, some of them had a weird hold over Brian. There were a lot of chicks there, they were having a party. I don't know man, I just don't know what happened to Brian that night." When Greenfield asked Richards if he believed that Brian Jones was murdered in his swimming pool, Richards said, "There was no one there that had wanted to murder him. Somebody didn't take care of him. And they should have done because he had somebody there who was supposed to take care of him. Everyone knew what Brian was like, especially at a party. Maybe he did go in for a swim and have an asthma attack. I'd never seen Brian have an attack. He was a good swimmer. He was a better swimmer than anyone else around me. He could just dive off these rocks straight into the sea. He was really easing back from the whole drug thing. He wasn't hitting them like he had been, he wasn't hitting anything like he had. Maybe the combination of things. It's one of those things I just can't find out. You know, who do you ask? Such a beautiful cat, man. He was one of those people who are so beautiful in one way, and such an asshole in another. 'Brian, how could you do that to me, man?' It was like that." (pg 17, #6)

When asked about his feelings regarding Brian's death, Richards explained, "We were completely shocked. I got straight into it and wanted to know who was there and couldn't find out. The only cat I could ask was the one, I think, who got rid of everybody and did the whole disappearing trick, so when the cops arrived it was just an accident. Maybe it was. Maybe the cat wanted to get everyone out of the way so it wasn't all names involved, et cetera, et cetera. Maybe he did the right thing, I don't know, I don't know. I don't even know who was there that night, and trying to find out is impossible. Maybe he tried to pull off one of his deep diving stunts and was too loaded and hit his chest and that was it. But I've seen Brian swim in terrible conditions in the sea, with breakers up to here. I've been underwater with Brian in Fiji. He was all right then. He was a goddamned good swimmer and it's very hard to believe he could have died in a swimming pool. But goddamnit, to find out is impossible. Especially with him not being officially one of the Stones then, none of our people were in direct contact then. So it was trying to find out who was around Brian at that final moment. It's the same feeling with who killed Kennedy. You can't get to the bottom of it." (pg 19, #6) Anita Pallenberg said about Brian, "He was surrounded by the wrong kind of people." (pg 19, #6) Marianne Faithfull was deeply saddened by Brian's death, but she had stated how concerned she was at the time that none of the other Stones seemed to care. (pg 112, #7) Faithfull said of Brian, "I did understand why they behaved like that, and Brian was asking for it. I do understand why they loathed him. But I saw him as another person, with low self-esteem, who needed to be helped. Not to be destroyed or humiliated and around under foot. Because that's what was going on." (pg 267, #8) Brian's father, Lewis Jones, said of his son after his death, "We had our violent disagreements, but we never stopped loving him." (pg 346, #5)

In Rich Cohen's book *The Sun & the Moon & the Rolling Stones*, he says that Jones, on the final day of his life, had been drinking all day while also being under the influence of the drugs Tuinal and Mandrax, and that he combined all of these with six or seven brandies. Cohen states that this combination was enough to cause Brian's drowning death that night, and does not put stock in the sinister circumstances of murder, as some have reported. Cohen further states, "In fact, the only person with a reason to kill Brian Jones was Brian Jones. Sad, unhealthy, overweight, addicted, discarded, done." (pg 203, #9) According to author Laura Jackson, " during the investigation of Brian's death, all three witnesses, Janet Lawson, Frank Thorogood, and Anna Wohlin, had given different accounts of circumstances leading to Brian's death." (pg 212, #10) But despite these discrepancies, there was never enough evidence to reopen the investigation into Brian's death, which was officially ruled as "death by misadventure" due to drowning. (pg 175, #1) Keith Richards analyzed Brian's Achilles heel regarding his being a member of the Rolling Stones: "Brian just didn't have it in him to be the 'successful rock musician.' He never held anything in reserve. He just wasted himself so quickly, and you knew that he wasn't going to last, that he wasn't going to reach anywhere near middle age." (pg 163, #11) Marianne Faithfull further comments on Brian, "Brian was too proud and too cool to discuss his inner turmoil. He just wasn't that kind of person, he kept it all in." (pg 185, #1) George Harrison said of Brian, "I don't think he had enough love or understanding." (pg 529, #12)

Ronnie Wood, Brian's eventual replacement in the Rolling Stones after Mick Taylor's departure in 1975, said that Brian was consumed by drugs and rock & roll. (pg 94, #13) But Brian's impact on the band he created was palpable, and as former Rolling Stones bass player Bill Wyman says, "If Keith and Mick were the mind and body of the Stones, Brian was clearly the soul." (pg 532, #12) Anna Wohlin points out that Thorogood would constantly hit on her when Brian wasn't around, and that Thorogood was constantly trying to get Wohlin to leave Brian for him, despite Wohlin being significantly younger than Thorogood and having no interest in him romantically. When Jones had passed away, according to Wohlin, Thorogood warned her to cooperate with the story of accidental death, and Wohlin says that she feared reprisal if she didn't. Because she wasn't outside at the pool, she couldn't prove that Brian's death wasn't accidental. Wohlin's inner inhibitions were telling her otherwise, but Wohlin feared that she might end up like Brian if she didn't cooperate with the story of an accident. So Wohlin went along with it because Thorogood had told her to, and she felt threatened by Thorogood. (pg 205, #2)

In contradiction to Fitzgerald's story of Tom Keylock being present at Cotchford Farm at the moment of Brian's death, Wohlin says that Keylock showed up sometime after Brian's death to take control of the situation, despite Jones no longer being in the Rolling Stones at the time of his death. Keylock had promised Wohlin that she could return in a few days to collect the remainder of her belongings, and he arranged for a car to transport Wohlin back to Cotchford Farm. She was instructed to pack only one bag of belongings to take with her ("things I needed") once she got there. (pg 208, #2) Wohlin, after she left Cotchford Farm, was taken to the Stones' office, where Les Perrin paired her up with Astrid Lundström to stay at the Londonderry Hotel in a private suite on July 3, 1969. Wohlin ultimately did not attend the Hyde Park concert, instead remaining in her hotel suite. Les Perrin made Anna sign an agreement saying that she would not talk to the media without Perrin's explicit approval. Wohlin agreed to these terms. Shortly after Wohlin's return to Sweden after Brian's death, she miscarried the baby that she and Brian were to have. It was a baby girl that Brian and Anna had decided was going to be named Johanna. Wohlin blamed the miscarriage on her overpowering grief at Brian's death. Wohlin did not attend Brian's funeral in Cheltenham on July 10, 1969, because the Rolling Stones themselves didn't want her to speak there. (pg 228, #2)

Brian's funeral was meant to be a private, family affair, but due to the amount of fans that showed up to pay their respects, it turned into a chaotic situation. More than 500 people packed into the church for the relatively quick ceremony, followed by many mourners who went to Brian's gravesite in Prestbury, U.K., approximately three miles down the road from the church. Brian's telegram to his parents after his 1967 drug bust was read aloud during the funeral, in which Brian wrote, "Please don't worry. Don't jump to hasty conclusions and please don't judge me too harshly." Photographers who attended Brian's arrival to the cemetery were heavily criticized for pushing people out of the way during the ceremony and when Brian's casket was lowered into his grave. Besides Brian's immediate family, other members of the Rolling Stones organization attended Brian's funeral, including Tom Keylock, Les Perrin, Bill Wyman, Charlie Watts, and Ian Stewart, as well as former girlfriend Suki Potier. However, Mick Jagger and Keith Richards did not attend, nor did Anita Pallenberg. Shortly after Brian's death, all of his possessions were cleared out of his house at Cotchford Farm and disappeared from sight. The payments that were promised to Brian—100,000 pounds plus yearly annuities on his agreement to leave the Rolling Stones in June 1969—never materialized.

CHAPTER 14

THE 1969 NORTH AMERICAN TOUR

Meanwhile, the Rolling Stones' new single, "Honky Tonk Woman," went to no. 1 in both the U.K. and America. During Brian's funeral week, Mick Jagger and Marianne Faithfull had flown to Australia to film the movie *Ned Kelly*, in which Jagger was selected to play the Australian outlaw. Many Australians protested the fact that Jagger was picked to play the title character, who was a folk hero to many in the country, but it didn't stop production of the film or Jagger's role in it. During this time, Faithfull had overdosed on 15 Tuinal pills, and she came close to death as a result. She was hospitalized in Australia, with Jagger at her side.

Immediately following Brian's death, in July and August 1969, the Beatles recorded what would become their last studio album, called *Abbey Road*. This album was eventually released on September 26, 1969, and was widely acclaimed as a very strong and high-quality record. It spent 11 weeks at no. 1, and it was considered to be a happy album for the Beatles in the recording studio. It should be noted that *Abbey Road* was not the last Beatles album to be released. *Let it Be* was released in May 1970, despite being recorded in January 1969. But this would mark the end of the Beatles as a band. As the Beatles were not going back on the road to promote *Abbey Road*, this was a fortuitous moment for the Rolling Stones to go back on tour in America before the release of their next album, *Let it Bleed*.

It was exciting for the Stones to go back on the road and play live again, with a new guitarist and sound amplification powerful enough to truly penetrate the crowd noise. Previously, like the Beatles, the Stones' music had been drowned out completely by the audience's screaming and the accompanying mania. But by the 1969 tour, the sound equipment was loud enough for the band to be heard clearly by an audience. This made the concerts a much different experience. After the birth of Keith and Anita's son Marlon on August 10, 1969, the Rolling Stones began their sixth tour of the United States on November 7, 1969, in Fort Collins, Colorado. They would crisscross the country in what was considered to be a very successful tour. There were, however, many complaints of exorbitant ticket prices for Rolling Stones shows, despite the tour selling out in every city they visited. Even though the band hadn't played live in America for three years, they brought their enthusiasm and professionalism to every stop on the tour. Their opening acts included such legendary performers as B.B. King, Ike and Tina Turner, Terry Reid, and Chuck Berry. The Rolling Stones broke attendance records literally everywhere they went.

But the Rolling Stones still had problems getting properly paid by their then- manager, Allen Klein. Klein controlled their money, and he continuously failed to pay the band members what was owed to them while himself accumulating vast wealth. This included $2 million from the North American tour alone. So, the Stones took matters into their own hands. It was decided that they would give a free concert as a way to say thank you to their American fans. It was intended to be similar to the Stones' Hyde Park show in England on July 5, 1969 that introduced Brian's replacement guitarist, Mick Taylor. It would also be the last date of the 1969 tour in America, meant to coincide with the release of their new album, *Let It Bleed*, released in the U.K. on December 5 (but released in America in November 1969). This free show was scheduled for December 6, 1969, initially at Golden Gate Park in San Francisco, California—but City Hall did not approve the request. Next on the list was the Sears Point Raceway in Sonoma County, California, but a concert was not approved there, either. Lawyer Melvin Belli was brought in to negotiate a location on which all sides could agree in order to pull off this free concert. Finally, the Altamont Speedway, located 50 miles east of San Francisco on an 80-acre plot that could accommodate up to 80,000 cars, was chosen. (pg 351, #5) Once all sides had agreed, the concert was on, and it was also agreed that the San Francisco chapter of the Hells Angels would be brought in as security for the event. And so we come to Altamont.

CHAPTER 15

ALTAMONT

BRIAN'S REVENGE?

Former Rolling Stones bass guitarist Bill Wyman later said of the Altamont show, "Altamont was the end of the swinging sixties, the dream was over." (pg 360 #5) Altamont was described as egos mixed with immaturity in its planning and execution. Other acts at this festival included Santana, Jefferson Airplane, Crosby, Stills & Nash, the Flying Burrito Brothers, and the Grateful Dead, and all performed except the Grateful Dead. Santana, led by Carlos Santana, went on first, and that's when all hell broke loose between the Hells Angels and the crowd, exploding into violence. The Hells Angels were paid in beer for their security services at the event. The Angels were expected to properly control a crowd of approximately 350,000 people, and things got out of control quickly. During Jefferson Airplane's set, band member Marty Balin was knocked out cold by one of the Hells Angels when Balin protested one of its members beating up audience members and tried in vain to break it up. The Angels were hitting people with cue sticks in a merciless fashion. By the time the Rolling Stones were ready to take the stage later that evening, the Hells Angels were literally plowing through the crowd on their motorcycles in order to clear a path towards the stage so that the Rolling Stones could go on.

Problems with violence started again once the Stones went on stage and began their set, forcing the band to stop playing several times. Meredith Hunter, an 18-year-old African-American in the audience that night, got into a physical fight with several of the Hells Angels near the stage. While this altercation was commencing, Hunter pulled out a gun and was promptly stabbed in the back by one of the Angels. He died shortly thereafter. This attack was caught by the video recorders while filming the Rolling Stones playing "Under My Thumb." Keith Richards, shaken by what he had just witnessed from the stage, warned the Hells Angels to stop attacking the crowd or they wouldn't play. No charges were ever brought against the Hells Angel who stabbed Meredith Hunter, because Hunter had a gun in his hand and was approaching the stage, so the Angels instantly reacted. Those who were with Hunter proclaimed that he was just trying to defend himself, but due to the quick speed of the events that led to Hunter's death, no charges were ever filed. Two other fans were killed when a Plymouth convertible plowed through the crowd. Both victims were 22 years old. Another fan fell into an irrigation channel and drowned. At the end of this controversial performance in Altamont, 4 babies were born, 4 people died, and all were forever affected. The Hyde Park show on July 5 was a happy counterpart to the violence and carnage of the Altamont concert. However, it was also clear that the London Hells Angels were quite different from the Northern California Hells Angels. Was this incident at Altamont an example of Brian Jones' revenge from beyond the grave against his former bandmates?

After the show at Altamont, the Rolling Stones were criticized for penny-pinching in hiring the Hells Angels in the first place, and then for paying them with beer. Promoters thought that too little consideration had been given to the concertgoers, including from legendary promoter Bill Graham, who called Mick Jagger "a selfish prick." (pg 119, #7) Keith Richards stated about the Altamont experience, "I thought the show would have been stopped, but hardly anybody seemed to want to take any notice. The violence just in front of the stage was incredible. Looking back, I don't think it was a good idea to have the Hells Angels. But the Grateful Dead, who've organized these shows before, thought they would be best." (pg 97, #14) In truth, Richards did blame the Grateful Dead band members, who suggested that the Hells Angels should provide security for the Altamont concert. The fiasco taught them a valuable lesson about what can go wrong at an event with so many people, and how to successfully play at events of that magnitude in the future. (pg 360, #5) After all, there was no road map or guide book on how to properly navigate venues and obtain adequate security for free concerts, like the ones in Hyde Park and Altamont, featuring an act as big as the Rolling Stones. They had to learn by experience.

In an interview I conducted with Dr. Allan Hunter, a professor of English Literature at Curry College in Milton, Massachusetts, I asked him about the fallout from the disastrous Altamont concert upon the Rolling Stones and how it affected their career. When asked what the contributing factors were that led to the Altamont concert the Stones gave in December 1969 becoming such a controversial part of their legacy, Hunter said, "The Altamont concert was a strange, scrambled episode. The Stones have massaged their own version of what happened over the years, and even the film taken at the time shows a very chaotic scene. The satanic aspects have been played up, of course—security provided by the Hells Angels and the band playing 'Sympathy for the Devil' when an audience member was killed by the Angels. This all puts a bit of a spin on it, that the Stones themselves seem to like. After the peace and love that we associate with Woodstock, this turned out to be the exact opposite. So what happened? I think the Stones went to Altamont because they thought it might be another Woodstock, and they were eager to be in on the action. When they got there, of course, is was chaotic. They could barely move on stage from hangers-on, Hells Angels, and others. It was, as they saw right away, a very dangerous situation. They'd had fans rush the stage before this, and here the fans were already on stage before they began! *Crossfire Hurricane* [the film] does a good job of showing this. In this instance, the Stones hadn't done their homework, usually casing the place beforehand. They turned up trying to boost their U.S. appeal and ran into disaster. What they learned was that their rough, tough, bad-boy image, carefully developed over the years, was not actually a match for a real rough and dangerous situation with real thugs. It was never intended to be. Still, I can't help thinking that by being associated with the disaster even in a negative way (they got out as fast as they could), their prestige was somehow enhanced."

At the time, Mick Jagger had ended his relationship with Marianne Faithfull. Their joint drug possession arrest earlier in 1969 had resulted in a conviction and fine for Jagger and an acquittal for Faithfull. After this court proceeding, Jagger and Faithfull had gone their separate ways. Faithfull next ended up with Italian painter Mario Schifano.

With the end of the 1960s, established music festivals like Woodstock or the Isle of Wight began to dominate the music landscape. Brian's friend Jimi Hendrix won Performer of the Year in 1969 with his memorable live performances. A group formed by

Jimmy Page, after the Yardbirds had disbanded in 1968, called Led Zeppelin, went on to great success in 1969, with their first two albums going multiplatinum. The Who found great success with the release of their album *Tommy* in May 1969, and they played it everywhere, including the Isle of Wight and Woodstock. Brian's friend Bob Dylan also performed at the Isle of Wight in 1969 to a crowd of approximately 150,000 people, including John Lennon, George Harrison, and Ringo Starr—but not Paul McCartney. Eric Clapton, after leaving the band Cream in 1968, formed Blind Faith with Steve Winwood (formerly of the band Traffic), Ric Grech, and Ginger Baker on drums (former drummer of Cream).

In 1970, Jagger's film *Ned Kelly* was released to the public. The Rolling Stones were due to get out of their Decca recording contract that year, and also began to break away from their manager Allen Klein, with whom the Stones had grown increasingly dissatisfied over time. Klein had taken $29 million more from the Rolling Stones than he should have, and the time for the break between the two parties had come. (pg 431, #15) Klein had convinced all members of the Rolling Stones to put their money into a company they mistakenly thought they owned, called Nanker Phledge USA, which in fact was owned by Klein. As a result, Klein owned all of the Rolling Stones' recordings prior to 1970. (pg 108, #7) To counter this, Mick Jagger brought in his friend Prince Rupert Loewenstein as the Rolling Stones' financial advisor in order to check Klein and his reckless theft. (pg 107, #7) By May 1970, the estate of Brian Jones was reported to be in debt to the tune of approximately $400,000, with his assets estimated to be valued at $75,000.

While the Rolling Stones were planning to tour Europe later in 1970, they felt the need to address their immediate contractual and managerial problems with both Decca Records and Allen Klein. When Klein first became co-manager of the Rolling Stones in August 1965, the Rolling Stones and Andrew Oldham created their own company in England called Nanker Phledge Music. But Klein formed his own company, Nanker Phledge USA, which was entirely separate from Nanker Phledge Music. Klein was the president and sole stock holder. Klein further tricked the Stones into signing away the publishing rights to all of their songs until the expiration of their contract with Decca Records in 1971. (pg 199, #16) This included all of Brian Jones' contributions to the band.

It was planned by Jagger and Loewenstein that the Rolling Stones would move to France for tax reasons, until their personal finances could be straightened out. This was due in large part to England's very high tax rate at the time. It was agreed that the Rolling Stones would be in exile in France for 21 months. (pg 351, #5) This was the plan to liberate them from Klein's grip and give them the opportunity to form a more favorable contract with Ahmet Ertegun's Atlantic Records, which they eventually did. Trevor Marshall was the label's manager, and Marshall Chess, who was the son of Leonard Chess and CEO of Chess Records, was brought in as the general manager for Atlantic. Decca Records insisted that the Rolling Stones owed them one more album on their contract. So, the album *Cocksucker Blues* is what they got. It would never be released by Decca Records.

Before leaving for their planned exile in France, the Rolling Stones went on tour in Europe from August to October 1970. During this time, on September 18, 1970, Brian Jones' close friend and guitar legend Jimi Hendrix passed away at age 27 in England. Hendrix was with his girlfriend, Monika Dannemann, at the time of his death. His cause of death was attributed to choking on his own vomit after overdosing on the drug Vesparax, which he mixed with alcohol. He was buried in Seattle, Washington.

On a happier note, Jagger's second film, which he starred in, *Performance*, was released on August 3, 1970 to mixed reviews at first. It has gained cult popularity in the time since, however, and is generally viewed favorably, despite its violence. This was Jagger's last acting role for a long time, until the early 1990s. In November 1970, Mick Jagger's girlfriend Marsha Hunt gave birth to his first child, a daughter named Karis. But by then, Jagger was already in a new relationship, with 25-year-old model Bianca Pérez-Mora Macías, whom he would later marry.

With their lawsuit well under way against Allen Klein, the Rolling Stones released their new album, *Sticky Fingers*, on April 23, 1971 on their new imprint, Rolling Stones Records. *Sticky Fingers* is widely considered to be one of the very best albums in their illustrious catalog, and reached no. 1 on the charts in both the United Kingdom and America. Mick Jagger asked artist Andy Warhol to create the album cover, with Jagger specifically aiming for shock value. Warhol gave Jagger exactly that. The Rolling

Stones played a short farewell tour of England in March 1971, and then they moved to France.

It was there, on May 12, 1971, that Mick and Bianca got married, at St. Anne's chapel in St. Tropez. Reportedly, Mick and Bianca argued all the way to the moment they got married over the prenuptial agreement. (pg 141, #7) The guest list included Paul and Linda McCartney, Ringo and Maureen Starr, Ronnie Lane, Kenney Jones, Jimmy Miller, Marshall Chess, Ahmet Ertegun, and Ronnie Wood. Bianca was four months' pregnant at the time of her wedding. In an ironic twist of fate, Marianne Faithfull was arrested on the same day in London for drunk and disorderly conduct and fined as a result. (pg 382, #5)

CHAPTER 16

THE PIPES OF PAN AT JAJOUKA IS RELEASED, EXILE IN FRANCE

Meanwhile, by June 1, 1971, both the album *Sticky Fingers* and the single "Brown Sugar" were no. 1 in America. In 1971, the Rolling Stones signed a $5 million, six-album deal with Ertegun's Atlantic Records, who distributed these records in partnership with Rolling Stones Inc. Atlantic also had other major rock groups on their label, such as Genesis, Queen, and Led Zeppelin. (pg 138, #7) On August 31, 1971, Mick Jagger, Keith Richards, Charlie Watts, Bill Wyman, and Lewis Jones (on behalf of Brian) filed a lawsuit against Andrew Oldham and Eric Easton for the deal that Brian Jones had signed with them, which gave the Rolling Stones only 6% of record sales. In contrast, Decca gave Oldham and Easton 14%—on top of the 25% management contract that Oldham and Easton were already getting from the band. The Rolling Stones and Lewis Jones also sued Klein for $29 million to compensate for the money the Stones estimated he had wrongly stolen from them while he managed the band. The lawsuit accused Klein of falsely representing Nanker Phledge USA to be the Rolling Stones' company, when it really belonged to Klein, and purposely misleading the band. The Stones accused Klein of flagrantly stealing their music and of poor management representation.

While this contentious legal battle was going on, Klein's company ABKCO released the album *Brian Jones Presents the Pipes of Pan at Jajouka* on October 8, 1971, the Jajouka being the master musicians that Brian had discovered in Morocco. All music on the album was written and performed by the Master Musicians of Jajouka, and it was recorded in Morocco on July 29, 1968. The album was produced by Brian Jones. The music features percussion-based African rhythms and melodies that, although perhaps not possessing the Top 40 sound of the Rolling Stones, border on psychedelia and take the listener on a journey into a new world of sound. Brian himself was very enthusiastic about this music during his life.

The songs on the album came from the annual, week-long Rites of Pan festival. Jones, recording engineer George Chkiantz, (#25) and Brion Gysin went to the village in Morocco to record the musicians in 1968. This was the same Brion Gysin who was with Brian in the market square when Keith Richards, Anita Pallenberg, and the whole entourage abandoned Brian in February 1967, thus leaving him all alone in Morocco and resulting in Pallenberg effectively dumping him for Richards. According to Wikipedia, Pan is the Greek god of "wild shepherds and flocks, nature of mountain wilds, rustic music, and companion of the nymphs. Pan is also the god of fields groves, wooded glens, and often affiliated with sex because of this. Pan is connected to fertility, and the season of spring." (#17) Pan's fertility skills were something that Brian Jones could relate to and identify with, despite not taking care emotionally or financially of any of his five offspring. Perhaps Brian, like Pan, felt that he could reproduce as he saw fit and viewed it as a badge of honor to have that ability and power. *Brian Jones Presents the Pipes of Pan at Jajouka* contains the following tracks: "55," "War Song/Standing + One Half," "Take Me With You Darling Take Me With You," "Your Eyes Are Like a Cup of Tea," "I Am Calling Out," and a repeat of "Your Eyes Are Like a Cup of Tea" but with a flute accompaniment. The discovery of the Master Musicians of Jajouka showed that Brian Jones had musical visions outside the Rolling Stones that he could have kept exploring, had he lived. He could have created another sound and experience that could have possibly rivaled the Rolling Stones. Sadly, we will never know whether that would have happened.

Meanwhile, Jade Sheena Jezebel Jagger was born to Mick and Bianca on October 21, 1971. Jagger was criticized at the time for ignoring his other daughter, Karis, whom he had with Marsha Hunt. In regards to the Rolling Stones' pursuit of breaking ties completely with manager Allen Klein, Mick Jagger said, "We'd been working hard, we were a very successful band, we'd sold a lot of records, but we weren't getting paid for it, because the record contracts were giving us such a low royalty. What we found out was that we had a bad managerial company guy [Klein] who claimed that he owned everything we were doing in the past and always would in the future: touring, records, publishing, songs, everything, he said he owned. So we had to get rid of him and try to get out of

this ridiculous Byzantine mess that you've created for yourself."
(#18) Bill Wyman said about their then-financial predicament, "We
were supposed to live this life, you know, of limousines, you had to
have this, that or the other. The money just flew, so you were always
in debt. None of us paid tax we thought we had, we thought that it
had been dealt with. And it hadn't. Tax under the Labour
government then was 93%." (#18) So the Rolling Stones relocated
to France to live and work on the next album, which would become
Exile on Main St., in April 1971.

The Stones were officially in exile. One of the advantages this
provided was that no one knew or recognized the Stones while they
were in the south of France, so they could live normally there,
without the hassle of fame. Keith and Anita bought a house called
Villa Nellcôte in Ville Franche-sur-Mer, which would become the
main recording studio for the album, in addition to their mobile
truck, because other local studios in France did not work out due to
sound issues. Keith didn't like any of the recording studios available
in southern France, so it was decided that they would record at
Keith's house.

Speaking about his new home, Villa Nellcôte, Keith Richards
said, "Admiral Byrd built it. He was an English admiral with steps
down to his own private boating dock. So I bought a speed boat."
(#18). Richards further explained, "That whole era, just before we
moved to France, we were all kinds of jittery. So in a way, it was
quite a relief to get to France and have that off your back and start
learning French." (#18) Anita Pallenberg agreed: "Until I had
Marlon, we were just living in hotel rooms, moving around
constantly. So for me, going to the south of France was great. It was
a wonderful place. It was very romantic. I totally lost my sense of
time there. It was like a kind of dream, you know." (#18) One of
Anita's responsibilities in France was to argue with the cook, Fat
Jacques—no one else dared. Fat Jacques was described by Keith
Richards as a "junkie."

According to Mick Jagger, "In those days, if a band was big in
England, and then left England, that's the end of them. You didn't
like them anymore. It's fucking curtains! And when you leave for
tax reasons, it's really not very cool. I had to get out of the country
to pay the tax incurred for me. That's why I had to leave." (#18)
Certainly, not every member of the band was happy about this

migration to France. According to Bill Wyman, "I hated leaving England. I did, because when you get there, you had to replace everything that you loved, because it wasn't there. Then you had to deal with French milk, which wasn't the same." (#18) Wyman had to import all of the British tea that he liked. Saxophonist Bobby Keys went with them, playing saxophone in concert and, now, also in the recording studio.

Because Charlie Watts' house in France was approximately a seven-hour drive to Nellcôte, he often stayed at Keith's house overnight during the recordings. Andy Johns was the record engineer. At the time, the Rolling Stones were technically an 8-piece band with the aforementioned Bobby Keys on saxophone, Jim Price on horns, and Nicky Hopkins on piano. Ian Stewart also played piano on some recordings. The band recorded material in separate rooms in Keith's basement. Charlie Watts said, "A lot of *Exile* was done how Keith works: which is play it 20 times, marinate it, and play it another 20 times. Keith's very like a jazz player in lots of ways. I mean, he knows what he likes, but he's very loose, Keith's a very Bohemian and eccentric, in the best of terms, person." (#18) Richards said of these sessions, "I never plan anything, which is probably the difference between Mick and myself. Mick needs to know what he's going to do tomorrow, and me, I'm just happy to wake up and see who's hanging around. Mick's rock and I'm roll." (#18) There were a lot of drugs being consumed at Nellcôte, including substantial amounts of heroin by Keith and Anita. Other people who were just there hanging out and living at the house (the "hangers-on") were also strung out by heroin. On October 1, 1971, burglars stole 9 guitars belonging to Keith, one of Bill Wyman's bass guitars, and Bobby Keys' saxophone form Keith's house while they were watching television. (pg 385, #5)

Yet *Exile on Main St.* began to take shape and character, spurred by extra excitement from the band, as if they knew they were making an exemplary album that would stand out in their catalog. Bill Wyman said, "We started off jamming, really casual. Hung together. It always ended up great. That was the great thing about it." (#18) Richards concurs by saying, "I don't think we ever said, 'let's make this kind of album or that kind.' They take on their own character once you start to get into it. Since we'd left the country and we were recording in a totally different way, I just wanted to go back to basics." (#18)

It was said that the Rolling Stones reintroduced black music to America. Keith said, "We'd absorbed so much different kind of music since we'd become the Rolling Stones. Maybe we'd missed America, I don't know. Mick and I always loved country music anyway. You're playing the Midwest in 1964-65. You ain't gonna hear much else. It's the other side of rock & roll. Rock & roll, basically, is your blues and they put it under a little bit of white hillbilly melody, it's the coming together, it's that lovely, which music's always about, is one culture hitting another. Hillbillies' ideas of subject matter are, like, really interesting." (#18) The song "Sweet Virginia," on which Bobby Keys plays saxophone, is an example of this. Richards explains, "One of the things about *Exile*, I think, was that a lot of stuff we'd picked up on the road and along the way came out. You've drawn from whatever you've listened to since you were a child. Probably some of the things I write or play are things that I listened to in 1947. Rock & roll in its basic sense is a mixture. What I always loved about it when I thought about it is that it's a beautiful synthesis of black and white music, and it's just a beautiful cauldron to mix things up." (#18) Anita Pallenberg complained that the Stones were too loud when they practiced in the basement, and that the whole town heard them when they practiced at Keith's house. Keith said of his house at Nellcôte, "Once you're into the recording, everything else is a bit peripheral. We'd be down in the basement working, but the odd time you'd come up to the surface, oh they'd be partying up there. So you never knew quite what you were going to meet. Nellcôte was never empty. There were people all over the place. Some people sprawled out and said, 'I can't make it home.' I used to say, 'have the couch, have the big couch.' " (#18)

Pallenberg said, "Everybody would go in and out of the place as they wished, so I kind of got really paranoid, it was unbelievable. I walked into the living room and there was this guy sitting on a sofa, [and] he pulled out a bag full of smack. The whole thing kind of disintegrated and we got heavily into drugs, like breakfast, lunch and dinner." (#18) Richards said, "I did it [heroin] basically to hide from fame and be this other person, because all I wanted to do was play music and bring my family up. With a bit of smack, I could walk through anything and not give a damn." (#18) In fact, Keith and Anita were almost killed when a fire broke out in their bedroom, with both of them out cold in a heroin stupor, but they were successfully rescued. After the burglary of Keith's house, the Stones were ready to leave Nellcôte and France altogether, especially after it was rumored that they were about to be arrested by French police. So the Stones went to Los Angeles, California to finish the record.

CHAPTER 17

STONES CLAIM FULL CONTROL OF MUSIC AND TOURING, BRIAN'S REPLACEMENT DEPARTS

Exile on Main St. would become the first double album released by the Rolling Stones. Mick Jagger said of this period, "I remember Keith saying, 'I'm so burned out on this record.' But we still got loads of unfinished songs, some of them had fragmentary lyrics, some had none at all. So we had a big mountain to climb. It's weird where your lyrics things come from. In 'Tumblin' Dice,' I sat down with the housekeeper and talked about gambling. She liked to play dice and I didn't know much about it. But I got it off of her and I made a song out of that." (#18) While in California, the Stones recorded at Sunset Studios in Los Angeles. It was Mick Jagger and Charlie Watts who picked the photos that were on the cover of the album, which had a very Americana influence. Richards said that as they had officially moved out of England, they had better make this album work. So, that provided extra motivation.

Jagger said of *Exile on Main St.*, "It's a different kind of record. It's a very sprawling, gutsy piece of work. Criticism of *Exile*, it didn't have direction, but then there's something very laudable about it that it exhibits all these styles and even multiple styles in one song. Does it have a ton of hit singles on it? No, this isn't that kind of record." (#18)

This enormously successful album propelled the Stones through a very successful 1972 North American tour, on which Stevie Wonder was the opening act. The *Exile on Main St.* album was released on May 26, 1972 and reached no. 1 in both the United Kingdom and America. The Rolling Stones' North American tour opened on June 3, 1972 in Vancouver, Canada, (pg 114, #14) and finished at Madison Square Garden in New York City on July 26. The U.S. magazine *Billboard* voted the Rolling Stones as the best band of 1972. (pg 120, #14)

But drugs and internal strife were still ravaging the band. Both Keith and Anita flew to Switzerland to try to get clean from their heroin addictions. Even Mick Taylor was abusing heroin during this time, and he started to express his unhappiness about his role in the Rolling Stones. He was frustrated with the Stones not allowing him to write any songs to record, and criticizing him for not moving around on stage enough. Taylor seemed to be looking for a way out of being Brian Jones' replacement. Later, in 1973, Keith, Anita, and Brian's friend Stash were arrested at Keith's house, Redlands, by the drugs squad for possession of marijuana and were released on bail. Keith and Anita would be fined for their marijuana charge but not imprisoned.

Before this bust, Keith and Anita had a baby girl named Dandelion, also known as Angela, in 1972. (pg 392, #5) The Stones settled their lawsuit with former manager Allen Klein for $2 million: $1 million to Jagger and Richards for songwriting and publishing, and the other half to be shared between each of the other band members and the estate of Brian Jones. They were finally free of their contract with Klein, though it came at an enormous price. Yet they enjoyed a very successful North American tour in 1972. In total, the Stones grossed $4 million from 51 shows in 32 cities. It was reported to be the most lucrative rock tour of its time. (pg 398, #5) Their next album *Goats Head Soup* was released on August 31, 1973, peaking at no. 2 and remaining in the charts for nine weeks.

Meanwhile, Bill Wyman released his first solo album, *Monkey Grip*, in May 1974 on Rolling Stones Records. The next Rolling Stones album was *It's Only Rock 'n' Roll*, which reached no. 1 in America and stayed on the charts for 13 weeks in 1974. (pg 134, #14) The Stones were starting to spend more time with Faces guitarist Ronnie Wood, whom Keith Richards moved in with in 1974. In fact, Ronnie Wood's solo album *I've Got My Own Album to Do* was released on September 27, 1974 and featured Mick Jagger, Keith Richards, and Mick Taylor, with two Jagger/Richards compositions included on the album. On December 12, 1974, Mick Taylor officially quit the Rolling Stones at a party at Robert Stigwood's house to join the Jack Bruce Band, and Jagger desperately turned to Wood on the spot to ask him if he'd join the Stones and take Taylor's place. As much as Wood wanted to accept, he still was the lead guitarist for Faces, with whom he was still under contract to perform. According to Ronnie Wood, "As fate had it, I was at a party at Robert Stigwood's with Mick and Mick Taylor, and I remember being next to Mick Jagger while Taylor came up and handed his resignation in. And Mick Jagger turned to me and says, 'What am I going to do? Mick's just left the band!' I said, 'Oh no!' He says, 'Yeah, he's really serious this time.' He said, 'Would you join?' I said, 'Of course I would, in a minute, but I don't want to let the Faces down,' and he said, 'No, I don't want to split that up either, but I'm in a real predicament.'" (#19)

Taylor had quit the Rolling Stones due to his frustrations over his perceived inability to grow within the band, and felt that the Jack Bruce Band would be a better fit for him musically. Once word of Taylor's resignation got to Keith Richards, he favored Wood also in taking that spot in the band, despite Wood's commitment to Faces. In fact, Keith had already lived with Ronnie before Ronnie was a member of the Rolling Stones and was very familiar with his guitar work. So, when Ronnie auditioned for the Rolling Stones, Keith said, "When Ronnie walked in the room, just played one number, hey, that's it, it's obvious and everyone else up for the gig agreed." (#19) Although many different guitarists did audition for the spot in the band, including Jeff Beck and Eric Clapton, the spot ultimately went to Ronnie Wood as the permanent replacement for Mick Taylor. The only logistical problems were that Wood had to tour with both Faces and the Rolling Stones in 1975, and he also had to learn approximately 200 songs for the Stones' tour alone. (pg 120, #13)

PART TWO: THE AFTERMATH

CHAPTER 18

RONNIE JOINS THE BAND, BUST IN TORONTO 1977

The Rolling Stones' 1975 North American tour opened in Baton Rouge, Louisiana on June 1, and it was Ronnie's stage debut. As fate had it, the band Faces ended after their last tour in 1975, much to the anger lead singer Rod Stewart, though he would go on to have a successful solo career after Faces broke up. Faces drummer Kenney Jones temporarily replaced Keith Moon in the Who after Moon's death in September 1978, staying with the band until the Who's first break-up in 1982. Wood was the catalyst who kept the Rolling Stones on track to continue their lucrative touring schedule and studio albums from then on, in the spot once occupied by Brian. At this point, it is valuable to examine more of Wood's musical history before he joined the Rolling Stones and his background as a musician.

Ronnie Wood was born on June 1, 1947 (pg 6, #13) into a musical family, with his older brother Art singing and playing in Alexis Korner's group Blues Incorporated. Blues Incorporated then featured Korner and Art on guitar, Dick Heckstall-Smith on saxophone, Jack Bruce on bass guitar, and Charlie Watts on drums. (pg 29, #13) Occasionally, Mick Jagger would sit in and sing with them. Among Wood's big musical influences was Big Bill Broonzy, who also influenced musicians such as Keith Richards, Eric Clapton, and Jimmy Page with his Chicago blues sound. Iconic blues artists who dominated the musical scene then included Memphis Slim, Washboard Sam, Sonny Boy Williamson, Tampa Red, and Blind Willie McTell. (pg 27, #13) Ronnie, like Keith, was also heavily influenced by Chuck Berry, whom, Ronnie said, "I later got to know as one of the greatest nut cases on the planet." (pg 24, #13) As a youth, Ronnie lived in Yiewsley, England, just outside of London near Heathrow Airport. (pg 3, #13) Wood began his musical career playing washboard in a skiffle group, then progressed to playing guitar for a band called the Birds. Later, Wood played for Jeff Beck's group after Beck left the Yardbirds in

1966. Wood initially played bass guitar for Beck's group, with Rod Stewart on vocals and Nicky Hopkins on keyboard. (pg 65, #13) Wood also once shared a house with Brian Jones' friend Jimi Hendrix at Holland Park, London in 1966.

Peter Grant managed the Jeff Beck Group, as well as the Animals and the Yardbirds. Grant would later gain infamy as the no-nonsense and quite intimidating manager of Led Zeppelin, reaping millions of dollars on their behalf from both their Atlantic Records contract and touring schedule. In fact, Ronnie Wood says that he was offered a spot in Led Zeppelin when they initially formed, but he declined. Wood referred to Led Zeppelin's legendary drummer John Bonham as "rude." (pg 68, #13) Wood claims to have only met Brian Jones once, at Olympic Studios in Barnes, and Jones was stoned out of his head. Wood says that Jones had lost his drive to be in the Rolling Stones and was consumed by drugs and the rock & roll lifestyle. After initially missing his chance to replace Jones in the Rolling Stones in 1969, Fate gave Wood another opportunity to take that second guitar spot, and Wood couldn't turn it down this time. Wood debuted on stage with the Stones right before their 1975 tour in a unique way, by playing the song "Brown Sugar" on the back of a flatbed truck on Fifth Avenue in New York City, bringing traffic to a standstill in the process. With Faces officially finished after their 1975 tour, Wood could turn his full attention to his new band, the Rolling Stones.

The Rolling Stones played 58 dates on the 1975 North American tour, at the time reported to be their biggest and longest tour yet. (pg 138, #14) Jagger said enthusiastically of Wood's addition to the Rolling Stones at this crucial time, "Ron seems a natural in the respect that both he and Keith are brilliant rhythm guitarists. It allows a certain cross-trading of riffs not previously possible." (pg 138, #14) Ronnie's first studio album with the Stones was the *Black and Blue* record, which was released on April 30, 1976. *Black and Blue* would stay in the charts for 15 weeks, with its highest spot being no. 2. Sadly, during this time, Keith and Anita's son Tara died of respiratory failure at just 2 1/2 months old during the summer of 1976.

During this time, Mick and Bianca's marriage was beginning to unravel. Bianca said of her marriage to Jagger, "My marriage ended on my wedding day." (pg 503, #15) Mick and Bianca were described as very unhappy together and fought constantly. (pg 159, #7) Mick began an affair with singer Carly Simon, who would later go on to marry musician James Taylor. Jagger was known to frequent gay nightclubs, such as the 82 Club, Les Mouches, The Gilded Grape, and Galaxy 21 on West 23rd St., and also spent a lot of time at Studio 54 in New York City. Interestingly, Bianca also spent a lot of time there without Jagger. It was around this time that Jagger met and hooked up with 19- year-old Texas model Jerry Hall, who was dating rocker Bryan Ferry at the time.

From a business perspective, the Stones signed a new record deal, after their Atlantic contract had expired, with EMI for six albums. But Keith and Anita's heroin problems hit a dangerous high when they were arrested in Canada on February 27, 1977, and charged with possession of heroin with intent to distribute, which carried with it a possible life sentence for Richards if convicted. It was said of Keith Richards' mental state at the time that he never really dealt with the loss of Brian Jones, instead turning to heroin. Author Bill Janovitz describes Richards at the time: "Keith's way of reacting to Brian's death was to become Brian. He became the very image of a falling down stoned junkie hovering perpetually on the verge of death." (pg 257, #20) Anita Pallenberg was also subject to survivor's guilt from Brian's death, which included developing grisly compulsions like Keith did. Anita herself had been arrested at the Toronto airport on February 24, 1977 for possession of hashish and traces of heroin, found among her 28 bags of luggage. Keith, too, would be arrested, and was facing seven years in prison. Despite the new record deal, the future of the Rolling Stones, at this point, was very much in doubt.

The band thought that in the time between Keith and Anita's trials, they could realistically do one more studio and one more live album—and that might be the end of the band, depending on the outcome of Keith's trial. Keith and Anita certainly realized the trouble they were in, and knew that the penalty from the Canadian government might be quite harsh. On the morning of Keith's arrest in Toronto, he said, "They had to wake me up to formally arrest me. I woke up with rosy cheeks. 'Oh, he's awake. You are under arrest' (laughs). I thought great, I looked at the old lady and said, 'See ya in about seven years, babe.' ." (#19) Keith faced one charge for possession of heroin and two for possession of cocaine found by the

Royal Canadian Mounted Police. Mick acknowledged that if Keith
was given a long prison sentence, then the Rolling Stones might not
continue as a band.

The Stones played the El Mocambo nightclub in Toronto, a
show that was attended by Margaret Trudeau, whose husband
Pierre was the Prime Minster of Canada at the time. Margaret
Trudeau also got to ride in the limousine back to the Harbor Castle
hotel and attended a party there with the band. By 1978, Mick and
Bianca had split and Mick was now permanently with Jerry Hall. By
the end of 1977, with some music critics writing the Stones off in
favor of new punk-rock acts like the Sex Pistols and the Clash, the
Stones began recording the tracks that would end up on their next
album, *Some Girls*. The song "Miss You" would become an iconic
disco track that skyrocketed to no. 1 on the singles charts. (pg 336,
#5) When the album *Some Girls* was released in June 1978, it
reached no. 1 and stayed in the charts for an astounding 32 weeks.
(pg 448, #5) *Rolling Stone* magazine even named *Some Girls* as its
album of the year. The Rolling Stones' previous album, *Love You
Live*, was a live album released the previous year to decent success.
Sadly, Stones publicist Les Perrin passed away on August 7, 1978.
He was 57 years old. The Stones would appear on the "Saturday
Night Live" television show on October 7, 1978. Two weeks later, on
October 23, 1978, Richards went to court in Canada to face the
charges against him, with Austin Cooper as his representative. (pg
164, #14)

Keith explained the depths of his heroin addiction to the court,
which began in June 1969, and his treatment in America that had
helped him finally conquer his addiction. Judge Lloyd Graburn gave
Richards a one-year suspended jail sentence and ordered Keith to
give a concert for the blind in tribute to a blind fan named Rita
Bedard, who wrote the judge personally to ask him to spare
Richards a jail sentence. Bedard attended Rolling Stones concerts
despite her handicap. Richards, not surprisingly, gladly gave this
performance. Sadly, another rock legend passed away on September
7, 1978, when Who drummer Keith Moon overdosed on 33
chlomethiazole tablets that were supposed to keep him from
drinking and help him with alcohol withdrawal. Bill Wyman and
Charlie Watts were in attendance at Moon's funeral, as the Stones
considered him a good friend. (pg 453, #5) Although Moon was an

impossible act to replace in the Who, they decided to continue with Kenney Jones, who used to be the Faces' drummer and worked with Brian Jones on the film score for *A Degree of Murder*. But Who lead singer Roger Daltrey said that, though he liked Kenney Jones as a person and thought he was a great drummer, he felt that Jones was all wrong for the Who. (pg 190, #21) However, the Who would continue with Kenney Jones as their drummer through 1982, and he also played drums for their Live Aid performance in 1985. Jones' tenure as the Who's drummer included the tragedy that occurred at Cincinnati's Riverfront Coliseum in December 1979 at a Who concert, when 11 people were trampled to death trying to get in the venue. The stampede began when not all of the stadium doors had opened properly to let the fans into the concert, forcing all fans to an overcrowded entrance that resulted in horrific tragedy. The Who didn't even know until after the concert the extent of what had happened. Yet the Who, like the Rolling Stones, have continued on into the 1980s, 1990s, and the 21st century, with Zak Starkey, who is the son of Ringo Starr, on drums when the band plays either in studio or live. Fittingly, Keith Moon is Zak's godfather. Starkey also plays drums on Roger Daltrey's solo song in tribute to Keith Moon, called "Under a Raging Moon," which showed true similarities between Starkey's and Moon's drumming styles.

After Jagger had filed for divorce from Bianca in March 1978, Bianca eventually won custody of their daughter Jade and an astounding sum of $25 million from Jagger. (pg 194, #7) On March 20, 1979, Keith Richards fulfilled his promise to the Canadian court system by announcing two benefit concerts for the Canadian National Institute for the Blind, which took place on April 21 at Oshawa Civic Auditorium near Toronto. The New Barbarians, Keith's solo band that he formed with Ronnie Wood, played first, followed by the only Rolling Stones live performance that year. (pg 166, #14) The New Barbarians consisted of Keith, Ronnie, Bobby Keys, Stanley Clarke, Joseph Modeliste, and Ian McLagan. (pg 168, #14) Ronnie Wood's solo album, *Gimme Some Neck*, was released on May 11, 1979 on the CBS Records label.

Around this time, Keith Richards met striking blonde supermodel Patti Hansen, and began a relationship with her shortly thereafter. Keith's relationship with Anita Pallenberg had deteriorated badly by then, and Anita was getting into trouble on her own. Anita's 17-year-old lover Scott Cantrell committed suicide on July 20, 1979 by playing Russian roulette with a .38 Smith & Wesson revolver that was reported stolen from Ft. Lauderdale, Florida. Cantrell's suicide happened in South Salem, New York in a house that was owned by Keith Richards. The detectives who were sent to investigate Cantrell's death described the premises as surprisingly filthy and unsanitary. Keith and Anita would soon divorce after this event, and the Stones began recording again in Paris in June 1979.

CHAPTER 19

STONES BACK TO NUMBER ONE ENTERING THE 1980'S, THE CHECKERBOARD LOUNGE

The next Rolling Stones album, *Emotional Rescue*, was released in July 1980, and it went to no. 1 on the charts. This very successful album included the songs "Where the Boys Go," "Down in the Hole," "Emotional Rescue," and "She's So Cold."

Tragically, the rock & roll world would suffer two huge losses towards the end of 1980 that shook the music world to its very core. First, on September 25, 1980, legendary Led Zeppelin drummer John Bonham died after consuming large quantities of vodka at Jimmy Page's house while rehearsing for what was supposed to be Led Zeppelin's 12th North American tour. At the time of Bonham's death, he was nervous about touring the United States again after an incident in Oakland, California at a show in 1977, in which both manager Peter Grant and John Bonham were arrested after beating up a roadie for hitting Grant's son, who attempted to take a sign lying around backstage. This led to a substantial legal hassle for the band. Bonham was described as a nice, pleasant farmer at home in England, but an angry, violent alcoholic on the road with Led Zeppelin. Rather than continue, Led Zeppelin respectfully decided to end their run as a band in tribute to their legendary drummer. He was 32 years old. Led Zeppelin have only reunited a handful of times since, last appearing at London's O2 arena in 2007 with Bonham's son Jason on drums, filling in for his iconic father.

In another, even more shocking tragedy on December 8, 1980, former Beatle John Lennon was assassinated by a deranged fan at approximately 10:50 p.m. as he was entering his apartment building, the Dakota, in New York City. Lennon's murder happened shortly after the release of his comeback album *Double Fantasy*, after taking time off from the music business to raise his son Sean with his wife, Yoko Ono. *Double Fantasy* would go to no. 1 after Lennon's death. The whole music world was shocked at Lennon's assassination, and grief was expressed worldwide. Bill Wyman of the Rolling Stones shared his grief the following day by stating, "I was really shocked. I don't know what to say, really. It's the same thing as when I heard about Keith Moon or Brian Jones. It's not believable at first, it's very disappointing and very upsetting." (pg 464, #5) In a twist of tragic irony, in Cynthia Lennon's book *John*, she said that John was warned by a psychic in 1966 that he would be shot in the United States. Even John predicted that he would be shot. (pgs 8-9, #23) John Lennon's assassin also had Mick Jagger on his hit list of targets, and Jagger lived very close to Lennon in New York City. (pg 200, #7)

The New Barbarians played the 1979 Knebworth Festival, which was Led Zeppelin's final concert. (pg 192, #13) Although Keith Richards wanted the Stones to tour after the 1980 *Emotional Rescue* album, Mick Jagger did not. However, despite reported growing tension between Jagger and Richards, the Rolling Stones did agree to tour America in 1981. They had also been working on a new studio album that they were set to release at the same time as the 1981 tour. Yet Keith Richards failed to show up at a meeting of the Stones in New York City to discuss the tour and album—a meeting that Keith had insisted on in the first place. The Stones very much questioned their future at this point, with drummer Charlie Watts initially saying that he wasn't going on tour. (pg 464, #5) Wood was told by the band that he had to clean up his drinking and drug issues, which included cocaine and heroin abuse.

Ronnie Wood was failing to show up for practices, like Brian Jones did, and Keith and Ronnie would have arguments over this. (pg 468, #5) Despite this, in June and July 1981 the Stones were back in rehearsal for the tour, which began in August to coincide with the release of their new album, *Tattoo You*. This album and tour were very successful, with the album going to no. 1 in the United States. The album contained the successful singles "Start Me Up" and "Waiting on a Friend," which both did very well on the singles charts. The Stones were known then for opening tours in small clubs, and, true to form, they opened their 1981 tour under the name Blue Sunday and the Cockroaches in Worcester, Massachusetts to an enthusiastic audience. The official 1981 North American tour began on September 25, 1981 in Philadelphia, Pennsylvania's JFK Stadium and criss-crossed the States, ending on December 19, 1981 in Hampton, Virginia. The all-female group the Go-Go's opened for the Stones on parts of this tour. (pg 472, #5)

The Stones played 50 concerts in 28 cities to an estimated 2 million people, while grossing an estimated $38 to $50 million. The Stones accomplished this despite many acts feeling reluctant to tour at all after the death of John Lennon.

Yet the fighting from within the Rolling Stones increased during their time on the 1981 tour. Mick and Keith disagreed more and more about decisions regarding the Stones' business and practice schedules. But one of the more memorable and iconic moments of that 1981 tour took place on November 22, 1981, in Chicago, when Mick, Keith, Ronnie, and Ian Stewart went to the Checkerboard Lounge. Muddy Waters was performing with Buddy Guy and Junior Wells, singing blues classics from his catalog. During this set, Keith, Ronnie, and Mick got on stage with Muddy Waters and performed with him some classic blues numbers, such as "Mannish Boy" and "Hoochie Coochie Man." The absence of Brian Jones there was palpable, because Brian would have been in his element playing the Chicago blues with these icons—the very inspiration Brian had when he created the band in 1962. It's also easy to see Brian on stage that night at the Checkerboard Lounge, either playing slide guitar or blues harmonica with these blues legends. This music was what Brian loved and performed well, and it's what the Rolling Stones owe their very existence to. Ian Stewart, technically the second-ever member of the Rolling Stones, performed boogie-woogie piano that night, while Buddy Guy and Junior Wells played with Keith and Ronnie on blues numbers with the band. A great performance by all, even though technically not all of the Rolling Stones were there: Bill Wyman and Charlie Watts didn't attend. Yet this was advertised as the Rolling Stones and Muddy Waters live at the Checkerboard Lounge, and in a strange way it seemed to be an unspoken tribute to Brian Jones: it was what he wanted the Rolling Stones to be.

PART TWO: THE AFTERMATH

CHAPTER 20

FRICTION FROM WITHIN THE STONES

In the 1982, the Rolling Stones were preparing for the European leg of their tour. The tour began on May 26, 1982 in Scotland and concluded on July 25, in Leeds, UK. Also in 1982, the Rolling Stones released a new live album called *Still Life*, recorded at the Hampton, Virginia show at the conclusion of the 1981 tour. During the show, a fan had rushed the stage while a huge amount of Rolling Stones balloons were dropped from above as part of the spectacle. With the death of John Lennon fresh in the minds of the Stones, especially while touring the same country where Lennon was shot, Richards took matters into his own hands and swatted his guitar at the fan's head to get him off the stage. Once Richards did this and the fan was caught by security, he calmly put his guitar back on to finish the song. In 1983, the Rolling Stones released the album Undercover, and Keith rounded out the year on December 18 by marrying Patti Hansen on his 40th birthday.

Earlier in August 1983, the Rolling Stones signed a very lucrative record deal with CBS, after their contract with Atlantic had expired. (pg 180, #14) This deal would cover the Rolling Stones' next four albums and would pay them $6 million, but the deal also included extra promotional expenditures that could potentially raise their compensation to $28 million. (pg 190, #14) A new single from the album, "Undercover of the Night," was released on October 31, 1983 and would become a top-10 hit in the United States. Also in 1983, Bill Wyman separated from his long-time partner Astrid Lundström.

On January 1, 1984, Brian's friend and blues inspiration Alexis Korner died at the age of 55 in London. As Bill Wyman stated, "Without Alexis, it is arguable that there would be no Rolling Stones." (pg 478, #5) Korner's ties with the Stones, and particularly with Brian, were a huge inspiration to the original concept of what Brian wanted the Rolling Stones to be. (pg 192, #14) Meanwhile, on March 2, 1984, Jerry Hall gave birth to Jagger's daughter, Elizabeth Scarlett. The deal the Rolling Stones had signed with CBS Records was for 4 albums and 3 solo albums by Mick Jagger. (pg 531, #15)

Keith Richards was pissed off about the solo album deal for Mick. (pg 208, #7) By May 1984, Jagger recorded with Michael Jackson a song called "State of Shock," which began to fuel Jagger's desire to venture into the world of a solo artist, a notion to which Keith Richards was vehemently opposed. Jagger wanted his solo work to be distinct from his work with the Rolling Stones. The Stones met in June 1984 in New York to discuss plans for their next album, but the meeting was overwrought with tension regarding Mick's solo work schedule, which conflicted with the Stones' plans; Keith felt that work with the band should be more important than Mick's solo work. Yet the plans were still on for the Stones' next album, *Dirty Work*, despite the obvious tension between Keith and Mick.

Mick's first solo album, *She's the Boss*, was released on the CBS label. This album did have some modest success, reaching the top-10 in the charts in both the United Kingdom and United States. The event Live Aid took place on July 13, 1985 at both Wembley Stadium in London and JFK Stadium in Philadelphia, and raised money for Ethiopian famine victims. (pg 198, #14) For logistical reasons, the Stones were unable to perform as a band, but Mick Jagger did perform a set with Tina Turner, while Keith Richards and Ronnie Wood played with Bob Dylan at the end of the show. Mick Jagger and David Bowie's song "Dancing in the Street" enjoyed top-10 success on both sides of the Atlantic. But the Rolling Stones suffered a big loss on December 12, 1985, when Ian Stewart passed away of a heart attack while waiting to see a doctor in a London clinic. He was just 47 years old. All of the Stones attended his funeral on December 20, and Eric Clapton and Jeff Beck also attended. The first two members of the Rolling Stones, Brian Jones and Ian Stewart, were now gone. Richards said that Stewart's importance in the band was the glue that held everything together over the years, an opinion held by every band member.

In March 1986, the Rolling Stones released *Dirty Work* to the public. This album would reach no. 4 in both the U.K. and U.S. charts (pg 483, #5). Tensions were high between Jagger and Richards, which culminated in a fictitious fight scene between the two in the video for the song "One Hit (to the Body)." Keith was still upset about Mick's solo career, and he said, "If Mick tours without this band, I'll slit his throat." (pg 483, #5) At the time, Keith wanted to tour with the Stones but Mick did not. It was a tense time for the whole band, and even Charlie Watts was doing speed and heroin by then, and drinking too much. (pg 242, #13) Watts soon quit everything drug related shortly after that, including drinking.

By then, Mick and Keith had stopped talking to each other and communicated through Ronnie Wood. (pg 246, #13) Richards said to Wood, "Mick's my wife whether I like it or not. We can't get a divorce." (pg 247, #13) Previously, Bill Wyman and Keith had stopped talking to each other over all the drugs that Keith was doing at the time. Wood's creative influence in the band was growing, and he contributed four songs to *Dirty Work*, an opportunity that neither Brian Jones nor Mick Taylor got. It was clear that since the Stones would not be touring for this album, the band's future was very much in doubt, and rumors of their break-up were prevalent. Were the Rolling Stones actually breaking up, as the Beatles had before them?

After Mick Jagger's album *She's the Boss* went platinum, his second album, *Primitive Cool*, was released in 1987. Richards turned his attention to Chuck Berry, working on Berry's concert film, *Hail! Hail! Rock 'n' Roll*, as a musician. This led to some tense moments between Richards and Berry in practice, but the film was still a success. In 1987, Mick and Keith worked independently on solo projects. Wood returned to painting, and he displayed his artistic works at art galleries in England. Mick Jagger said, "I was feeling very stultified within the Rolling Stones and I felt that I had to go and work with other people to get a bit revitalized, and I think it actually worked but it created a tremendous ruckus within the Rolling Stones, which was totally unnecessary, really. I think that everyone made much [too] much of a fuss about it, and I think that everybody should have been much more indulgent. So I was surprised when Keith was so upset that I wanted to do something outside of the band, he'd already done this with New Barbarians." (#19) Mick's album *Primitive Cool* had modest success, but not the numbers he was hoping for to establish himself as a permanent solo act. Keith Richards, on the other hand, who was the most ardent band member about keeping the Rolling Stones together, finally started working on solo projects outside the Rolling Stones.

Richards said of the experience, "Hell, we needed a break. Mick needed to find his own feed out there and see what it's like, he thought he could live without us, and I had to find out and do it myself too, and we both grew up a lot doing and finding out certain realisms. It's easy to go a little crazy inside the Rolling Stones bubble if that's all you do. One thing I never wanted to do was a solo record, until I started doing it. By then, working with all these cats, I found the nucleus of another great band." (#19)

Richards' solo album, *Talk Is Cheap*, was released on October 4, 1988, and he went on tour to support it with his new band, the X-Pensive Winos, until the end of the year. By then, Jagger was touring in Japan. However, Jagger's solo tour of the United States was canceled due to poor ticket sales. (pg 215, #7) By May 1988, Richards and Jagger had buried the hatchet, and all five Rolling Stones met to discuss a new album and tour, their first since 1982. It was agreed that the album and tour would occur the following year, beginning at the Rock & Roll Hall of Fame ceremony in January 1989, then held in New York City, where the Rolling Stones were to be inducted into the Rock & Roll Hall of Fame. The Who guitarist and songwriter Pete Townshend inducted them that night. Mick Jagger, Keith Richards, Ronnie Wood, and Mick Taylor showed up on behalf of the Rolling Stones. It was the first time that Mick Jagger and Keith Richards had appeared on stage together in public for some time, and everything once again seemed friendly between the two.

Jagger, when accepting the award, said to the audience, "You know, it's slightly ironic that tonight you see us all on our best behavior, but we're being rewarded for 25 years of bad behavior." Jagger continued, "I'm very proud to have worked with this group of musicians for 25 years. The other thing I'm very proud of is the songs that Keith and I have written over the last 25 years." Then came a very poignant and memorable moment in his acceptance speech regarding the first two members of the band, introduced in backwards order in terms of their actual longevity in the band. Jagger said, "I'd like to pay tribute to two people who couldn't be here tonight. One ... Ian Stewart, a great friend, a great blues pianist whose odd but invaluable musical advice kept us on a steady, bluesy course most of the time. And to Brian Jones, whose individuality and musicianship often took us off the bluesy course with often marvelous results." This statement goes to show the importance of the two men in the ultimate success of the band, but for different reasons. Stu was the rock that served the band as road manager, piano player when needed, and overall positive influence on the very foundation of the band. Brian Jones, on the other hand, was the founding member and was much more in favor of keeping the band a rhythm & blues outfit, as he had originally intended. Yet Jagger stated in the acceptance speech that it was Brian's individuality that had taken the band off its bluesy course; this may not have been completely accurate. However, by then, Mick Jagger and Keith Richards had been the undisputed leaders of the band for a long time, with Jones just a memory of what the band once was.

Richards, in his book *Life*, credits Stewart with the creation of the Rolling Stones, when research shows that the band was 100% Jones' creation. Jones' importance has been largely diminished by the current incarnation of the Rolling Stones. By March 1989, all five members of the Stones were in Barbados, recording a new album and openly planning a new tour thanks to a new contract with Toronto promoter Michael Cohl, the chief of Concert Productions International, to promote the 1989 tour and handle all the merchandising through his company Brockum. (pg 214, #19) Cohl is responsible for making the Stones an estimated $66 to $70 million from this venture. By the end of March 1989, the Rolling Stones relocated to Montserrat from Barbados to continue work on the new album, *Steel Wheels*. Also in March 1989, Bill Wyman proposed to his girlfriend, model Mandy Smith, who had only just turned 18. Wyman was 52 at the time. All members of the Rolling Stones attended Bill and Mandy's wedding on June 5, 1989, although the two had already been secretly married several days before at the registrar's office in Suffolk. (pg 215, #14) The only wedding guests were Bill's son Stephan and Mandy's sister Nicole. Even Wyman's own mother, Kathleen Perks, wasn't told of the wedding until it was over, though she was subsequently invited to the luncheon afterwards. Four years earlier, another member of the Stones tied the knot in a more traditional manner, when Ronnie Wood and Jo Howard were married on January 2, 1985 in Gerrard's Cross, Buckinghamshire. All of the Stones, except Mick Jagger, were present, as were guests such as Jeff Beck, Rod Stewart, Peter Cook, Peter Asher, and Ringo Starr.

PART TWO: THE AFTERMATH

CHAPTER 21

STEEL WHEELS TO THE RESCUE! AND MICK IS KNIGHTED

On July 11, 1989, in their usual grandiose style, the Stones announced to the world, at Grand Central Station in New York City, that they were planning a North American tour and the release of their new album, *Steel Wheels*. The *Steel Wheels* tour encompassed 115 shows and opened at Veterans Stadium in Philadelphia, Pennsylvania, then criss-crossed the country. The Rolling Stones made approximately $140 million from that tour alone, an impressive feat for any band. The album *Steel Wheels* went double platinum and featured several successful singles, including "Mixed Emotions," "Rock and a Hard Place," and "Almost Hear You Sigh," as well as Richards' noteworthy contributions on vocals on "Can't Be Seen," and "Slipping Away."

One very interesting track on the *Steel Wheels* album was a song called "Continental Drift," in which Jagger, Richards, and Wood flew to Tangier, Morocco to record with the Master Musicians of Jajouka. This song was an unspoken tribute to Brian, who had been out of the band for 20 years at that point. These were the same musicians with whom Brian Jones recorded in 1968, producing a subsequent album. Speaking of Brian Jones right before the 1989 tour, Jagger said of Brian's crippling drug problems, "If we'd all been a little more mature, it could have been avoided. It was a malaise of the time. Let everyone do what they want, don't worry about people killing themselves. I was too smart to go that far with drugs. But what happened to Brian seems such a tragic waste now. It was almost the same with Keith as well." (pg 210, #14)

Mick Jagger also returned to acting for the first time since the film *Performance* in the science fiction film *Freejack*, co-starring Emilio Estevez and released on January 17, 1992. However, the film didn't receive great reviews. It seemed that Jagger's attempt to establish himself as an actor, in addition to his role as a singer (either in the Rolling Stones or as a solo act) didn't work out as he had hoped it might.

After this successful album and tour, the band signed a three-album, $45 million record deal with Virgin Records. Jagger was very much involved with the details that were successfully negotiated in this contract. The Stones would go on to tour Canada, Japan, and Europe into the year 1990 after touring the United States. It is estimated that approximately 2.5 million people saw them on the European leg of the *Steel Wheels* tour alone. (pg 494, #5) Mick Jagger and longtime girlfriend Jerry Hall finally got married on March 21, 1990. It was at this time that bass player Bill Wyman decided that he had grown tired of touring and the demands of being in the Rolling Stones, and formally announced his retirement from the band, much to Mick and Keith's chagrin. Wyman's last show with the Rolling Stones was at Wembley Stadium in London. (pg. 276, #13) Despite the rest of the band trying to talk him out of this decision, Wyman decided that he wanted to pursue other opportunities, to work with other musicians, such as Terry Taylor and Gary Booker, and to form a new group called Willie and the Poor Boys. Wyman was also dealing with the consequences of marrying a much younger partner, Mandy Smith, and their relationship ended fairly quickly. As a consequence, the Rolling Stones decided to carry on without Wyman, with a new bass guitar player named Darryl Jones joining their line-up. Jones was the first African-American member of the band and had previously worked with Miles Davis, Peter Gabriel, and Madonna. (pg 291, #13)

Jones started playing bass guitar with the Rolling Stones full-time in 1994, for both the *Voodoo Lounge* album and its supporting North American tour. The Stones played 108 shows for that tour, grossing approximately $359 million, in 26 countries. (pg. 243, #7)This tour began in Washington, D.C. at RFK Stadium and would be wildly successful for the band. The album *Voodoo Lounge* went to no. 1 on the charts and sold 4 million copies, proving the Stones staying power in popular culture. It is definitely a quality album in their collection. Sadly, though, on September 6, 1994, pianist Nicky Hopkins passed away. Hopkins had performed often in the studio and live with the Rolling Stones, and was a huge part of the band during their most successful years.

In August 1997, the Rolling Stones released their new album,

Bridges to Babylon, followed by a 153-venue tour that went on for the next 20 months, making it the longest tour the band had ever done to date. The Rolling Stones started using "B" stages and catwalks to get themselves on stage during that tour. By then, Mick's marriage to Jerry Hall was in shambles, compounded by Jagger having public affairs with Carla Bruni and actress Uma Thurman, who is 27 years younger than Jagger. Nonetheless, Hall delivered Jagger's sixth child, Gabriel Luke Beauregard Jagger, in December 1997, despite Jagger's infidelity. Mick's seventh child, a boy named Lucas Maurice Jagger, was born to Mick's girlfriend Lucianna Gimenez Morad on May 17, 1999; DNA testing had proven Jagger to be the father. As a consequence, Jagger and Hall would officially divorce in 1999, with Hall receiving $15 million in the divorce settlement, plus the mansion in Surrey, England that was valued at approximately $7 million, plus a deposit of $1.5 million in each of Jagger and Hall's four children's trust accounts. (pg 255, #7) Mick Jagger's own estimated worth by the year 2000 was approximately $300 million. (pg 281, #7)

Meanwhile, Ronnie Wood's lifestyle of overspending and drug addiction was a cause of great concern among the other Stones. Notably, Mick Jagger was growing increasingly concerned about Wood's drinking and drug habits, which included both cocaine and heroin abuse. Ronnie had bought a nightclub called Harrington Club, and he was in debt from it. Ironically enough, Wood checked himself into the Priory Clinic in Roehampton in July 2000 to curb his drinking and drug habits, the same clinic that Brian Jones had checked himself into in the late 1960s.

After the tragedy of the September 11, 2001, terrorist attacks on the United States, both Mick Jagger and Keith Richards played the October 20, 2001 Madison Square Garden concert to raise money for 9/11 victims and their families. Thy played "Salt of the Earth," and "Miss You" for that emotional performance. The Rolling Stones were also deeply saddened by the death of former Beatle George Harrison, who had passed away on November 29, 2001. Harrison succumbed to cancer, as well as injuries sustained from a knife attack by a deranged fan who broke into his house in England in 1999. Harrison was 58 years old.

The same year, Jagger's solo album *Goddess in the Doorway* was considered to be a total flop, and that month Jagger became involved with 6'3" model L'Wren Scott (Luann Bambrough). It was reported around this time that Jagger had pursued Britney Spears also, but failed in that endeavor. (pg 278, #7) though Mick did apparently hook up with actress Angelina Jolie. (pg 243, #7) In fact, Jagger claims to have slept with over 4000 women. (pg 226, #7) At the end of the day, Jagger has been accused of being incapable of being faithful to any of his wives or girlfriends, and Richards even advised Jagger to get psychiatric help for his sexual addictions.

Sadly, the world lost another rock legend in 2002 when Who bass guitarist John Entwistle passed away in Las Vegas, Nevada, the night before the Who were to begin a 27-show tour of the United States and Canada. Entwistle died after snorting cocaine, in room 658 of the Hard Rock Hotel and Casino, in bed with a hooker. (pg 221, #21) He was 57 years old. Despite this gigantic loss of a vital musician and friend from the beginning of the band, the Who decided to go on with the tour as scheduled, and have continued on as a band ever since. The Who and the Rolling Stones developed a very close bond over the years, and both bands began as R & B groups. In 2002, the Rolling Stones performed their *Forty Licks* tour to commemorate the 40th anniversary of the band by playing 127 shows in 73 cities. The band earned approximately $300 million from this tour, but there were complaints of expensive ticket prices from fans throughout that tour. By the beginning of the 21st century, the Rolling Stones had successfully grossed approximately $1.7 billion in total concert revenue, and the *Forty Licks* tour by itself beat out artists U2, Michael Jackson, and Madonna in gross ticket sales.

In 2003, Jagger was knighted by British royalty at Kensington Palace, but not by the Queen herself, as is normally the case. Apparently, Queen Elizabeth II opposed the idea of Jagger becoming knighted, as he was denied this honor five times before finally being accepted. Jagger was nominated for knighthood by then English Prime Minister Tony Blair. Part the controversy over Jagger being nominated for knighthood involved rumors of him being once romantically involved with the Queen's sister, Margaret. (pg 4, #7) When the day came for Jagger's knighting, Queen Elizabeth II made sure that she had her scheduled surgery to remove cartilage from her knee. In Her Majesty's place, her son Prince Charles knighted Jagger. Ironically enough, there had been some past drama between Prince Charles and Jagger when his late wife Princess Diana had invited Jagger to Kensington Palace for tea and Jagger had accepted. When Prince Charles found out about this, he expressed his dismay and disapproval of the idea, and the result was that Jagger's invitation was canceled. In Jagger's place, artist Phil Collins was invited to the palace for tea. (pg 6, #7)

On the day of Jagger's knighting, he wore a pair of $55 Adidas sneakers to Buckingham Palace, and brought his beaming-with-pride father Joe Jagger, who was overwhelmingly proud of the true accomplishment by his son moving up in the English hierarchy. Keith Richards, on the other hand, was pissed off and angry at Jagger's acceptance of knighthood, and instructed Jagger to stick it up the Queen's ass. (pg 7, #7) Richards found it too hypocritical after all the problems the Rolling Stones had encountered from the English government, having wanted the band jailed or killed, and thought that being knighted by royalty was not what the Rolling Stones were all about. It is worth noting that former Beatle Paul McCartney was knighted without any debate from the Crown, likely due to his cleaner image and mostly (but not entirely) staying out of trouble. In recent years, former Beatle Richard Starkey (Ringo Starr) was also knighted by the Queen. Nevertheless, the Rolling Stones were back on the road in 2003, playing in China for the first time, in both Shanghai and Beijing. (pg 292, #7)

In 2004, the Rolling Stones were inducted into the short-lived U.K. Music Hall of Fame. They were back on the road again in 2005 to support their album *A Bigger Bang*, which was produced by Don Was. (pg 299, #7) This very successful and lucrative tour began on August 21, 2005 at Fenway Park in Boston, Massachusetts and ended in 2007, grossing the band an astounding $550 million worldwide and a spot in the Guinness Book of World Records. In October 2006, the Rolling Stones played the Beacon Theatre in New York City to film a concert movie called *Shine a Light*, directed by Martin Scorsese. (pg 582, #15) Although the concert was filmed in October 2006, it would not be released until 2008. This concert film had guest appearances by artists such as Buddy Guy, Jack White, and Christina Aguilera. The film was given a PG-13 rating. In the beginning of the film, Mick and "Marty" (Mick's nickname for Scorsese) openly have disagreements over the stage size and set-up. The Rolling Stones themselves were just introduced as four

members: Mick. Keith, Ronnie, and Charlie, minus bass player
Darryl Jones, who is regarded as a hired musician. Scorsese asked
Jagger for a copy of the set list for the show, and he didn't receive it.
The Stones conducted meticulous rehearsals in preparation for the
show.

Former President Bill Clinton visited the Stones backstage
before the show and hugged every member of the band. Hillary
Clinton, then a Senator from the state of New York, was also in
attendance. President Clinton got to introduce the Rolling Stones
on stage that night at the Beacon Theatre. Backstage, before the
start of the show, Keith Richards joked, "Hey Clinton, I'm Bushed!
." The Stones put on a magnificent performance that night, with
Jack White on guitar and vocals for the song "Loving Cup," Buddy
Guy on guitar and vocals for the song "Champagne & Reefer," and
Christina Aguilera singing "Live With Me" quite impressively with
Jagger. The movie shows that even in the year 2006, the Rolling
Stones were at the height of their game and vast abilities to
entertain a crowd, including former Presidents of the United States.
Scorsese's film shots throughout the movie were also exceptionally
well done, including footage from the past that included the Brian
Jones years, Keith's drug bust in Toronto, and Mick Jagger
predicting in 1964 that he thought the Stones would last for at least
another year. The film reminded me of Led Zeppelin's concert film
The Song Remains the Same, in which they were filmed performing
at nearby Madison Square Garden during the height of their touring
fame in 1973 after the release of their *Houses of the Holy* album.
That film merged concert footage with fantasy dream sequences
featuring each individual member of Led Zeppelin, including their
manager Peter Grant. Perhaps the difference between these two
films is the status of each group at the time of filming: although Led
Zeppelin was an enormously popular band and touring act during
their time together, they didn't have the touring longevity that the
Stones have, and Scorsese's directorial touch made the quality of his
film much higher than Led Zeppelin's. *Shine a Light* ends with a
memorial to Ahmet Ertegun of Atlantic Records, who fell down
after leaving the Beacon Theatre that night (October 29, 2006) and
succumbed to his brain injuries in December.

Sadly, Mick Jagger's father Joe passed away at the age of 93 in
November 2006. Joe Jagger is very much credited for establishing

discipline and a strong work ethic in his son. (pg. 308, #7) Mick described Joe as a good father. (pg 309, #7) On February 4, 2006, at Super Bowl XL in Detroit, Michigan, the Rolling Stones gave a magnificent and memorable performance at the halftime show to an estimated television audience of 89.9 million people. Since 1989, it has been estimated that the Rolling Stones have earned 2 billion pounds. They have done this through song rights, merchandising, touring, and sponsorship. (pg 594, #15) After the Super Bowl performance, the Rolling Stones played a free concert (they could afford to do so) at Copacabana Beach in Rio de Janeiro to an estimated 1 million people. Unlike the Altamont show in 1969, there was no violence reported at Copacabana Beach. After the Stones performed in Rio de Janeiro, they played Japan, China, New Zealand, and Australia in March and April 2006. Then, the band took a break before heading to Europe. Keith Richards was hospitalized in Fiji when he fell out of a tree, requiring cranial surgery. This caused a six-week delay in preparations for their European tour. The Stones played the Isle of Wight festival on June 10, 2007, with guest Amy Winehouse singing "Ain't Too Proud to Beg" with them on stage. (pg 351, #13)

Former manager Allen Klein passed away on July 4, 2009; his influence and the controversy he generated still affect the Rolling Stones to this day. In what may be the irony of all ironies, former driver/road manager Tom Keylock, one of the first members of the Stones' front office to arrive at Cotchford Farm on the night of Brian's death, also died on July 2, 2009, in England. He was 82 years old. On a happier note, the song "Moves Like Jagger" was a top-10 hit for the group Maroon 5 in 2011. (pg 324, #7) Mick Jagger performed to President Barack Obama and the First Family on February 21, 2012 in the White House, even getting President Obama to sing parts of "Sweet Home Chicago." After a long break from each other, the Rolling Stones got back together for rehearsals in Weehawken, New Jersey in preparation for another world tour in 2012. The Stones also released a greatest hits compilation album, along with two new singles, "Doom and Gloom" and "One More Shot," on November 12, 2012. They also published a book called *The Rolling Stones 50* and a documentary called *Crossfire Hurricane*, which was released on November 15, 2012 and featured interviews with all six surviving members of the Stones. In 2012 and 2013, the Stones criss-crossed America and played some European dates.

Yet tragedy would strike with a vengeance on March 17, 2014, when Mick Jagger's girlfriend L'Wren Scott was found dead in her apartment in the Chelsea neighborhood of Manhattan. The cause of death was determined to be suicide after a long bout with depression. She was still a model and designer at the time of her death, and she was dealing with financial problems, which were cited as a possible reason for her suicide. Jagger was on tour with the Rolling Stones at the time of Scott's death, and he was completely devastated by the news. Scott was 49 years old. In addition, the Rolling Stones and the music world lost another friend and icon when saxophonist Bobby Keys died on December 2, 2014. Keys not only recorded with the Stones, but also worked with such artists as Lynyrd Skynyrd, Harry Nilsson, Delaney & Bonnie and friends, John Lennon, George Harrison, Eric Clapton, and Joe Cocker. In fact, Keys was with Lennon on his "lost weekend" in Los Angeles after Yoko Ono had kicked him out, and he recorded saxophone on Lennon's anthem "Power to the People." He died of cirrhosis of the liver. He was 70 years old, and the Stones were devastated by his death.

CHAPTER 22

RETURN TO THE BLUES

The Stones once again made history when they appeared in Havana, Cuba to perform in March 2016. It was clear that the Rolling Stones' music was breaking down barriers in a world once very much against their message and performances, proving it to be a universal language. In December 2016, the Rolling Stones released an album that only took them three days to record, once again produced by Don Was. For this album, the Rolling Stones returned to their basic rhythm & blues roots, covering great blues standards. *Blue & Lonesome* went to no. 1 on the charts, and seemed to be the album of strictly blues cover songs that Brian Jones had envisioned for the band. The album includes four songs written by Walter Jacobs (Little Walter): "Just Your Fool," "Blue and Lonesome," "I Gotta Go," and " Hate to See You Go," one Chester Burnett song (Howlin' Wolf) called "Commit a Crime," "Little Rain" by Ewart G. Abner and Jimmy Reed, "Hoo Doo Blues," by Otis Hicks and Jerry West, "All of Your Love," by Samuel Maghett (Magic Sam), and two songs from Willie Dixon called "Just Like I Treat You" and "I Can't Quit You Baby." It is interesting to note that the Rolling Stones' version is slightly different from that of Led Zeppelin, with both songs featuring significant amplification and distortion compared to Willie Dixon's original. Yet the Stones' version, with Mick Jagger's vocals, is of very high quality, and the Rolling Stones put their stamp on this blues classic, making it one of the strongest tracks on the album. It's clear that the Rolling Stones are still on top of their game professionally and have the luxury of going back to their roots to play the music they were meant to play (according to Brian Jones). As Muddy Waters says in so many words on the sleeve of this album, rock & roll is the baby of rhythm & blues, and without R & B, there would be no rock & roll. Ironically, while recording this album, it just so happened that Eric Clapton was recording at the same studio, and was convinced by the Stones to play on two tracks, further giving the album an authentic bluesy character, just what the Stones were looking for.

In my opinion, this is the best album the Rolling Stones have produced since *Emotional Rescue*, and it showed that the blues, if performed at a very high level, could be sold to the public and be appreciated in the commercial world of popular music. It is interesting and ironic to note that neither Brian Jones nor Ian Stewart are mentioned on the album, and don't receive credit for their roles in the early (and now current) musical inspiration of the Rolling Stones. However, when listening to the album, both of their influences are felt in the selection and progression of the songs, especially Brian Jones. The album feels almost like a tribute to him without mentioning his name, Jones being the one who got them all together in the first place to pay homage to the American Chicago and Delta blues songs that they heard and fell in love with as youths. Despite Brian's physical absence on the album, you can feel his presence on every track, as if he were spiritually guiding the selection of the songs and laying harmonica or slide guitar on every track.

In 2017, the Rolling Stones released a double CD of prerecorded tracks called *On Air*, which was a recording the Rolling Stones did early in their career for the BBC. These tracks included Chuck Berry's songs "Come On," "Roll Over Beethoven," and "Carol," and other cover songs like "Cops and Robbers," "Hi-Heel Sneakers," "Walking the Dog," and "I Just Want to Make Love to You." This album has the feel of Brian Jones' leadership, when the band was heavily influenced by the Chicago blues sound, with some Chuck Berry rock & roll thrown in to speed up the tempo. It also shows the Rolling Stones' state of mind at the time, when they were young and hungry to break into the music market as a rhythm & blues band, but with definite rock & roll influences as well. The album sold well and made it to no. 4 on the Billboard chart. There was an accompanying book that was published at the same time as the release of the CD, called *The Rolling Stones: On Air in the Sixties, TV, and Radio History as It Happened*, written by Richard Havers. In it, the period of 1963 until 1969 is covered.

This book illustrates how much Brian Jones was the driving force in the band, although his power would be severely diminished over time. It was Brian's love of American rhythm & blues, combined with Mick and Keith's love of Chuck Berry that morphed into the sound of what the early Rolling Stones were. Over time, the band evolved into more of a rock & roll group, with occasional returns to rhythm & blues music. The album also featured all five original members of the Rolling Stones, including Bill Wyman and Brian Jones. This showed that the Rolling Stones' music, even from over 50 years ago, is still popular today.

The most recent tour that the Rolling Stones embarked on is the No Filter tour, a three-part tour that covered European dates, followed by a North American tour that was scheduled to start in April 2019. This leg of the tour was delayed by an unexpected ailment that Mick Jagger was suffering from, requiring a replacement to a valve in his heart, which was successfully completed on April 5, 2019. This is where the story takes an unexpected turn for me. The show that was initially scheduled for FedEx Field in Landover, Maryland, which would have been the closest location to me on that tour, would have been on May 25, 2019. While I was still contemplating going to this exciting yet expensive event, I hesitated to buy a ticket until a date for the postponed May 25 concert was announced. As fate had it, the make-up show for FedEx Field would be July 3, 2019, the 50th anniversary of Brian's death.

Initially, I had considered flying over to Cheltenham, England to possibly visit Brian's grave, even obtaining my passport earlier in the year in preparation for this potential pilgrimage. However, the rescheduling of the Rolling Stones concert to July 3 appeared to be a sign from God that I was meant to be at that particular Rolling Stones concert in Landover, Maryland, to see the very band Brian Jones created perform on stage in front of me. It seemed to be too good an opportunity to turn down, especially on the 50th anniversary of Brian's death.

Opportunity came my way again when a good friend of mine offered me a ticket at face value (thanks, Alev), which was a standing-room-only ticket for $200. It is well known how expensive Rolling Stones concert tickets usually are, so this price was about the absolute limit I was willing to spend on a ticket, even to see a band of the quality of the Rolling Stones. Accordingly, with my high school friends Alev Sezer- Jacobs and Janet Tropea, and my friend from work Reggie Braddy, we headed off to FedEx Field on July 3, 2019 to literally witness history.

On that night, the Rolling Stones were about to give the FedEx Field audience a memorable and high-quality show that ranks as truly one for the ages. I was also curious how they were going to treat the anniversary of Brian's death, despite him largely being written out of history. True to form, the Rolling Stones didn't even mention his name that night.

However, the set list and quality of their performance were truly spectacular and mesmerized the sold out audience. The set list was not too out of the ordinary, packed with hits and classic live numbers. The set list, in order, from that night was:

1. Jumpin' Jack Flash
2. It's Only Rock and Roll
3. Tumblin' Dice
4. You've Got Me Rocking
5. Mercy, Mercy
6. Rocks Off
7. You Can't Always Get What You Want
8. Angie
9. Let It Bleed
10. Sympathy for the Devil
11. Honky Tonk Woman
12. Slipping Away
13. Before They Make Me Run
14. Miss You
15. Paint It Black
16. Midnight Rambler
17. Start Me Up
18. Brown Sugar
19. Gimme Shelter
20. (I Can't Get No) Satisfaction

All in all, this concert by the Rolling Stones, despite their ages, was exceptional, and the band gave their all to the audience. The sold-out crowd at FedEx Field was fully in unison with the Rolling Stones that night, singing note for note (myself included) throughout every memorable song from the set chosen by the band. It certainly made standing in line after the show to buy a Rolling Stones tour T-shirt for $50 a bit more bearable, proving that I, too, was there that memorable night. The Rolling Stones are still one of the best musical acts in the world.

Yet, the fact that Brian Jones was not even mentioned by the band on the 50th anniversary of his death also spoke deafening volumes about their position on Brian decades after his departure from the band he created. It is said that the current incarnation of the Rolling Stones considered Jones not to be an important piece of the band's history, but simply just a former member who, like Mick

Taylor, Ian Stewart, or Bill Wyman, was just part of the band's past, with no bearing on the current line-up or sound of the band. This shows that not all wounds have healed since Brian's departure from the band. It is hard to imagine Paul McCartney or Ringo Starr not mentioning and paying tribute to their former Beatle bandmates John Lennon and George Harrison at every concert they perform together, especially on the anniversaries of their passing (December 8 and November 29, respectively). It is also hard to imagine Pete Townshend and Roger Daltrey of the Who not paying tribute to either Keith Moon or John Entwistle on the anniversaries of their deaths, due to the enormous impact both musicians had on the overall sound of and live performances by the Who. Surely, Brian deserves to be in this category—after all, the band that he created still enjoys tremendous success 58 years later. Unfortunately, the answer seems to be a clear and unambiguous "no" from the current members of the band, who seem to have the most to gain by not mentioning Brian Jones at all.

According to *27: A History of the 27 Club*, Howard Sounes says of Jones, "Despite his talent and achievements, history has not been kind to Brian. He formed the Rolling Stones. He was a key part of the band's look and sound in the early years of its success, and precious few bands have been more successful." (pg 11, #4) Yet if Brian is remembered at all, it is as a casualty of fame, a weak, foolish, and unpleasant person who couldn't cope with its restrictions. Sounes says that, of the members of the "27 Club" of famous deceased musicians, "least remembered is Brian Jones, whose part of the Rolling Stones story has been effaced by the success of the surviving members. Brian went without mention as the Stones celebrated their 50th anniversary tour in 2012. It was partly his own fault. He was the least likeable of the principal members, neurotic, weepy, and sometimes violent, and he was always going to be less iconic than Mick Jagger." (pg 285, #4) Jones' eventual replacement in the Rolling Stones, Ronnie Wood, says he found it easy to adapt and change styles to follow the opportunities that came his way, in both Faces and the Rolling Stones. But for his predecessor, Brian Jones, such opportunities ultimately proved to be elusive. Ronnie also credits being at the right place at the right time in joining the Rolling Stones when he did. (pg 353, #13)

The Rolling Stones have certainly carried on with great success, touring the world and grossing huge amounts of money in the process. In Chris Andersen's 2012 biography of Mick Jagger, he stated that at the time of his book's publication, the Rolling Stones held five of the top 10 richest-grossing tours of all time, occupying spots 1, 3, 4, 5, and 9. (pg xiii, #7) According to Wikipedia, however, on December 16, 2019, the numbers now have the legendary Rolling Stones tours only occupying two spots in the top 10, with the *A Bigger Bang* tour at no. 4 and the ongoing No Filter tour at no. 9, and two more in the top 20, with the 1994 *Voodoo Lounge* tour coming in at no. 19 and the *Forty Licks* tour at no. 20. (#26) Author Chris Andersen credits Jagger's education at the London School of Economics for helping build the financial juggernaut that helped the Rolling Stones earn billions of dollars and Jagger earn a fortune estimated to be approximately $400 million.

Sadly, Brian's close friend and rock drumming legend Ginger Baker passed away on October 6, 2019 at the age of 80. As for the Rolling Stones in the year 2020, the rest of the No Filter tour has been put on hold due to the global coronavirus pandemic, but they could possibly record and release a new album with all the surviving members of the band, including Wyman, Taylor, and Darryl Jones, with another world tour (assuming a vaccine to the COVID-19 virus is found) to follow. Nevertheless, the legend of the Rolling Stones, the band Brian Jones created, continues into 2020 and, perhaps, well beyond.

BIBLIOGRAPHY

1. *Paint It Black: The Murder of Brian Jones*, by Geoffrey Giuliano. London, UK: Virgin Books, 1994.

2. *The Murder of Brian Jones: The Secret Story of My Love Affair with the Murdered Rolling Stone*, by Anna Wohlin and Christine Lindsjoo. London, UK: Blake Publishing, 1999.

3. *Brian Jones: The Inside Story of the Original Rolling Stone*, by Nicholas Fitzgerald. New York, NY: Putnam, 1985.

4. *27: A History of the 27 Club Through the Lives of Brian Jones, Jimi Hendrix, Janis Joplin, Jim Morrison, Kurt Cobain and Amy Winehouse*, by Howard Sounes. Boston, MA: De Capo Press, 2013.

5. *Rolling with the Stones*, by Bill Wyman (with Richard Haver). New York, NY: DK Publishing, 2002.

6. *Keith Richards: The Ultimate Guide to His Music & Legend. Rolling Stone* Special Collectors Edition. New York, NY: Penske Media, 2018.

7. *Mick: The Wild Life and Mad Genius of Jagger*, by Christopher Andersen. New York, NY: Gallery Books, 2012.

8. *Brian Jones: The Making of the Rolling Stones*, by Paul Trynka. New York, NY: Penguin/Random House, 2014.

9. *The Sun & the Moon & the Rolling Stones*, by Rich Cohen. New York, NY: Spiegel + Grau, 2016.

10. *Golden Stone: The Untold Life and Tragic Death of Brian Jones*, by Laura Jackson. New York, NY: St. Martin's Press, 1993.

11. *Brian Jones*, by Alan Clayson. London, UK: Sanctuary Publishing, 2003.

12. *Stone Alone*, by Bill Wyman (with Ray Coleman). New York, NY: Viking Penguin, 1990.

13. *Ronnie*, by Ronnie Wood. London, UK: Macmillan, 2007.

14. *The Rolling Stones Chronicle: The First Thirty Years*, by Massimo Bonanno. New York, NY: Henry Holt, 1990.

15. *Mick Jagger*, by Phillip Norman. New York, NY: HarperCollins/Jessica Productions, 2012.

16. *Beatles vs. Stones*, by John McMillian. New York, NY: Simon & Schuster, 2013.

17. "Pan (god)." Wikipedia. https://en.wikipedia.org/wiki/Pan_(god)

18. *Stones in Exile* (DVD, 61 minutes). New York, NY: Passion Pictures, 2010.

19. *25 x 5: The Continuing Adventures of the Rolling Stones* (VHS tape, 130 minutes). New York, NY: CBS Music Video Enterprises, 1989.

20. *Rocks Off: 50 Tracks That Tell the Story of the Rolling Stones*, by BIll Janovitz. New York, NY: St. Martin's Press, 2014.

21. *Thanks a Lot Mr. Kibblewhite: My Story*, by Roger Daltrey. New York, NY: Henry Holt, 2018.

22. *No Quarter: The Three Lives of Jimmy Page*, by Martin Power. New York, NY: Overlook Omnibus Books, 2016.

23. *John*, by Cynthia Lennon. New York, NY: Crown Publishing, 2005.

24. *The Rolling Stones: On Air in the Sixties, TV, and Radio History as It Happened*, by Richard Havers. New York, NY: HarperCollins, 2017.

25. *"Brian Jones Presents the Pipes of Pan at Joujouka."* Wikipedia. https://en.wikipedia.org/wiki/Brian_Jones_Present s_the_Pipes_of_Pan_at_Joujouka

26. "List of Highest-Grossing Concert Tours." Wikipedia. https://en.wikipedia.org/wiki/List_of_highest-grossing_concert_tours

PART THREE
THE LEGACY

PART THREE: THE LEGACY

27 Club

CHAPTER 23

BRIAN JOINS THE 27 CLUB

What is the legacy of Brian Jones, a.k.a. Elmo Lewis, now over 50 years after his death? How should he be remembered? Should he be remembered at all? Or does he deserve vastly more recognition and respect than he got? Could Brian have started another band that would be as successful as the Rolling Stones, or even more so? Had Brian lived, would he have become a more successful husband and parent to the five children he already had, and any future ones? Will Brian ever receive true appreciation and recognition from his former band, or will he continue to be written out of existence by them? Could Brian have conquered his inner demons that led to his

PART THREE: THE LEGACY

failed relationships with family, girlfriends, bandmates, and children? Could he have redeemed himself in their eyes? Should Brian have his own spot in the Rock & Rol Hall of Fame? How about the Blues Hall of Fame? Can Brian be forgiven for the mistakes he made when he was alive? Will Brian's influence re-emerge over time, with future musical generations? Where do we go from here?

Brian Jones' legacy was destined to be a complex paradox due to the controversial issues that plagued his short life of 27 years. His legacy is well documented, with many successes and many failures, and he is either praised or dismissed, depending on whose opinion you ask. There are many speculations about what Brian could have become musically and artistically in the years since his death. The main reason that I chose to write about Brian Jones is that I feel that his story may have been told incorrectly—and, to be frank, I also feel that Brian got a raw deal from music history. Although Brian was very self-destructive, he was also a musical genius in that short time period. It was his vision, and his alone, that led to the formation of the Rolling Stones, one of the most successful and influential bands in history.

Despite the fact that his power and influence were stripped from him within the Rolling Stones, I believe that there is evidence that he could have created another band that could have competed with the Rolling Stones—or any other band of the time. Apparently, even though it was just a discussion at the time of this death, Brian did talk to Jimi Hendrix, John Lennon, and Alexis Korner about forming a new band after his departure from the Rolling Stones. In fact, Jimi Hendrix was possibly a free agent at the time of Brian's death, with his former band, the Jimi Hendrix Experience, having played their last show with Noel Redding and Mitch Mitchell at the Denver Pop Festival in 1969. Brian and Jimi remained friends all the way until Brian's death.

It is impossible to predict whether Brian could have pulled off the genesis of this super group had he been given more time to accomplish the feat. However, there is skepticism that John Lennon would have joined another band that he did not fully control, as he did with the Plastic Ono Band after the break-up with the Beatles. Instead, Lennon would have had to clear his ideas with Hendrix, Jones, and Korner, which seems very unlikely. After the Beatles went their separate ways in 1970, Lennon's passions seemed clearly focused on creating his own sound and art displays with his wife, Yoko Ono. The same could be said for Hendrix, who would go on to shine with his new band, Band of Gypsys, featuring his Army buddy Billy Cox on bass guitar and Buddy Miles on drums. Hendrix also reunited with Mitchell for his performances at Woodstock in August 1969, shortly after Brian's death, and at his memorable Isle of Wight Festival appearance in 1970, shortly before his own death on September 18, 1970.

However, it seems clear that Alexis Korner very well could have embarked on a new musical project with Brian that could have been extraordinary. This could have been a case of history repeating itself, with Korner again taking Brian under his wing in London and introducing him to the new music scene there. It could be argued that Jones and Korner could have created a new group, sticking to a more traditional rhythm & blues sound in contrast to what the Rolling Stones had become, and possibly giving the Stones real competition in the charts and in record sales. And if Brian was given the opportunity to write songs in a band where he had a fresh start as the musical leader, it is quite possible, if not likely, that he could have developed into a successful writer and composer on his own.

Because Brian's life was cut short at such an early age, it is difficult to determine what the future might have held. Any band that Brian started after his departure from the Stones would have been compared to his original band. As the record shows, the Stones went on to greater success without Brian, in both album creation and global touring. Yet, there are many people—myself included—who feel that Brian, despite his many shortcomings, should be better honored and recognized for his contributions to music and pop culture. I feel that Brian Jones should be more recognized as a true musical genius whose influence can still be felt across a broad range of music more than 50 years after his death.

Brian Jones is a member of the "27 Club," which boasts an impressive list of more than 50 famous musicians who, like Brian, met an untimely death at this age, including music's most iconic stars. How does Brian Jones' story compare to the other members of the 27 Club? What about other famous rock & roll and rhythm & blues musicians either before or after the age of 27? Did the lives of these stars compare to the tragedy and wastefulness of Brian's life? Is the music business a pathway to an early grave, with artists given no roadmap to guide them through the pressures of road life, including drug and alcohol addiction and the other traps that come with fame? Or is it the fault of these individual musicians, including Brian, who were too weak to survive the rough-and-tumble world of pop stardom? In order to answer these questions, I have reviewed a long list of deceased music stars from before, during, and after Brian Jones' life, from both the 27 Club and outside of it, and compared their lives to that of Brian's. Some of these artists, like Brian, burned both ends of the candle to live their extravagant lifestyles, but experienced both adulation and loneliness, mixed with isolation, that often eventually led to self-destruction.

As for members of the "27 Club" itself, there are many notable names on it besides the obvious ones: Brian Jones, Jimi Hendrix, Jim Morrison, Janis Joplin, Kurt Cobain, and Amy Winehouse. However, this "club" is far more extensive and inclusive than the six members listed above. The list includes Russian singer and songwriter Alexander "Sasha" Bashlachev, who perished in February of 1988 after falling from his apartment window in Leningrad, and Alan Wilson of the band Canned Heat, who was one of its founding members but passed away on September 3, 1970 in Topanga, California after overdosing on barbiturates. Ronald McKernan, also known as "Pigpen," was one of the founding members of the Grateful Dead, and their original keyboard player. After years of very heavy drinking on the road and in the studio, Mckernan died on March 8, 1973 of a gastrointestinal hemorrhage. Pete de Freitas was the drummer for the band Echo & the Bunnymen, and tragically died after a motorcycle accident in 1989. All of them were 27.

In reviewing the life of Brian's close friend Jimi Hendrix, although their individual paths to fame were quite different, their untimely deaths were eerily similar. Both Jones and Hendrix were in love with the blues, and both achieved the height of music stardom as a result. But, as is often the case with the blues, the story does not end well for those involved with unlocking its secrets.

The fatal mistake that Hendrix made on the night of his death was mixing alcohol with the drug Vesparax, while also being under the influence of heroin. He took nine Vesparax tablets when the prescription was clearly only for one, and the results proved to be fatal. (pg 198, #1) Hendrix choked to death on his own vomit during the night of September 18, 1970. Hendrix was with his then-girlfriend Monika Dannemann, who discovered his body. Hendrix's body was taken back to the United States, and he was buried in Seattle after his funeral on October 1, 1970. (pg 198, #1)

Another member of the 27 Club, Kurt Cobain, was born on February 20, 1967 in Aberdeen, Washington. Cobain was a singer, songwriter, and guitar player who rose to great prominence in the band he created, Nirvana. Their album *Nevermind* has sold over 30 million copies and became a staple of the grunge rock movement that originated in Seattle. Cobain wore strictly inexpensive garments, mostly from thrift stores. Although Nirvana is largely credited with establishing the Seattle grunge music sound in the 1990s, Cobain lived most of his life 2 hours away, in Aberdeen. Other Seattle bands that scored chart success after Nirvana include Pearl Jam, Soundgarden, and Alice in Chains. (pg 2, #2) One major difference between Brian Jones and Kurt Cobain should be noted: although Brian Jones created the Rolling Stones, he didn't receive any songwriting credit for the band's illustrious catalog of songs. Cobain, however, was the main songwriter for Nirvana, and he successfully wrote over 100 songs for the band during his time in Nirvana.

Kurt began dating his eventual wife, Courtney Harrison, later known as Courtney Love, in 1991, with whom he would have a daughter, Frances Bean, in August 1992. Tragically, Cobain began his downfall with heroin addiction in 1991, which continued all the way until his death. Yet in late 1993, Cobain and his bandmates gave an unforgettable acoustic performance on the MTV show "Unplugged," which showed a global audience the true genius of the band and its songwriter. Nirvana covered Lead Belly's song "Where Did You Sleep Last Night?" at that performance, showing their deep appreciation of the Delta blues that had once inspired a young Brian Jones.

Cobain was diagnosed with attention-deficit disorder and bipolar disorder as a child and was treated with the drug Ritalin. Cobain was also very affected by his parents' divorce when he was 9 years old. Despite his enormous success with Nirvana and the music scene it was an integral part of, Cobain was very unhappy with the demands and rigor of touring, and he was very uncomfortable with being constantly pressured by his label to perform. Like Brian Jones, Cobain was easily overwhelmed by feelings of self-doubt and jealousy, especially when it came to his wife, Courtney. Cobain had complained of bad stomach pains while promoting what would be the last Nirvana album, *In Utero*, in late 1993. Cobain had claimed that the heroin he was using was helping him cope with the stomach pains he was experiencing.

Tragedy struck in July 1993 when the singer of the band The Gits, Mia Zapata, was raped and murdered while she was on her way home from a Seattle nightclub. (pg 225, #1) In response to this atrocity, Nirvana helped raise money for the investigation into her murder by performing a concert. However, like Janis Joplin, Cobain was teetering on death literally every day with his rampant abuse of heroin, which showed no signs of slowing down. He was spiraling out of control, and Cobain's slide towards suicide had begun. He initially attempted suicide in March 1994 while in Rome, by swallowing 60 tablets of Rohypnol, and left a suicide note. (pg 231, #1) As a result, the rest of the European leg of Nirvana's tour was canceled. Cobain was found dead in a room above his garage at his house in Seattle on April 8, 1994. He had committed suicide with a shotgun, and again left a note. His inner demons had finally caught up to him.

James Douglas Morrison, or Jim Morrison, was an American singer, songwriter, poet, and stage presence who was born on December 8, 1943 in Florida. His father George was an admiral in the U.S. Navy, and as a result the Morrison family moved around a lot in Jim's youth. His family moved from Florida to Fairfax, Virginia, where Morrison attended elementary school, then to Kingsville, Texas, followed by San Diego, California, then a return to northern Virginia, settling in Arlington, just outside Washington, D.C. Morrison went on to UCLA for his bachelor's degree, which he would earn in 1965 with a degree in filmmaking.

Morrison lived in Venice Beach after graduation, and met up with Ray Manzarek, whom he knew from UCLA. Morrison recited some of his lyrics and poetry to Manzarek, and Manzarek was very impressed. Once Robby Krieger and John Densmore joined the band, they were complete. The band's name was inspired by Aldous Huxley's book *The Doors of Perception*, and Krieger shared songwriting duties for the Doors. They recorded six successful albums with Jim Morrison as the lead singer, with a seventh, *An American Prayer*, containing Morrison's poetry combined with the Doors' music overdubbed to Morrison's words, released after his death.

Morrison had cut off his family completely after he became famous. This included refusing to see them backstage after a concert they had attended in an effort to communicate with him. Morrison got into serious legal trouble when, on March 1, 1969, while on stage in Miami, Florida, and after becoming severely intoxicated, he asked the audience if they wanted to see his private parts to which he supposedly then exposed himself on stage. This act caused a huge uproar from within the Miami Police Department, whom immediately stopped the concert, consequently leading to the cancellation of the entire tour, and resulted in Morrison being charged with six felonies. After his trial had concluded, Morrison was convicted by the jury and faced 6 months in prison, with a $500 fine. Morrison's attorneys immediately appealed the decision, and Morrison was released on bail. Consequently, Morrison decided to fly to France in March 1971 to be with his girlfriend, Pamela Courson, who was already there looking for a place for them to live. The Doors had honored their contract with Elektra Records, and Jim told the band that he would be gone for a while and would possibly return to the Doors, but not with certainty. Once Morrison had moved to France, he was struck by the art and culture the country offered, and he could live his life in relative anonymity, due to the Doors being less well known in France.

However, Morrison's alcohol consumption was, as usual, out of control and slowly doing irreparable damage to his body. According to Morrison's girlfriend, Pamela Courson, she and Morrison were snorting heroin on his last day, which might explain why he was in a bathtub at the time of his death—a tub of cold water is often used to revive those who have overdosed on the drug. Yet evidence shows that Morrison's was filled with warm water. Tragically, Morrison died on July 3, 1971 in the Paris bathtub, two years to the day after the death of Brian Jones.

Because he died in France and because French law didn't require it, no autopsy was performed on Jim Morrison, and his cause of death was listed as heart failure. Morrison is buried at Père Lachaise Cemetery in Paris, which is the final resting place of many accomplished artists, including Oscar Wilde.

In an interview I conducted with huge Doors fan Daniel Schwarz, I asked him some questions that pertained to Morrison's impact on music and his legacy in the music business.

QUESTION: What is Jim Morrison's legacy on music after his death?
ANSWER: I think all artists are immortal. Whether musician, novelist, painter, etc., someone will rediscover your work after you're deceased; your name will always be spoken, making the artist eternal. Jim always pushed the limits; he'll always be remembered as a "wild child."

Q: What is your favorite Doors album?
A: My favorite Doors album is *Live in Europe 1968*. "Five to One" and "When the Music's Over" sounded awesome live. It's hard to choose a favorite album, so many great songs.

Q: Was Jim Morrison one of the greatest singers and frontmen of all time?
A: Tough question: Morrison was one of the most unpredictable frontmen of all time, wrecked on booze or drugs most of the time. Unpredictable was an understatement, but he was certainly entertaining and gave it all to his audience.

Q: Could Morrison have cleaned himself up and lived a sober life?
A: I don't know if Morrison could have gotten sober. His father was a very rigid, career military man in the Navy. Jim moved a lot in his youth, and he didn't take kindly to conformity or religion or strictly imposed limits. In fact, I believe he looked for ways to test limits whenever he could, so I don't think it was possible for him to change.

Q: How does the Doors' music affect you spiritually?
A: His music speaks to me on many levels. First, Ray Manzarek played a Vox Continental combo organ, which created a unique

sound for the Doors. Jim was a poet above all, and their timing was impeccable. Listen to "The Severed Garden" by Jim. Read his poetry books: *Wilderness*, *An American Prayer*, and others. So incredible for a man who only lived until 27.

His girlfriend Pamela Courson died in her Los Angeles apartment of a heroin overdose on April 25, 1974. She, too, was 27 years old. Morrison's bandmate in the Doors, keyboardist Ray Manzarek, went on after the Doors and formed a band called Nite City, and did several reunion projects with the surviving members of the Doors. Manzarek also wrote several books, including *Light My Fire: My Life with the Doors*. He was diagnosed with cancer and passed away in Germany on May 20, 2013. He was 74 years old.

Amy Winehouse, was a uniquely talented and gifted singer who rose quickly to the heights of fame early in her career. However, Winehouse had a disastrous dark side that led her to an early grave. Although Winehouse achieved tremendous success and high record sales with her 2006 *Back to Black* album, which won 5 Grammy awards, Winehouse's gargantuan drinking problem, coupled with heavy drug abuse, resulted in her fall from grace and global success. These demons only intensified her wild mood swings and unpredictable temper, which affected her relationships with her managers, the press, and her boyfriends. Her popular song, "Rehab," on which she sang "No, no, no," was her reaction to being advised to go back to a rehabilitation hospital by her management team. Her relationship with husband Blake Fielder-Civil was contentious and destructive, and they both abused crack cocaine and heroin. (pg 140, #1) Winehouse always hated being alone, and would drink and party with anyone who had the stamina to stay up late with her. This included connecting with people on Skype. Winehouse had a history of harming herself when she had too much to drink, and was on a path of self- destruction that no one had the power to stop or control. (pg. 148, #1) Her drug arrests, similar to Brian Jones' immigration issues, led her to being denied a visa to tour the United States in 2007. She would never tour the United States again, which definitely hurt her career. By 2008, Winehouse had attempted to quit all of the hard drugs that she was abusing, but she attempted this feat by switching to purely alcohol consumption, with episodes of binge drinking. Winehouse self-medicated for her anxiety issues by taking diazepam, as well as Librium for her alcohol withdrawal issues. (pg 6, #1) Winehouse also suffered from bulimia. After her divorce from Blake Fielder-Civil, Winehouse eventually ended up with filmmaker Reg Traviss, with whom she remained until her death. Winehouse also had an unhealthy love/hate relationship with the paparazzi, who hounded her on a continuous basis. She would often lash out at them publicly via the press.

Winehouse was described as "a heavy binge drinker until she died." (pg 257, #1) Her final concert in Belgrade, Serbia on June 18, 2011 was a complete disaster in front of 20,000 fans. Winehouse was in no condition to perform due to being severely intoxicated and was loudly booed by the audience. She never performed live again, and the planned concert tour of Europe was canceled. Winehouse drank herself to death on July 23, 2011 in her home at Camden Square. Her body was found in her bedroom with three empty vodka bottles on the floor.

Janis Joplin, was born on January 19, 1943, in Port Arthur, Texas. Joplin's early musical influences led her to pursue a career in music and included Bessie Smith, Ma Rainey, and Lead Belly. Joplin suffered from severe bullying at school in Texas, and she was ostracized from her peers in the community. This led to Joplin's feeling of being secluded in her Texas town. Joplin left Texas in 1963 after dropping out of school at the University of Texas at Austin, and moved to San Francisco, California to become involved in the blues music scene there. Soon, Joplin joined the band Big Brother and the Holding Company, and became their lead singer. Joplin's drug experimentations began to pick up steam, including heroin use. Interestingly, Joplin had a short relationship with fellow member of the 27 Club Ron "Pigpen" McKernan. She gave an epic performance at the Monterey Pop Festival in 1967 to great success, and can be seen performing her classic cover of the song "Ball and Chain" in the documentary film version of the festival. *Time* magazine called Joplin, "probably the most powerful singer to emerge from the white rock movement" in 1968. (#21) Joplin released her second album with Big Brother and the Holding Company that year, *Cheap Thrills*, which included the hits " Piece of My Heart" and "Summertime." This album went to no. 1 on the charts and went gold. When Joplin left Big Brother and the Holding

Company, she formed a new band called the Kozmic Blues Band.

However, by early 1969, Joplin was shooting up about $200 worth of heroin a day, which in 2016 money was approximately $1300 a day. Joplin appeared at the legendary Woodstock festival at 2:00 a.m. on Sunday, August 17, 1969. Because she arrived at the festival well before the time she'd be going on stage, Joplin shot up heroin and drank alcohol before performing. She still gave an epic performance. Joplin's third band was formed in 1970, called Full Tilt Boogie Band. Joplin's last show was on August 12, 1970, at Harvard Stadium in Boston, Massachusetts. Joplin's heroin habits had her on the verge of death on a daily basis, and she knew it. The end came for Joplin on October 4, 1970, by way of a lethal dose of heroin mixed with alcohol. The coroner's investigation into Joplin's death concluded that it was an accident. (#3)

Robert Johnson, was an American Delta blues singer, songwriter, and performer. He was born on May 8, 1911. Despite the fact that Johnson was a seasoned and accomplished performer, he only made two recordings in his career, in 1936 and 1937. Yet Johnson would go on to have a huge influence on future musicians, including Eric Clapton, Bob Dylan, Keith Richards, Robert Plant, and Brian Jones. Johnson was accused of "selling his soul" by not following a proper, traditional career, instead making a living by singing the blues. (#3) Johnson was heavily influenced by Eddie "Son" House. In fact, after some criticism from House about his playing, Johnson completely reversed course and became a brilliant guitarist— seemingly overnight. "Sweet Home Chicago" is a Robert Johnson song, "Love in Vain" is a Robert Johnson number that the Rolling Stones covered on their *Let it Bleed* album in 1969. "Traveling Riverside Blues," which Led Zeppelin recorded, is also a Robert Johnson song. Eric Clapton described Johnson as literally the most important blues musician who ever lived. Frontman Robert Plant of Led Zeppelin said that they owed their very existence to Robert Johnson and the songs he had created. Johnson himself was influenced by boogie-woogie styles of piano playing and incorporated them into his guitar work, including his rhythm, bass, and slide guitar playing, while he sang. Johnson died on August 16, 1938 near Greenwood, Mississippi. The official cause of his death was ruled as congenital syphilis. It is also rumored that Johnson was murdered by a jealous husband of a woman he was flirting with at a country dance. She supposedly gave Johnson a bottle of whiskey that was poisoned by her husband and that Johnson later drank, leading to his death. As in Jim Morrison's death, no autopsy was ever conducted to officially determine the cause of Johnson's death. After his death, Johnson became a huge legend of the blues and a massive influence for many musical generations to follow.

CHAPTER 24

ROCK'S GREATEST ICONS
WHO MET AN EARLY GRAVE

There are many others in the music industry, though outside the 27 Club, who have passed away and whose impact on music was similar to that of Brian Jones.' Charles Hardin Holley, also known as Buddy Holly, was a very successful and influential singer, songwriter, and performer. Holly had signed with Decca Records after opening for Elvis Presley. Holly's songwriting talent had influenced the Beatles to write their own songs, who in turn had influenced the Rolling Stones and countless other performers to do the same. Holly's story ended tragically in a plane crash on February 3, 1959 near Clear Lake, Iowa that took not only Holly's life, but also those of the pilot and musicians Ritchie Valens and Jiles Perry "The Big Bopper" Richardson. Holly was just 22 years old.

Duane Allman of the Allman Brothers Band was a talented guitarist and musician who had also recorded with Derek and the Dominos. He was killed in a motorcycle accident in Macon, Georgia on October 25, 1971. He was 24 years old. Hillel Slovak was the original guitar player for the band Red Hot Chili Peppers and played on two of the band's first three studio albums: *Freaky Styley* and *The Uplift Mofo Party Plan*. These two early Chili Peppers albums showed the band at their most funky and even most punk, truly encapsulating the great sound of their Los Angeles roots. Slovak met Anthony Kiedis and Michael Balzary, otherwise known by his stage name Flea, in high school in Los Angeles, California. They went on to great success with the band and became a dominant force on the music scene. Sadly, Slovak became massively addicted to heroin and died of an overdose on June 25, 1988 in Los Angeles. He was 26 years old. (#3)

Musician Jerry Garcia was one of the founding members of the Grateful Dead, along with the previously mentioned Ron McKernan. Garcia was a singer, songwriter, performer, and (some would argue) cultural icon whose influence extended into ice cream and ties named after him. Garcia was born on August 1, 1942 in San Francisco, California. When Garcia was four years old, he lost two thirds of his right middle finger in a wood splitting accident with his brother, Clifford. Less than a year later, his father, Jose Ramon Garcia, died in a fly-fishing accident. Garcia became a musician who was influenced by Chuck Berry and Bo Diddley. Garcia met lyricist Robert Hunter in 1961, bass guitarist Phil Lesh in 1962, and guitarist Bobby Weir on New Year's Day 1963, and then "Pigpen" McKernan. Drummer Billy Kreutzmann joined the band in 1965, followed by percussionist Mickey Hart in 1968. The band was originally called Mother McRee's Uptown Jug Champions, and later the Warlocks, but would later be known as the Grateful Dead. Garcia first tried LSD in 1964, which would later become very influential in his songwriting and lifestyle. The Grateful Dead became one of the largest and most successful touring bands of all time, logging an astounding 2,314 concerts in their illustrious touring career. Garcia also worked on many successful solo projects, including his work with jazz keyboardist Merl Saunders on the widely acclaimed album *Blues From the Rainforest*. Garcia was also a successful painter, and had a successful collection of neckties that were introduced to a wide, new audience in the fashion industry. After McKernan's death in 1973, the Grateful Dead also lost keyboardist Brent Mydland, who died from a speedball overdose in July 1990. He would be replaced by Bruce Hornsby and Vince Welnick, who both took over keyboard duties for the band. Garcia would have health scares and issues of his own. For example, he slipped into a diabetic coma in 1986. While he did recover from this and succeeded in losing weight, he returned to his old bad habits over time, including smoking, unhealthy eating, weight gain, and an inability to free himself from heroin abuse. Garcia died of a heart attack at a California drug rehabilitation center in August 1995. He was 53 years old. (#3)

Syd Barrett of the British band Pink Floyd was the singer, songwriter, guitarist, and creator of the band. Like Brian Jones, Barrett at the time was the undisputed leader of Pink Floyd, which he started in 1965, and the band relied on his material, similar to the role of Brian Jones in the Stones. However, unlike Jones, Barrett wrote all the original songs Pink Floyd recorded during his time in the band, including almost all the tracks from the first album, *The Piper at the Gates of Dawn*. He also wrote part of the band's second album, *A Saucerful of Secrets*. Barrett, like Brian Jones, was heavily into LSD and took huge quantities of the drug. Sadly, Barrett did permanent damage to his mental health by taking LSD and was forced to leave the band as a result. Guitarist David Gilmour took over for Barrett, and Pink Floyd went on to even greater success after Barrett's departure, much like the Rolling Stones did after Brian left. The legendary albums that Pink Floyd created after Barrett's departure include *Meddle*, *The Dark Side of the Moon*, *Animals*, *The Wall*, and *Wish You Were Here*. In fact, the band dedicated *Wish You Were Here* to their former leader, the man who co-founded the band in the first place, Syd Barrett. Barrett did complete a couple of solo projects, but he remained in seclusion for the rest of his life. Barrett passed away in England on July 7, 2006. He was 60 years old. (#3)

Otis Redding was a very exceptional soul singer who had great talent for his (or any) time. He is considered to be one of the greatest singers in American music history. Redding had performed a brilliant set at the Monterey Pop Festival in 1967 that won the admiration of both Jimi Hendrix and Brian Jones. Tragically, Redding died in a plane crash on his way to a show in Madison, Wisconsin on December 10, 1967. Redding was 26 years old. (#3)

Aaliyah Dana Haughton, known to her fans as Aaliyah, was born on January 16, 1979 in Brooklyn, New York. Aaliyah was a successful singer, model, and actress who began her ascent to fame at the age of 10 on the television show "Star Search." Aaliyah released just three albums in her career, beginning with *Age Ain't Nothing but a Number*. That album would go on to sell 3 million copies and went double platinum. In total, Aaliyah sold anywhere from 24 to 31 million albums worldwide. She tragically died in a plane crash, along with 8 others, on August 25, 2001 in the Bahamas after filming a music video for her song "Rock the Boat." The pilot of this doomed flight, who was unlicensed, had traces of alcohol and cocaine in his system. Aaliyah was 22 years old. (#3)

Iconic singer and performer James Brown was born on May 3, 1933 in Barnwell, South Carolina. Brown was blessed with natural, God-given talent that included singing, songwriting, producing, band leading, and, most of all, dancing. Among his many musical accomplishments, Brown had 17 no. 1 songs on Billboard's R & B charts. He also was inducted into the Rhythm & Blues Hall of Fame in 2013, and the Rock and Roll Hall of Fame in 1986. Brown's original music consisted of R & B mixed with soul, and later morphed into more of a funk sound in an effort to make his music more "Africanized," which also included adding more social commentary to his lyrics. These later songs include "Say It Loud, I'm Black and I'm Proud" and "The Payback." After a legendary 50-plus-year career as an entertainer, Brown died on Christmas Day 2006 after a bout with pneumonia. He was 73 years old. (#3)

Bernie Worrell was one of the founding members of the group Parliament- Funkadelic and played keyboard. He was instrumental in creating the sound and live act that they became known for throughout many countries and generations. He was part of all of their successful albums and live shows through 1980, and would occasionally appear with them in concert or on albums after that. He worked independently with many different acts after Parliament, both as a producer and musician. He died of cancer in 2016 at the age of 72. (#3)

Peter Edward "Ginger" Baker was the legendary drummer for both supergroups Cream and Blind Faith. His impact on music was far reaching, impactful, and profound. Baker was born on August 19, 1939 in England. Baker was a member of Alexis Korner's band Blues Incorporated, where he met bass guitarist Jack Bruce. Baker knew Brian Jones personally, and he respected his work and his undisputed role as leader of the Rolling Stones. He and Jones spoke at length very often during the formation and early days of the band. Baker and Eric Clapton formed the band Cream alongside bass player Jack Bruce after Clapton had left the Yardbirds. Clapton had quit the Yardbirds after the single "For Your Love" became a hit. Clapton felt the song was too pop sounding and strayed too far from the rhythm & blues that the Yardbirds were committed to playing when they were initially formed. Surprisingly, when Clapton, Bruce, and Baker got together in the studio, it was Baker and Bruce who clashed and argued constantly during their time together. This would ultimately lead to the band's break-up, after four albums, in 1968. Baker then became the drummer for the new band Blind Faith, with fellow Cream alumnus Eric Clapton on guitar, Ric Grech on bass guitar, and Steve Winwood on keyboards and vocals. After this album, Baker moved to Lagos, Nigeria to live and record music on his own. Baker struggled mightily with his addiction to heroin, which took a great toll on the musician. Baker was known for having a violent temper, and he had many confrontations with fans and fellow musicians alike. Despite these struggles, Baker will always be remembered as one of rock music's most talented drummers. Yet Baker preferred to be remembered as a jazz drummer. Baker died on October 6, 2019 at the age of 80. His former bandmate Jack Bruce died of liver disease on October 25, 2014. He was 71 years old. (#3)

Keith Moon, the infamous drummer for the Who, was born on August 23, 1946 in Alperton, which is a suburb of Wembley in Middlesex in the United Kingdom. Moon began his musical career as the drummer for a surf band called the Beachcombers that played surfing, Beach Boys–style music. Moon later approached a member of the Who one night at a club, after their drummer Doug Sandom had left the band and his replacement had trouble keeping up with the rest of the band. Moon said to the band that he heard they were looking for a new drummer, and he was much better than the one they had. Therefore, Roger Daltrey, Pete Townshend, and John Entwistle invited Keith to join them on stage for the second set. They described Keith's appearance that night by saying that he looked like a little gingerbread man, with dyed ginger hair to match his ginger clothes. When Moon took the stage at the drum kit, he proceeded with a blistering performance, breaking the drum set. Moon became the Who's permanent drummer that night, although Moon had joked that he was never officially asked to join the band, but merely asked by the band what he was doing the next Saturday night. Moon was recognized by the music world as a phenomenal drummer who truly enhanced the sound and quality of the Who, especially during his masterful live performances for the Who at festivals like the Monterey Pop Festival, the Isle of Wight Festival, Woodstock, and for their legendary album *Live at Leeds*. However, with Moon's immense musical talent came also his dark side, and his unpredictable, outlandish, and outright dangerous behavior, which often times proved to be very costly to the band.

According to Roger Daltrey, the lead singer of the Who, in his book *Thanks a Lot Mr. Kibblewhite: My Story*, Moon became the master of upstaging because he couldn't sing despite wanting to do so anyway. The Who had taken over the Tuesday night slot at the

Marquee on Oxford St. in London that the Rolling Stones had left vacant and gained huge popularity there. (pg 66, #4) The more success that came the Who's way, however, the crazier and more self-destructive Moon became. Moon was a self- described "connoisseur of booze," and became known for blowing up hotel toilets with cherry bombs when he was asked by management to keep it down. (pg 92, #4) Moon was also known for jumping off hotel roofs into swimming pools. And speaking of swimming pools, at his infamous 21st birthday party on August 23, 1967, Moon made history—but probably not exactly in the correct manner.

Moon began his party in a hotel room, including with members of the band Herman's Hermits, and it promptly turned into a food fight with his birthday cake. When the hotel management came into the room to order that the noise be turned down, Moon proceeded to throw the remaining parts of the birthday cake into the manger's face, and then stormed the hallways in a drunken rampage. He managed to knock out his two front teeth in this incident, followed by his famous climb into a Cadillac, which he drove into the hotel swimming pool. This infamous night in the history of the Who would result in the band being banned from every Holiday Inn on Earth. Moon was arrested that night and, after being booked, was taken back to the airport by the sheriff of Flint, Michigan (where they were at the time), who told him never to come back to town again. (pg 92, #4)

These antics cost the Who a great deal of money in damages. Daltrey would eventually book himself into different hotel rooms to avoid Moon, after his many cherry bomb incidents got the band thrown out of many hotels, including the Hilton, some Sheratons, and the aforementioned Holiday Inn. These incidents happened because of Keith's uncontrollable behavior. Daltrey blamed Moon's severe alcoholism on his terrible case of nerves and anxiety before every show they performed. Daltrey said Moon threw up before every show because of his nervousness. In describing Moon in his book *Sound Man*, engineer Glyn Johns said, "There are many stories about Keith Moon's extraordinary behavior, most of which sound amusing when told. In reality, these incidents were anything but funny to witness, as they very often involved some degree of violence or destruction of someone's property. He was capable of being very funny. Unfortunately, it rarely stopped there, and what started out being amusing ended up being extremely unpleasant." (pgs 229-230, #5) Moon was known for destroying every hotel room he stayed in, including once forcing the band to delay their journey to the airport and return to the hotel because he exasperatedly insisted that he'd left something behind. When they finally got to the hotel and let him back into the room, upon his return to the car, he informed the band that he had forgotten to destroy the television. Moon even made a brief cameo appearance as a drunken nun in Frank Zappa's film *200 Motels*.

Tragically, things turned from bad to worse when, in January 1970, Moon ran over and killed his friend and chauffeur Neil Boland outside Keith's friend's pub in Hatfield. A bunch of skinheads had attacked Keith's car with Keith and Neil in it, with Neil driving and Keith in the back. After Boland had gotten out of the car to confront the attackers, Moon jumped into the driver's seat and accelerated. After Boland had fallen to the ground, Moon then ran over and killed his friend in the calamity. Despite Keith's obvious alcohol consumption that night, he was not charged with a crime involving Boland's death. However, Moon was deeply affected, upset, and shaken by this incident. Moon's drinking problem became much worse after this. (pg 122, #4) Moon even referred to himself, in a conversation with Daltrey, as a murderer. This was exacerbated by the fact that Moon partied too hard when he was not on the road touring with the Who, because he didn't practice drums at all when he was home. (pg 123, #4) Keith drove another car into a pond at his house. (pg 134, #4) Moon's wife Kim and their daughter Mandy finally left him after not being able to deal with Moon's antics, and Kim began a relationship with musician Ian McLagan of Faces. This resulted in Moon going absolutely berserk. Due to the overwhelming jealousy Moon had toward his wife, he couldn't handle the break-up at all, and ended up destroying his entire house and everything in it. He did get physically violent with Kim by breaking her nose in a fight during this incident. That was it for Keith and Kim's marriage, with Kim filing for divorce from Keith soon thereafter. Keith never got over Mandy leaving him for the rest of his life.

Then came the November 20, 1973 incident at the Who concert near San Francisco, California at the Cow Palace. Moon was dealing again with his stage fright issues, and drank a bottle of brandy before the show, coupling it with also taking a horse tranquilizer that someone had given him. Consequently, midway through the set, Moon was out cold, unconscious on his drum kit. In his place, guitarist Pete Townshend called for anybody in the audience who could play the drums, and 19-year-old Scot Halpin filled in for three songs. Moon moved to California after his divorce from Kim, where, according to Daltrey, he went completely insane. Moon's physical health was suffering greatly from his severe alcohol addiction, and his physical stamina playing the drums suffered greatly as well over the last 18 months of his life. Moon's natural talent was deserting him. (pg 185, #4) Moon died on September 7, 1978 after attending a film the night before, *The Buddy Holly Story*, at an event hosted by Paul McCartney. After returning home, Moon took 33 chlomethiazole tablets that were used to control his drinking and alcohol withdrawal symptoms. Daltrey said that he had been expecting Moon's death for 5 years before it actually happened. Moon is regarded as one of the greatest rock drummers of all time. He was 32 years old at the time of his death. As Daltrey explained in a television interview shortly after Moon's death, the Who would never be the same again, no matter how they tried to carry on without him.

John Henry Bonham, born on May 31, 1948, was the iconic drummer for the band Led Zeppelin. He is universally ranked no. 1 in most polls as the greatest rock drummer ever, and this title is very difficult to argue against. Bonham was recommended to Jimmy Page by singer Robert Plant for the group Page was forming after the breakup of the Yardbirds in May 1968. Once Page and manager Peter Grant saw Bonham play the drums live, they just knew they had to have him join the band. While Bonham was being courted for his percussion services by other local groups, because of Page's and Grant's constant telegrams, he was convinced to join the band that became Led Zeppelin. The band consisted of Robert Plant, Jimmy Page, John Baldwin (John Paul Jones), and Bonham, who first got together to practice in mid- August 1968 in London. The session displayed the immense talent that this band had, separately and in combination. According to John Bonham, in describing their first session, "The playing was good, even the first time we played together. There's a feeling, you know, when you're playing in a group whether it's going to be any good or not, and it was good, very good indeed. And it went on from there. We had a good play that day and it went quite well, it got together very quickly. We made the album straight after coming back from Scandinavia. How long had we been together then, a month? By that time, I don't think I had any idea the group was going to achieve what it did. You could tell it was going to be a good group, you know?." (pg 16, #6) Bandmate John Paul Jones concurs by saying, "From that moment we first played together in a tiny rehearsal room lined with wall to wall amplifiers, I knew that I was about to be involved in something very special. The energy generated by the four musicians was immediate and the connection magical and, although we had no notion of what the future would hold for us, there was a heady sense of anticipation and excitement." (pg 15, #6) As a result, Led Zeppelin, managed by Peter Grant, would take the world by storm on the Atlantic Records label, owned by Ahmet Ertegun, and went to no. 1 on the charts with their first, self-titled album in January 1969. They were also selling out stadiums in America and throughout the world.

Despite the band's success with albums and ticket sales, John Bonham would very often become a handful on the road, causing problems along the way. Author Martin Power says, "Often at the head of the storm was John Bonham, whose titanic beer consumption in combination with homesickness and crushing between gig boredom saw him pass the hours by terrorizing fellow band members, road crew, and hotel staff alike. For Bonzo's birthday, the group gave him a motorbike, whom they recall promptly riding it down the hotel corridor." (pg 300, #7) By 1975, Bonham seemed to hate the prospect of leaving his family even for the shortest time. This explains why his drinking was reaching new levels of danger, with heavy drug abuse to match. As the band became very rich from touring and record sales, it was clear that Bonham was self-destructing under the pressure. Bonham attacked a stewardess on a plane while he was drunk, and got the band into serious trouble with the airline. According to Power, "By late 1977, both John Bonham and Jimmy Page were struggling with various addictions. Bonzo's alcohol problem had now escalated far beyond a few beers in his local pub, the drummer's increasing fondness for vodka a cause for growing concern for those around him. More, one could clearly see it in his appearance. Though still only just 30 years old, Bonham began to resemble a man at least a decade older, the T- shirts and sunglasses unable to disguise his aging pouch or baggy eyes." (pg 433, #7) After a roadie hit Peter Grant's son Warren for trying to take a sign backstage, Bonham and Grant beat up the security guard in Oakland, California at a concert in 1977, which resulted in both men's arrest and the arrest of Richard Cole and John Bindon, who worked for Grant.

Led Zeppelin was planning a North American tour in the fall of 1980, for which the band gathered at Jimmy Page's house in Windsor to rehearse. The tour was scheduled to begin on October 17, 1980 in Montreal, Canada. Bonham expressed to Robert Plant on the last day of his life that he didn't want to play drums anymore, and instead wanted to sing. On Bonham's last day, September 24, 1980, he drank for 12 hours straight, consuming approximately 40 units of vodka. Bonham eventually passed out and was taken to a couch, where he was put on his side to sleep. At some time during the night, Bonham experienced pulmonary aspiration by choking to death on his own vomit. He perished officially on September 25, 1980. He was 32 years old.

Bandmate John Paul Jones called Bonham's death a dreadful accident. Bonham had died at Jimmy Page's Old Mill House, where he was officially pronounced deceased. As a tribute to Bonham, Led Zeppelin ceased functioning. John's son Jason Bonham sat in with a reunited Led Zeppelin for several events over the years, including the 2007 concert Zeppelin performed at London's O2 arena, but the band never again released another album or toured.

Neil Peart, the legendary drummer for the band Rush, wrote many songs for the band, and he was known for his great skills and ability while playing the drums. Peart was also an author, and wrote seven nonfiction books. Peart's style included jazz, rock, blues, funk, and all points in between, and he was heavily influenced by Buddy Rich. Peart replaced the original Rush drummer, John Rutsey, in 1974.

The band Rush consisted of Geddy Lee on bass guitar and vocals, Alex Lifeson on guitar, and Peart on drums. Rush had many successful albums and tours in their epic career, and Peart's drumming skills were a vital part of the overall sound of the band. *Rolling Stone* ranked Peart the fourth best rock drummer of all time in 2016 (#22), and he was a gifted talent who cemented his legacy in rock history. Peart passed away on January 7, 2020 in Santa Monica, California after succumbing to brain cancer. He was 67 years old. (#3)

Mitch Mitchell, the former drummer for the Jimi Hendrix Experience, was born on July 9, 1946 in Ealing, UK. In addition to being the legendary drummer for Hendrix's band, he also played one gig for John Lennon's band The Dirty Mac at the "Rolling Stones Rock and Roll Circus" show in December 1968. Mitchell also reunited with Hendrix in his Band of Gypsys, with Billy Cox on bass guitar, shortly before Hendrix's death. Mitchell died on the road in Portland, Oregon on November 12, 2008. He had just finished a tour called the 2008 Experience Hendrix Tour, featuring Mitchell, Billy Cox, Buddy Guy, Jonny Lang, Robby Krieger, and a host of other artists. His amazing drumming skills entertained audiences for many years, and his impact on drumming is profound. Mitchell was 62 years old. (#3)

The bass guitarist for the Jimi Hendrix Experience, Noel Redding, was born on December 25, 1945. Redding was the first to join the Jimi Hendrix Experience (after Hendrix himself, of course), and wrote songs for the band, including "She's So Fine" and "Little Miss Strange." Redding died on May 11, 2003 from cirrhosis of the liver. He was 57 years old. (#3)

PART THREE: THE LEGACY

CHAPTER 25

POP AND HEAVY METAL'S STARS WHO DIED YOUNG

Sam Cooke was born on January 22, 1931 in Clarksdale, Mississippi. He would later migrate to Chicago, Illinois. Cooke is known as one of the all-time greatest singers in the history of music, who sang many classic hits, including "Wonderful World," "Twistin' the Night Away," and "Chain Gang." Cooke had 30 top 40 hits in his illustrious and successful career. He, too, was managed by Allen Klein, who also managed the Rolling Stones from the mid-1960s until the early 1970s. Cooke was tragically killed by a hotel manager named Bertha Franklin after he had been locked out of his hotel room on December 11, 1964. Cooke was with a woman in his hotel room he had met earlier that evening, who was identified as Elisa Boyer, at a local nightclub. Boyer claims that Cooke was trying to rape her, so she fought him off and ended up locking herself in the bathroom. Boyer then escaped by climbing out the bathroom window to freedom, with all of Cooke's possessions, which she apparently took by mistake. Cooke chased the woman unsuccessfully outside the hotel. After re-entering the hotel, he then confronted Bertha Franklin at the front desk. Cooke apparently then physically attacked Franklin, forcing Franklin to shoot and kill Cooke in the front office of the Hacienda Motel in Los Angeles, California. The police did investigate Franklin's actions on the night of Cooke's death, and she was cleared of any wrongdoing in a case that was declared a justifiable homicide by Franklin. And just like that, one of the all-time greatest singers was gone forever. He was 33 years old. (#3)

Stevie Ray Vaughan was born on October 3, 1954 in Dallas, Texas. Vaughan was a singer, songwriter, guitarist, and producer. Vaughan was also considered to be one of the greatest rock guitarists of all time, and was primarily known as a blues guitarist. He went on to form the band Double Trouble, consisting of himself, drummer Chris Layton, and bass player Tommy Shannon. Vaughan's family moved around a lot in his youth, and his father

Jimmy was a severe alcoholic. Jimmy Vaughan died on August 27, 1986, four years to the day before Stevie Ray's death in 1990. Among the lists of credits in his career, Vaughan was the guitar player for David Bowie's album *Let's Dance* in 1983, to great success. Vaughan's album *Texas Flood* sold half a million copies and was widely considered to be a success. At Vaughan's worst, though, he was drinking one quart of whiskey a day, coupled with a quarter ounce of cocaine. (#23) Eventually, Vaughan got clean and sober, and he remained so for some time before his death. Vaughan tragically died in a helicopter accident on August 27, 1990. He was 35 years old. (#3)

Farrokh Bulsara, better known to the world as Freddie Mercury, was born on September 5, 1946 to Parsi parents in Zanzibar, which is now part of Tanzania. His family remained there during Freddie's youth, then they decided to permanently move to England after a revolution broke out in Zanzibar. Mercury received a degree in graphic art and design in 1969. The band that would become Queen, featuring Brian May on guitar, John Deacon on bass guitar, Roger Taylor on drums, and Mercury as the singer and frequent songwriter, went on to truly phenomenal success, with many no. 1 songs. These include "Bohemian Rhapsody," "We Will Rock You," "We Are the Champions," "Another One Bites the Dust," and " Crazy Little Thing Called Love." Mercury's vocal talent alone earned him praise from all over the music industry as one of the best and most talented singers and performers in the business, including his incredible vocal range that he could tap into any time he was performing. Queen sold an astounding 170 to 300 million albums during their career, and became a legendary live act internationally. Their successful appearance on July 13, 1985 at Live Aid in Wembley Stadium in London, broadcast to a global audience, was one of their greatest triumphs on the stage, and Mercury performed masterfully. Tragically, Mercury was diagnosed with the AIDS virus in April 1987, and he passed away from the disease on November 24, 1991. Truly one of rock's greatest frontmen was taken away when he was only 45 years old. (#3)

Richard Shannon Hoon was the lead singer and songwriter for the band Blind Melon, which formed in Los Angeles, California in 1990. They were a psychedelic rock band, and although they were not from Seattle or the Northwest, they were described as having

elements of grunge rock in their music and style. The band
consisted of Hoon on vocals and musicians Brad Smith, Christopher
Thorn, Rogers Stevens, and Glen Graham. Hoon met Axl Rose
through a family friend, and got to sing backing vocals on several
tracks on the Guns N' Roses albums *Use Your Illusion* (volumes 1
and 2). Blind Melon served as the opening act for Guns N' Roses,
Ozzy Osbourne, and Soundgarden. They released their self-titled
debut album in 1992, which would eventually go multiplatinum. In
the summer of 1993, they began filming the video for their song "No
Rain," which included a great performance by actress Heather
DeLoach as the kid in the bee costume who performs tap-dancing
routines to an audience who pays no attention to her. She finally
finds some like-minded people who accept her and her ideas, unlike
the previous people. Hoon's performance showed the true strength
of Blind Melon and where it could go in the future. Blind Melon did
perform at Woodstock in 1994 for the festival's 25th anniversary.
Sadly, shortly after his daughter Nico Blue was born on July 1, 1995,
Hoon's problems with cocaine addiction would force him into rehab
in an attempt to stop its damaging effects. Blind Melon had a new
album to promote called *Soup*, and they had fall concert dates
already scheduled for 1995. On October 20, 1995, after what the
band had considered to be a subpar performance in Houston,
Texas, Blind Melon traveled to New Orleans, Louisiana to perform
at the legendary club Tipitina's the next day. Hoon, possibly due to
the poor performance the night before in Houston, went on an all-
night cocaine binge. The band's sound engineer went onto the tour
bus to retrieve Hoon for the customary sound check, but found him
completely unresponsive. When the ambulance arrived, Hoon was
pronounced dead on the bus, from a cocaine overdose. He barely
made it to age 28, having done so less than a month before his
death. (#3)

Andrew Roy Gibb, or Andy Gibb, was born on March 5, 1958 in
Manchester, England. He was the younger brother of Barry,
Maurice, and Robin Gibb, who formed a group called the Bee Gees.
His family moved to Australia when Andy was six months old, but
moved back to England in 1967 when his brothers were starting to
achieve chart success with their songs. Andy moved back to
Australia in 1974, at the urging of his brother Barry, to start his
career and build success before taking his act to an international

audience. Gibb did have success in Australia and became well known there. He married his girlfriend Kim Reeder on July 11, 1976 but got divorced on January 15, 1978. They had a daughter named Peta. Gibb's big break came when Robert Stigwood signed him to RSO Records in early 1976. He recorded a song written by his brother Barry, "I Just Want to Be Your Everything," which would become his first no. 1 hit in Australia and the United States. It peaked at no. 3 in England. His next single, "Love Is Thicker Than Water," co-written by Andy and Barry Gibb, also went to no. 1. His next album, *Shadow Dancing*, would also go to no. 1.

But with success came many problems for Gibb, such as his addiction to cocaine and increasing unreliability. Stigwood had let him go because of it. He was in a relationship with actress Victoria Principal, from the popular television show "Dallas," and in 1981 was hired to cohost a television show called "Solid Gold" with Marilyn McCoo. He was additionally hired to perform in the show "Joseph and the Amazing Technicolor Dreamcoat" as the lead. He was fired from both due to his crippling addiction to cocaine. Gibb's last appearance on the music charts was a cover of "All I Have to Do Is Dream," which he sang with girlfriend Victoria Principal. The romance between the two would soon end after Principal gave Andy an ultimatum: either quit drugs or they were over as a couple. Gibb chose drugs over his relationship with her. He went to many drug treatment facilities to try to cure his addiction, but none worked. He attempted a comeback in 1988, but his drug problems resurfaced and made him miss important meetings about his career. Gibb died on March 10, 1988 of myocarditis, or inflammation of the heart muscle, which was caused by years of cocaine abuse. He was 30 years old. (#3)

Selena Quintanilla-Pérez was born on April 16, 1971 in Lake Jackson, Texas. She was a singer, songwriter, model, actress, spokeswoman, and fashion designer. She was referred to as the Queen of Tejano music, and was very much a celebrated Mexican-American star. The world of Tejano music was mostly dominated by men, yet she would become very successful in it and win many awards in the process. Selena signed with EMI Latin Records in 1989 and released her debut album with the label that year, with her brother as producer. Her second album was *Ven Conmigo*, released in September 1990, which did very well in sales and in the charts. Her no. 1 albums include *Dreaming of You* and *Entre a Mi Mundo*. In addition to singing, Selena was a spokeswoman for Coca-Cola and designed a clothing line under her name. Selena became a very wealthy and successful star. Selena's assassin, whose name I will not mention, was initially hired by Selena's family to manage her boutiques. Her killer fired employees indiscriminately if she didn't like them, and many complaints about Selena's killer came to Selena's father. Her killer, who had stolen approximately $30,000 from Selena's fan club membership dues and her boutique, became obsessed with her. When Selena agreed to meet with her in a Texas hotel room on March 31, 1995, Selena confronted her assassin over the missing money that she was now becoming more convinced her killer had stolen. In fear that she was going to be fired as president of the fan club, and possibly have to face the police for embezzling money from it, her former friend and adviser pulled a gun from her purse and shot Selena, mortally wounding her. Before she died, Selena told police who had shot her. Selena passed away on March 31, 1995. She was 23 years old. Selena was one of the most influential Latin-American artists in history, and George W, Bush proclaimed April 16 to be Selena Day in Texas. (#3)

Cliff Burton was the bass guitar player for the American heavy metal band Metallica and was born on February 10, 1962. Burton played bass on Metallica's first three albums: *Kill 'Em All*, *Ride the Lightning*, and *Master of Puppets*. Burton met his future bandmates James Hetfield and Lars Ulrich at the Whisky a Go in Los Angeles, California in 1982. Metallica had signed with Elektra Records, the same label that signed the Doors. Burton was tragically killed in a bus accident while touring with Metallica on September 27, 1986 in Ljungby Municipality, Sweden. Burton was thrown out of the bus through a window, and the bus then ran him over. Bandmates Hetfield, Ulrich, and guitarist Kirk Hammett survived but were injured, and most of the road crew were also injured. The cause of the accident was initially blamed on the bus skidding on black ice, but Hetfield later accused the bus driver of being drunk at the time of the accident. Hetfield also said that he personally looked for black ice on the road immediately after the accident, but found none. The driver was also accused of falling asleep at the wheel, yet it was later determined, after an investigation, that the driver did nothing wrong, and no charges would ever be filed against him. Burton was 24 years old. (#3)

Burton's replacement, Jason Newsted, would eventually leave the band in 2001. He was replaced by Bob Rock and Robert Trujillo. Trujillo previously played with Ozzy Osbourne's solo band and for Suicidal Tendencies. In an interview I had with Metallica fan Joanna Corwin, I asked her how Burton should be remembered in the rock community as a musician. Corwin responded, "As an unsung hero? Seriously, I think he is well respected but perhaps under-appreciated, mostly due to his untimely death. I am not a musician, but I am a member of 'the community' and I know enough to know he was a bit of a maverick. He's certainly not the only finger-picking bass player, not the only bass player to write bass parts as if they were leads. But he was ahead of his time in his young age, and in his era, and probably influenced many. A good friend told me that Cliff was interested in experimenting with two bass players in a band, somewhat tracking the 'lead and rhythm' guitars, but on bass. That would have been really interesting to hear." When asked if Metallica was a better band with Burton in it, Corwin responded, "Ah, Metallica fans love to debate this. I try to [let] bands grow and change without judgment, but if I had to pick yes or no, I'd probably say yes. Their earlier albums are all my favorites, and I like what he brought to their song structures. He probably took the band further then they could have gone with Ron McGovney. Many speculate that if he had not died, he may have left the band for more avant garde pursuits in music. We'll never know. But I do think Metallica would not have enjoyed their continued success had Cliff not been part of the band for those formative years."

Ian Fraser Kilmister, also known as Lemmy, was the bass guitar player, singer, songwriter, and founder of the band Motörhead. Motörhead became one of the most influential heavy metal bands in the world. Lemmy was a strong influence in the world of metal until his death in 2015, and the band continued to release material until he died. Kilmister was a hard-rocking, chain-smoking, heavy-drinking, amphetamine-taking wild man who passed away from prostate cancer on December 28, 2015. He was 70 years old (#3). Corwin says of Kilmister's impact and legacy on music, "As God? Ha, just riffing on the 'Lemmy is God' trope from the metal world.

Lemmy was always fierce and uncompromising in every way. He attacked his bass and his vocals. He took no prisoners. He was one of the great-grandfathers of metal, a road dog, and it's a testament to his relentless drive that he lived so long while also living with no holds barred. Lemmy was an icon. From his characteristic clothing and appearance to his attitude, to his musicianship, he was his own man. And though he stood larger than life, I gather he was a super humble and down-to-Earth guy."

Darrell Lance Abbott, also known as Dimebag Darrell, was the guitarist and cofounder of the bands Pantera and Damageplan, with his brother Vinnie Paul. Abbott was considered to be one of the most influential heavy metal rock guitarists of all time. Abbott had great respect in the heavy metal community, despite some tensions from within Pantera, whose last studio album, was called *Reinventing the Steel*, was released in 2000. After Pantera dissolved, in 2003 Abbott and Paul formed the band Damageplan. But terrible tragedy struck on December 8, 2004, on the 24th anniversary of John Lennon's assassination in New York City, when Abbott was shot and killed by a deranged fan while performing on stage in Columbus, Ohio. Three other innocent people who were near the stage were also shot and killed in this horrible incident in rock history at the Alrosa Villa nightclub. Abbott was 38 years old. (#3)

Why was Dimebag Darrell murdered? According to Corwin, "Absolutely no good reason! Because people are crazy? I confess, I'm not really sure I recall at the time if the shooter had a reason. I really do think he was crazy. But anyone who would bring a gun to a live music event, let alone use it to kill not just Dimebag but others, is by definition 'crazy' in my book. Live music is transformative and a treat, and no one should go with hate in their hearts. Metal is cathartic, community open, and supportive. It was senseless killing of good people." When asked how Dimebag Darrell should be remembered, Corwin said, "To me, Dimebag Darrell is one of the original 'shredders' in bands. Sure, there were lots of virtuoso guitar shredders, but he was such a strong guitarist who made a big impression on me. To be honest, at first I found his tone almost hard to listen to, screaming and screeching. But totally dazzling. Of course, I didn't know him but got the sense that he was a fun-loving guy, but also one with a big heart that would have done anything for his brothers, true blood relatives or otherwise."

Randall William Rhoads, or Randy Rhoads, was born on December 6, 1956 in Santa Monica, California. He was the former lead guitarist for both Quiet Riot and Ozzy Osbourne's solo band. Rhoads was skilled as a lead guitarist in both classical and heavy metal styles. He was the youngest of three children, with an older sister and brother. His father Doug left the family when he was one year old. His mother was a music teacher, and she raised the family on her own. Rhoads had learned how to play piano from his mother. He was an excellent guitar player from an early age, and was once in a band called Violet Fox. He first formed the band Quiet Riot with bassist Kelly Garni, lead vocalist Kevin DuBrow, and drummer Drew Forsyth, and met Ozzy Osbourne in 1979 in Los Angeles, California after a show. Osbourne was apparently quite drunk for this meeting, but after Rhoads displayed his vast guitar skills in front of Ozzy, he was hired on the spot. Osbourne's first solo album, *Blizzard of Ozz*, became quite successful and included the hit song "Crazy Train." On his second album, *Diary of a Madman*, Rhoads again played quite excellently. Rhoads was due to part from Ozzy's band in 1982 after the end of his contractual obligations. He had many problems with how much Ozzy drank while on the road and in the studio. But Rhoads and two others died in a small plane crash when the plane clipped Ozzy's tour bus (with Osbourne and crew in it) in Leesburg, Florida. Rhoads was 25 years old. (#3)

Ronald Belford Scott, also known to the rock world as Bon Scott, was born on July 9, 1946 in Forfar, Scotland. Scott was the vocalist and lyricist for the Australian band AC/DC from 1974 until his death in February 1980. Scott's family moved to Melbourne, Australia from Scotland when he was six years old. His older brother Sandy died soon after he was born, but Bon did have younger siblings. He formed his first band, the Spektors, in 1964, and he was the drummer and occasional singer. Scott also knew how to play the bagpipes. He spent short stints in prison as a youth, and he was rejected from the Australian Army when he once attempted to join. Scott was inspired by American singer Little Richard. He performed with other bands, including the Valentines and Fraternity, before eventually replacing Dave Evans as the lead singer of AC/DC. Before that, however, on May 3, 1974, Scott got into a drunken argument with a bandmate, then decided to jump on a motorcycle, after which he got into a serious accident in which he was severely injured and ended up in a coma.

During his recovery, he was introduced by Vince Lovegrove to the band AC/DC, who were looking for a lead singer, their previous singer, Dave Evans, having been fired by the band. Scott was initially employed as the chauffeur, but became the lead singer after an audition. Their first album, *High Voltage*, was released in February 1975, and their second album, *T.N.T.*, was released that December. Their next album, *Dirty Deeds Done Dirt Cheap*, was released in 1976, followed by *Let There Be Rock* and *Powerage*. Their sixth album, *Highway to Hell*, was released in 1979 and did very well commercially, reaching no. 17 in the U.S. top 100. On February 15, 1980, Scott attended practice for what would eventually become the *Back in Black* album, practicing some of the songs already written. Then, on February 18, Scott went out to a nightclub in London for some drinks. He ended up passing out in a car, and he was found dead the next morning, February 19, 1980. He was 33 years old. He was rumored to have bought heroin that night, but the coroner had ruled acute alcohol poisoning as the cause of Scott's death, and the case was placed under the "death by misadventure" filing that Brian Jones had also been placed under. It is possible that Scott could have died of hypothermia that night, but it was never fully investigated. Brian Johnson was hired to replace Scott to complete the *Back in Black* album, but the band did discuss ending the whole thing after Scott's death. They decided, however, to go on without him and to dedicate *Back in Black* to Scott when it was released. The album did phenomenally well. Scott was inducted into the Rock & Roll Hall of Fame as a member of AC/DC, and in the July 2004 edition of *Classic Rock* magazine, in its rankings of the 100 greatest frontmen, Scott was listed as no. 1. (#3)

Tupac Shakur was born on June 16, 1971 in East Harlem, New York. His real name was Lesane Parish Crooks. Shakur was an actor, rapper, and performer who achieved the heights of superstardom from fairly modest beginnings. Tupac moved to Baltimore, Maryland in 1984, and went to Dunbar High School. Then he attended Baltimore School for the Arts, where he broadened his artistic horizons by studying acting, jazz, ballet, and poetry. There he met future superstar Jada Pinkett Smith, who remained friends with Shakur until his death. He was also once a back-up dancer for the band Digital Underground.

His solo album *2Pacalypse Now* concerned conditions of black youths and their community at the time. In late 1993, Shakur formed the group Thug Life, and their album *Volume 1* went gold the next year. His album *All Eyez on Me* was released by Death Row Records, run by Suge Knight. Shakur was released from prison after serving nine months for sexual assault in October 1995. Afterwards, Shakur verbally attacked The Notorious B.I.G., a.k.a. Christopher Wallace, and his associates, despite the fact that they had been on friendly terms in the past. He even claimed to have had sex with Wallace's wife, Faith Evans. While Suge Knight ran Death Row Records on the West Coast, Sean "P. Diddy" Combs ran Bad Boy Records on the East Coast, thus fueling the supposed East Coast-West Coast rivalry that fueled hip hop music at the time. Shakur was shot five times but survived a robbery by three men in a studio lobby in Manhattan on November 30, 1994. Shakur accused Wallace, Combs, and Uptown Records founder Andre Harrell of having him shot. He married his long- time girlfriend Keisha Morris on February 14, 1995, but they would divorce in 1996. Shakur was shot again, in an ambush-style attack, in a car with Suge Knight in Las Vegas, Nevada. Shakur was shot four times, and he died on September 13, 1996 at the age of 25. Shakur will always be remembered as a figure of resistance and a fighter of inequality. He sold over 75 million records during his illustrious career. Compton gang the Southside Crips were blamed for Tupac's death, although no one was ever arrested. (#3)

Christopher Wallace, a.k.a. Biggie Smalls, a.k.a. The Notorious B.I.G., was born on May 21, 1972 in Brooklyn, New York. He was a rapper-songwriter and actor. He signed with Sean Combs's Bad Boy Records in 1993. In 1994, Tupac and The Notorious B.I.G. were close and often traveled together. In the mid-1990s, Wallace worked with Michael Jackson on his *HIStory* album. Wallace's two albums, *Ready to Die* and *Life after Death*, sold well, and he was regarded by *Billboard* magazine as the greatest rapper of all time. On March 23, 1996, Wallace was arrested in Manhattan for threatening two fans who were seeking autographs, and he ended up punching out their taxi cab window and even hitting one of them. The next year, Wallace was murdered in a car at a stop light in Los Angeles, California when he was ambushed by another car. Wallace was shot four times and died at the hospital. He was 24 years old. (#3)

Ronnie Van Zant was the lead vocalist, primary lyricist, and founding member of the band Lynyrd Skynyrd. He was born on January 15, 1948 in Jacksonville, Florida. He formed a band in high school with friends Gary Rossington and Allen Collins that would eventually become Lynyrd Skynyrd, named in mock tribute to their infamous gym teacher, Leonard Skinner, who always gave them a hard time for having long hair. The group had great success as a live band and with studio tracks such as "Sweet Home Alabama," "Gimme Three Steps," and "Free Bird," which would elevate them to rock & roll elite status. Tragically, Van Zant died in a plane crash while the band was en route to a show in Baton Rouge, Louisiana on October 20, 1977. The crash also killed bandmates Steve and Cassie Gaines, roadie Dean Kilpatrick, and both pilots. The rest of the band was badly injured but survived. Van Zant was 29 years old. (#3)

Michael Jackson, one of the most successful pop stars of all time, came from a very talented family of brothers and sisters from rather humble beginnings in a place called Gary, Indiana. Their father Joseph was born on July 29, 1929 in Fountain Hill, Arkansas. Their mother Katherine was born on May 4, 1930. (pg 11, #8) Katherine suffered from polio. Although Joseph and Katherine had different personalities, they fell in love with each other anyway. They got married in Crown Point, Indiana on November 5, 1949. They settled on living in Gary shortly thereafter. They had many children together, including Maureen or Rebbie, Jackie, Tito, Jermaine, La Toya, Marlon, Janet, Randy, and, of course, Michael. Michael was born on August 29, 1958. The Jackson children lived in a strict household where all of them had chores to do, directed by the disciplinarian Joseph. Gary, Indiana was a rough place to live at the time, and the Jacksons didn't go outside at all. Their mother Katherine was a strict Jehovah's Witness, but their father Joseph was a Lutheran. The Jackson children would practice music at home and would rehearse up to three hours a day. By the time Michael was five years old, he was clearly the star of the brothers. (pg 19, #8) Yet Joseph used to viciously beat all of his children, especially Michael, as Michael graphically detailed in his controversial 2003 interview with Martin Bashir. The group of Jackson children began to be noticed for their obvious talent, winning many talent shows. The Jackson parents went into debt buying musical instruments for the band, even prioritizing them over food. Yet this sacrifice would pay off handsomely when they started getting booked for shows out of town and earning real money. Michael learned some new dance moves while on the road with James Brown himself, which he would later adapt. Of all the Jackson brothers Michael had, it was Jermaine who was hurt the most by Michael's ascendancy in the group as lead singer. Jermaine's star power wasn't going to pass Michael's from that point forward.

The Jacksons played at the famous Peppermint Lounge in Chicago. Their father Joseph would go out on the road with them and act as not only their father but also their manager. Joseph regularly cheated on his wife while he was on the road with the boys; she stayed home with her other children. The Jacksons first signed with the Steeltown Record Label. Next, the Jacksons auditioned for Motown in July of 1968, run by the legendary Berry Gordy, Jr. (pg 40, #8) Gordy, Jr. was the undisputed leader at the Motown label, and he ruled the company with an iron fist. After hearing the Jacksons audition, he agreed to sign them right away. The Jacksons signed a seven-year deal with Motown, even though the Jacksons thought they were only signing a one-year deal. Joseph didn't even read the contract that they all signed with the Motown executives, which heavily favored the interests of Motown instead of the Jacksons. It was Motown, and not the Jacksons, that picked which songs they would sing. (pg 47, #8)

Further, Motown owned the name the Jackson 5, agreed to when the contract was signed, and thereby controlled its use. Gordy discouraged his acts at Motown from writing their own songs, rather leaving that to his own hired songwriting staff, who were under his control. Michael became close to Motown star Diana Ross, eventually moving in with her. The Jackson family moved permanently to Los Angeles, California in November 1969, yet they still owned and rented their house in Gary, Indiana. Under the Motown label's strict control, Tito and Jermaine could only play their instruments on stage, not while recording in the studio.

Motown had its own musicians to record tracks for the album. (pg 73, #8)

The Jackson 5 played the "Ed Sullivan Show" on December 14, 1969. (pg 74, #8) Their song "ABC" was released in early February 1970 and went straight to no. 1. Soon the Jacksons were selling out concerts all over America. (pg 80, #8) Jermaine became romantically involved with Berry Gordy's daughter Hazel, and on December 15, 1973, they were married. (pg. 111, #8) Michael started doing solo work for Motown, including *Got to Be There*, to moderate success. Michael became more isolated from the group and began to develop traits associated with a loner.

Joseph and Katherine's marriage was beginning to crumble around this time, when she learned that Joseph had impregnated another girl. Her name was Cheryl Terrell, whose child Joh' Vonnie was born on August 30, 1974. Michael hated his father for the beatings that he and his siblings endured at home, and this new baby just added to the animosity Michael had felt for Joseph. Joseph and Katherine would reconcile over time, but the damage that had been done to their relationship because of this would take a long time to fix. In the meantime, Joseph had wanted his boys to leave Motown altogether, which they successfully did when they signed with the CBS label— everybody, that is, except for Jermaine, who re-signed his contract with Motown. Getting out of the contract with Gordy and Motown would certainly prove to be costly for the Jackson family. No longer would they be able to use the name the Jackson 5.

Also, the Jacksons were now being held financially responsible for the full cost of all of the recordings they did for Motown, including songs that were never released, which was estimated to be $500,000. (pg 142, #8) They had recorded 469 songs from 1969 to 1975. But as history would also prove, this was the best business decision that Michael could have made, for he achieved much greater superstardom on his own as a solo artist. In the end, the Jacksons paid Gordy almost $2 million to officially break their contract with Motown. (pg 147, #8)

The Jackson family filmed some variety shows for CBS before they could legally record with the label. Michael was cast as the Scarecrow in the movie *The Wiz* that, ironically, was produced by Berry Gordy, Jr. The film starred Michael's friend and mentor

Diana Ross as Dorothy, but the film would prove to be a box office flop. Quincy Jones then entered the picture and produced Michael's *Off the Wall* album, released to great success in 1979. Michael then began his many plastic surgeries with a rhinoplasty for a broken nose that he sustained in a dancing accident. Michael began work on what would be the *Thriller* album in August 1982. This album was again produced by Quincy Jones, at Westlake Recording Studios. Michael and Quincy had initially clashed when Jones predicted that, overall, it would sell about 2 million albums. It would instead end up selling about 66 million. *Thriller* spent an astounding 37 weeks at no. 1. (pg 226, #8) When Jackson was asked to perform with his brothers for the NBC television special "Motown 25: Yesterday, Today, Forever," he initially said no. However, when Gordy allowed Jackson to perform his song "Billie Jean," he agreed. The moonwalk that Jackson performed on that show was initially conceived, but abandoned, by "Soul Train" dancers. Yet Jackson seized the moment with this maneuver in front of a global audience, and made the most of it by making it his new signature dance move. Even Fred Astaire was impressed by Jackson's moonwalk.

Michael officially fired his father Joseph as his manager in 1983. (pg 254, #8) Despite this, the Jacksons Victory Tour was being planned, with Don King called in to help promote it. Michael didn't want to participate in the Victory Tour, and he didn't have a good relationship with King, whom he didn't like at all. However, Michael was eventually talked into participating after much pressure from his family.

Michael's unfortunate incident with his hair catching on fire while filming a Pepsi commercial occurred on January 24, 1984, which resulted in a frightening moment captured on camera, in which Michael was hospitalized with a burn about the size of a half-dollar on the back of his head. In February 1984, Jackson won 8 Grammy Awards for his album *Thriller*. This was a phenomenal accomplishment for any artist in the industry. Michael had hid a third plastic surgery after the Grammys in 1984, and he wanted to obtain a duplicate of the nose of his friend and mentor, Diana Ross. He met President Ronald Reagan and First Lady Nancy Reagan on May 14, 1984 at the White House. (pg 304, #8) The Victory Tour, meanwhile, went on as scheduled in 1984, which Michael was very unhappy with. He never toured with his brothers again after that.

In January 1985, Jackson bought the ATV music catalog that became available for sale. This valued catalog included work by the Beatles, some Elvis tunes, and songs by many other artists and equaled about 4,000 songs. The sale was final on August 10, 1985, which meant that Jackson now owned the rights to all the Beatles' songs for the price of approximately $47 million. Jackson later sold 50% of the ATV catalog to Sony for $95 million. Jackson achieved this coup after his then-friend Paul McCartney advised him to purchase the music rights of other artists. However, this permanently severed the relationship between McCartney and Jackson. Jackson participated in the "We Are the World" project in January 1985 to help raise money for famine victims in Africa, with a host of other artists recording on the song. Jackson's *Bad* album was released in July 1987. Although *Bad* did go to no. 1, it did not sell quite as many copies as his previous album, *Thriller*. (pg 372, #8) Although there were three no. 1 hits from the album, it did not win any Grammy Awards, unlike *Thriller*. However, Jackson did successfully gross over $125 million from the *Bad* tour.

Jackson bought the Neverland Ranch in 1988, where he developed the troubling habit of entertaining teenage friends at his house. Also, by then, Michael was bleaching his skin in an effort to look more white. As a result, Jackson developed vertigo from the constant bleaching. Trouble would surface in Jackson's life in the figure of a boy named Jordan Chandler, whom Jackson first met as a small boy. He became reacquainted with Chandler when he was about 12 years old. Jackson and Chandler became close, and Jackson moved the Chandler family, including his mother Jane and Jordie's other siblings, to his house at Neverland. Then he took them on the 1992 *Dangerous* tour. It wasn't long before Michael and Jordan were sleeping in the same bed, with Jackson proclaiming it to be innocent. Jordan's mother Jane even confronted Jackson to inquire if he was having sex with her son, to which Jackson replied no. Jordan's father Evan Chandler protested about these sleepovers at Neverland, and complained to his wife. Evan was a dentist, and one day, while extracting a tooth from his son's mouth and putting him under sedation with the drug sodium amytal, his son said that he had in fact been touched and molested by Jackson. (pg 486, #8) This occurred in August 1993. As a result,

Jackson was charged with perverse and lewd conduct with a minor. The Los Angeles Police Department opened a criminal investigation against Michael Jackson, and he was served with a search warrant on August 21, 1993 at the Neverland Ranch. Jackson was even subjected to a strip search by the police. In total, there were two grand juries and over 200 witnesses called for the Michael Jackson-Jordan Chandler investigation, including 30 children. (pg 541, #8) After a long and lengthy trial, Jackson claimed that he was innocent of the charges, but he just wanted desperately to get it over with and get on with his life. Jackson settled with the Chandler family for $22 million in January 1994.

During this time, Jackson began a relationship with Lisa Marie Presley, daughter of Elvis. They began their relationship as friends, while Presley was still married to her first husband, Danny Keough. After Presley's divorce from Keough, Jackson and Presley were married on May 26, 1994, and would remain married for 20 months. Presley was a Scientologist, and she already had two kids from her marriage to Keough, but she did not have any children with Jackson. Jackson and Presley had their infamous kiss at the 1994 MTV Music Video Awards. While still in his marriage to Presley, Jackson met nurse Debbie Rowe while being treated for a skin condition. Jackson would marry Rowe once his divorce from Presley was final, and Rowe carried two of Michael's children to birth: "Prince" Michael and Paris. His third child, Prince Michael II, was born to an unknown surrogate parent (not Rowe).

In February 2003, Jackson did that controversial Martin Bashir interview for a documentary in which he openly talked about sleeping with underage boys, although he claimed that it was non sexual. Jackson would be accused again of child molestation, this time by Gavin Arvizo, who said that Jackson had molested him at the Neverland Ranch. Arvizo was a cancer survivor and met Jackson at an event. Jackson then took great notice of him being sick and wanted to help. Despite Gavin and his family going on television to tell the public that Jackson was not a molester, they later said that they were forced to say that against their will. Arvizo later accused Jackson of serving him alcohol and showing him pornography. Ironically, Arvizo appeared in the documentary with Martin Bashir. In the trial that followed after the Arvizo accusations, Jackson was found not guilty in June 2005, and was freed of all charges. At the end of his life, Jackson was abusing the drug Diprivan, also known as propofol. Jackson had claimed to suffer from years of insomnia, and that he needed something strong to help him sleep. However, this drug should have never been prescribed for use outside of a hospital. Jackson overdosed on this drug and died on June 25, 2009 as one of the most successful entertainers of all time. Jackson's album *Thriller* sold 66 million copies, *Bad* sold 35 million, *HIStory* sold about 15 million, *Dangerous* sold about 27 million, and *Invincible*, released in 2001, sold about 10 million worldwide. (pg 614, #8) Jackson earned about $500 million in his lifetime. He was 50 years old when he died.

Ellen Naomi Cohen, also known by her stage name Cass Elliot or Mama Cass, was the former singer and actress who performed with the musical group the Mamas and the Papas. She additionally recorded five solo albums apart from the Mamas and the Papas. Elliot was born on September 19, 1941 in Baltimore, Maryland. She joined the Mamas and the Papas in 1965, when the group consisted of John and Michelle Phillips, who were married at the time, and Denny Doherty.

The group achieved tremendous success with hit singles like "California Dreamin'," and "Monday, Monday." The Mamas and the Papas played an iconic set at the Monterey Pop Festival in 1967. Elliot's advances towards bandmate Doherty were unrequited, but Doherty did have an affair with Michelle Phillips, which caused serious divisions within the band. Eliot was abusing heroin at the time, and she went into a tailspin after leaving the band in 1971. She still had some solo success, though, including her rendition of the song "Dream a Little Dream of Me." Mama Cass died in London on July 29, 1974 of heart failure. She was 32 years old. (#3)

Prince Rogers Nelson—also known to his fans as Prince, and briefly as The Artist Formerly Known as Prince, and who for seven years changed his name to a symbol—was born on June 7, 1958 in Minneapolis, Minnesota. Prince was a singer, songwriter, record producer, dancer, actor, and filmmaker who sold over 100 million albums worldwide. In 1984, his very successful album *Purple Rain* spent 24 weeks at no. 1 on the Billboard 200 chart, and Prince starred in a successful film of the same name. Prince changed his name to an unpronounceable symbol when he got into a heated dispute with his label, Warner Bros. He would be released from the terms of this disputed contract in 1996. Prince played the Super Bowl halftime show on February 2, 2007 in Miami, Florida to wide acclaim. Tragically, on April 21, 2016, Prince passed away from a fentanyl overdose at his Paisley Park home in Chanhassen, Minnesota. He was 57 years old. (#3)

"The King" of rock & roll, Elvis Aaron Presley, was an enormously successful singer, actor, and entertainer, whose influence on the music industry and popular culture was far-reaching and dominant over many generations. He was born in relative obscurity on January 8, 1935 in Tupelo, Mississippi, but relocated to Memphis, Tennessee when he was 13 years old. Presley clearly had prodigious and unmistakable talents for singing and playing the guitar, and by 1954 he officially signed with Sun Records and its producer, Sam Phillips. Presley was managed by Colonel Tom Parker. Presley's music was described as a rockabilly act with a backbeat-driven fusion of country music and African-inspired rhythm & blues. As Presley's popularity soared throughout the nation, he made three legendary appearances on "The Ed Sullivan Show" to enormous audiences across the country. Presley's first appearance was on September 9, 1956, with actor Charles Laughton filling in as host of the show while Sullivan was recovering from a car accident. Presley gave a powerfully energetic performance, displaying his skills in singing and performing with the accompaniment of his back-up singers and band. Elvis sang "Don't Be Cruel," "Love Me Tender," "Ready Teddy," and "Hound Dog" on the show. This appearance was followed by two more, on October 28, 1956 and January 6, 1957. These shows displayed Presley at the height of his musical power, and he was well on his way to international stardom as both a singer and an actor. His influence was extraordinary on multiple levels. Presley, like Brian Jones, was heavily influenced by African American music, including rhythm & blues. It is estimated that he sold approximately 1 billion records worldwide.

Presley served in the U.S. Army from 1958 until 1960, leaving the throne as rock's king for a little while. He married Priscilla Beaulieu on May 1, 1967. They had a daughter named Lisa Marie, born nine months to the day after their wedding on February 1, 1968. Presley's power and popularity would earn him an invitation to the White House to meet President Richard Nixon on December

21, 1970. This meeting, which brought together the most powerful man in the federal government with the King of Rock & Roll, covered a wide variety of topics, including illegal drug use among the population, to which both were vehemently opposed. They also discussed their opinion of the Beatles, whom they both deemed as anti-American. Nixon even presented Presley with a Bureau of Narcotics and Dangerous Drugs badge. This is ironic because Presley heavily abused drugs such as barbiturates.

His bodyguards were called the "Memphis Mafia" and responded to Presley's every wish with sycophantic obsession. The Memphis Mafia would get into trouble for roughing up fans, but they claimed that they would be eventually fired for being concerned about Presley's drug dependencies. Presley and his wife Priscilla separated in 1972, which led to great bouts of depression for the star. He would overdose on drugs and put himself into a coma. Over time, Presley became overweight and sluggish during his Las Vegas performances, which was blamed on his drug taking. His final concert was on June 26, 1977 in Indianapolis, Indiana. Presley passed away at his home, Graceland, on August 16, 1977 from a heart attack caused by prescription drug abuse. He was 42 years old. (#3)

Another successful musician who had similarities to Brian Jones was David Jones (no relation), who later changed his name to David Bowie. Bowie was born in south London on January 8, 1947. He formed his first band in 1962 at the age of 15. Some of Bowie's early bands included the Mannish Boys and the Lower Third. Bowie, like Brian, was influenced by American urban and Delta rhythm & blues. He changed his last name to Bowie after the success of the Monkees, who had a band member named Davy Jones. Therefore, he changed his name to Bowie after the 19th-century pioneer James Bowie. He released his first no. 1 album, *The Rise and Fall of Ziggy Stardust and the Spiders from Mars*, in 1972 to giant success. Bowie's androgyny as the character Ziggy Stardust was similar to Brian's androgyny that he occasionally displayed during his musical career. Bowie released another hugely successful album, *Diamond Dogs*, which included the song "Rebel Rebel," in 1974.

Bowie's 1983 *Let's Dance* album, produced by Chic band member Nile Rodgers, went platinum in both the United States and the United Kingdom. He released a cover version of the song "Dancing in the Street" with Rolling Stones frontman Mick Jagger in 1985, to great success. Bowie performed his classic song "Heroes" at Madison Square Garden in October 2001, after the 9/11 tragedy, to a sold-out crowd. Bowie tragically passed away from liver cancer two days after his 69th birthday, on January 10, 2016. Bowie will always be remembered as one of the most influential musicians of all time. (#3)

Music legend Aretha Franklin was born on March 25, 1942 in Memphis, Tennessee. Her parents were Rev. Clarence LaVaughn Franklin and Barbara Siggers. Her parents were from Shelby, Mississippi but chose to move from Memphis to Detroit, Michigan when Aretha was very young (pg 4, #9). Aretha's parents would separate when she was six. (pg 5, #9) Aretha got involved with her father's church by singing gospel songs with the choir. Clarence personally knew singing legends Sam Cooke and Jackie Wilson, while Smokey Robinson was a childhood friend of Franklin's in Detroit. Franklin signed with Columbia Records when she was 18 years old. She had some huge hits, with songs like "Respect" and "Chain of Fools." Franklin also became involved with civil rights and protesting the Vietnam War. Franklin signed with Ahmet Ertegun's Atlantic Records in 1967, where executive Jerry Wexler brought in Bobby Womack to assist with recording Aretha's music (pg 121, #9). By the end of the 1970s, in her time with Atlantic, Franklin had won 10 Grammy Awards—the most a female artist had won at that point. Franklin moved to Clive Davis's Arista Records in 1980, the same year she gave her iconic acting performance as Matt "Guitar" Murphy's wife in the film *The Blues Brothers*. Her gospel album *Amazing Grace* went gold upon its release (pg 152, #9), and she was also the first female artist inducted into the Rock and Roll Hall of Fame, in 1987. Franklin earned honorary degrees from various universities, including Harvard, Yale, Berklee College of Music, University of Michigan, and many others. She was known as the Queen of Soul. Franklin even performed at President Barack Obama's inauguration ceremony on January 20, 2009. Franklin would succumb to pancreatic cancer on August 16, 2018 at the age of 76. (#3)

Marvin Gaye, Jr., one of the all-time greats of the music industry, was born on April 2, 1939 in Washington, D.C. and raised in a Southwest neighborhood near the waterfront. Gaye started singing in church at the age of four, and grew more talented in his youth. His tumultuous relationship with his father led to many beatings suffered by Marvin, Jr. during his childhood. Gaye, Jr. attended Springarn High School before switching to Cardozo. While at Cardozo, Gaye's musical talent and experiences grew. He signed with Berry Gordy, Jr.'s Motown in 1960, and recorded the hit singles "I Heard It Through the Grapevine," "Ain't That Peculiar," and "How Sweet It Is to Be Loved by You." He married Berry Gordy, Jr.'s sister Anna, but they officially divorced in 1977. Gaye got into a heated dispute with Gordy over his song "What's Going On," which referred to the police brutality that was occurring in America, and Gordy refused to release it. Once it finally was released, it went to no. 1 anyway. Gaye, Jr. had tax and cocaine problems in the late 1970s and was left owing millions of dollars to the Internal Revenue Service in unpaid taxes. He moved to London to settle his finances, then to Belgium. He finally left Motown under acrimonious circumstances and signed with the CBS label in 1982. His song "Sexual Healing," released on CBS in 1982, turned out to be a huge hit and spent 10 weeks at no. 1. He would go on to win two Grammy Awards for his work. Gaye, Jr. sang the national anthem at the 1983 NBA All-Star Game. He also performed for "Motown 25: Yesterday, Today, Forever" that also featured Michael Jackson. On April 1, 1984, Gaye, Jr. was shot and killed by his father in a physical argument at the family's house in Los Angeles, California. Gaye, Sr. was initially charged with first-degree murder, but charges were reduced to manslaughter. Gaye, Jr. died the night before his 45th birthday. He was posthumously inducted into the Songwriters Hall of Fame, the Rhythm & Blues Hall of Fame, and the Rock and Roll Hall of Fame.

Iconic pop legend Whitney Houston was born on August 9, 1963 in Newark, New Jersey. Houston was a very successful singer and actress whose career catapulted her to the utmost heights of the entertainment industry. Houston began by singing in church as a child, where she honed her skills at the craft that would turn her into a superstar. Her first two albums, recorded in the mid-1980s, went to no. 1. She would follow this with a streak of seven consecutive no. 1 hits on the Billboard charts. She acted in the film *The Bodyguard*, costarring Kevin Costner, to great success and acclaim. Houston brilliantly sang "The Star-Spangled Banner" before Super Bowl XXV in Tampa, Florida in January 1991, just before the start of the Gulf War, and was widely praised for this performance. She married former New Edition band member Bobby Brown on July 18, 1992. Houston's single "I Will Always Love You" won a Grammy Award and sold approximately 20 million copies. Her subsequent films, such as *Waiting to Exhale*, *The Preacher's Wife*, and *Cinderella*, also had commercial success. In the late 1990s and early 2000s, Houston became more erratic and less dependable, showing up hours late for interviews or not at all. She was heavily abusing crack cocaine, marijuana, and alcohol with her husband, and it was definitely taking a toll on the pop star. Houston was busted for marijuana possession at an airport in Hawaii, but she managed to escape on a plane before the authorities arrived. No charges were filed against Houston for this incident. Houston signed a six-album, $100 million deal with Arista Records in 2001. However, her drug problems continued to escalate, and she looked frail and confused at musical events. Yet she was still producing hit albums, with *I Look to You* going to no. 1 in 2009.

Things took a tragic turn when, on February 11, 2012, Houston was found dead at a Beverly Hills hotel. She had drowned in her bathtub. Cocaine and alcohol were found in Houston's system by the coroner. She was 48 years old. Houston is the most awarded female artist of all time by the Guinness Book of World Records (#3). Like Brian, she was unable to truly escape her demons, no matter how great the amount of musical success they once had.

CHAPTER 26

BRIAN'S LIFE COMPARED TO THE THREE DECEASED BEATLES & REGGAE LEGENDS

Now I will compare Brian's legacy to those of three deceased members of the Beatles, starting with John Lennon. Like Brian Jones, Lennon was the undisputed leader of the band, originally called the Quarrymen, that would become the Beatles. Lennon was born on October 9, 1940 during the German bombing of Liverpool. His father Alfred, or Freddie, Lennon and his mother Julia were married in December 1938. Freddie was a merchant seaman and Julia was a free-spirited woman who influenced John's interest in music. When John's parents split up, they asked the six-year-old Lennon to choose which parent he wanted to be with, and this was very difficult to do for such a young boy who wanted both his parents in his life. It was decided that John would be raised by Julia's sister Mimi while Julia remained close by in Liverpool. Julia then became romantically involved with someone named Bobby Dykins and they had two children together: John's half-sisters Julia, born in 1947, and Jacqueline, born in 1949. Julia had a child with a Welsh soldier after she had left Freddie, but the child was given up for adoption.

Mimi's strict upbringing of John gave him a sense of both discipline and rebellion during his youth. When John became a teenager, his mother Julia encouraged him to pursue music, and she served a role model by playing the accordion at home. Julia had an extroverted personality while entertaining guests, singing, telling jokes, and doing impersonations. Julia also bought John his first guitar. (pg 31, #22) John liked top 20 music because of his mother, and became an enthusiastic fan of artists such as Elvis Presley, Lonnie Donegan, Richard Penniman (also known as Little Richard), Eddie Cochran, Buddy Holly, Chuck Berry, and Fats Domino. John was also influenced by the harmonies of the Everly Brothers (Don and Phil), whose blending voices added such strength to their songs. Although Lennon was heavily influenced by American rock & roll, he began his band The Quarrymen as a skiffle group. The Quarrymen would entertain at local parties and dance halls around the Liverpool area. John was the undisputed leader of this group, and he was the lead singer. (#3)

On July 6, 1957, Lennon was introduced to Paul McCartney by a mutual friend named Ivan Vaughan. Both McCartney and Vaughan had attended the Woolton village fête where the Quarrymen had performed. After the show, Lennon and McCartney talked, and discovered that they shared a mutual interest in musical influences. Lennon was impressed that McCartney could sing and play Eddie Cochran's song "Twenty Flight Rock" and could tune a guitar. Lennon asked McCartney to join his band at this first meeting, to which he said yes shortly thereafter. Two more additions would follow when Paul introduced John to his friend and neighbor from Liverpool, George Harrison. Although he was a couple of years younger than John, he could play the guitar well, and he played the song "Raunchy" on guitar to John and Paul one night on the top of a double-decker bus in 1958. George Harrison then officially joined the band. Also, John's friend from art college, Stu Sutcliffe, an exceptional artist and painter, joined the band. Sutcliffe was convinced by John and Paul to use the money that he had won in an art competition to buy a bass guitar and join the band as the new bass player, despite Sutcliffe not knowing how to play the instrument. John met Stu at art college and admired his obvious artistic skills. Sutcliffe payed 75 quid for the instrument.

John's mother Julia was killed after being hit by a car driven by an off-duty policeman near her house on Menlove Avenue on July 15, 1958. She was 44 years old. John was severely traumatized by this event, having built a stronger relationship with her over the last few years of her life. John was still 17 when this happened. John met his first wife, Cynthia Powell, in art college shortly after the death of his mother. Cynthia describes John as very much angry over the death of his mother when they first met each other. John and Cynthia had class together, and Cynthia described Lennon as a "Teddy Boy" and a troublemaker in class. (pg 18, #10) Cynthia further described him as aggressive, rebellious, and sarcastic. (pg 18, #10) Cynthia said that John had developed a hard outer shell to his personality that was a combination of cynicism, cruel wit, aggressiveness, and possessiveness. These traits were developed from John's painful childhood and his deep sense of insecurity. (pg 30, #10) Nonetheless, John and Cynthia would become a couple, and Cynthia said that she was John's first real relationship. John would explode toward Cynthia with his jealous rages, just as Brian did to all of his women.

The Beatles then-manager Allan Williams booked the group to go to Hamburg, Germany in 1960. They then became a five-piece band when they were introduced to Pete Best, the son of the owner of Casbar. Allan Williams owned the club the Jacaranda in Liverpool, where the Beatles frequented between gigs. After a fight that Stu got into with Paul McCartney on stage, coupled with being beaten up by a gang of Teds who stomped and kicked him in the head, Sutcliffe's interest in the band rapidly diminished. Crucially, Stu didn't know how to play the bass guitar, so he chose to quit the band and remain in Hamburg with his girlfriend, Astrid. In April 1962, Sutcliffe died from a cerebral hemorrhage that he had sustained earlier. He was 21 years old.

The deaths of his mother Julia and his friend Stu affected John greatly. When John met Joko Ono in 1966, and when he became reacquainted with her again in 1968, they became an intense couple, which would ultimately lead to the end of the Beatles in 1970. John started a new band with Yoko called the Plastic Ono Band, which included Klaus Voormann on bass guitar, Eric Clapton on guitar, and Ringo Starr on drums. In 1971, Lennon's album *Imagine* would prove to be successful in the U.S. and U.K. charts, rising to no. 1 in America and in England. In 1973, Lennon and Ono temporarily separated, with Yoko remaining in New York and Lennon traveling to Los Angeles. This exile would be called Lennon's "Lost Weekend." Lennon played on stage for the last time on November 28, 1974 in Madison Square Garden in New York City, during a concert given by Elton John. Lennon had lost a bet to Elton John by saying that his song "Whatever Gets You Thru the Night" wouldn't reach no. 1 on the charts, but it did. This meant that Lennon had to go back on stage with Elton John at a concert in New York City, which he did. It was at this performance that Lennon was reunited with Yoko Ono backstage. Shortly thereafter, they became a couple again and Ono became pregnant. On October 9, 1975, on John's 35th birthday, their son Sean was born. Lennon spent the next five years at home in The Dakota building raising his son and being a house husband. In July 1976, Lennon was granted a permanent visa and became a U.S. citizen after a long battle with immigration officials, who attempted to deny him a visa. After the release of his new album with Yoko Ono, *Double Fantasy*, in November 1980, Lennon was back on the charts again, with discussions of a potential tour to promote the album in 1981.

While returning home from the studio, on December 8, 1980, Lennon was assassinated in front of The Dakota building by a 25-year-old mentally deranged lunatic, whose name we must also never mention. Lennon was shot at approximately 10:50 p.m. and was pronounced deceased at Roosevelt Hospital at 11:07 p.m. In 1966, Lennon was warned by a psychic that he would be shot in the United States, and even John himself had predicted that he would be shot. (pgs 8-9, #10) He was 40 years old. His death left a gaping hole not just in the legacy of the Beatles, but also in pop culture.

Lennon's bandmate in the Beatles, George Harrison, was born on February 25, 1943 in Liverpool to Louise and Harold Harrison. George was the youngest of four siblings: he had an older sister named Louise and two older brothers named Harry and Peter. They lived at 12 Arnold Grove in Liverpool. In his youth, George was influenced by Lonnie Donegan, and he learned how to play guitar as a young teenager. George was encouraged by his mother Louise to learn to play guitar. Through his friendship with Paul McCartney, he met John Lennon and joined the band during the rough and lean years in Hamburg and Liverpool that would ultimately lead to global superstardom. In the beginning, Lennon and McCartney were the main songwriters in the band. However, over time, Harrison's original songs began appearing on the albums. Harrison began his relationship with model Pattie Boyd in 1964, and they would later get married in 1966. When the Beatles became hugely successful and Beatlemania was in full swing, it was George who was the most uncomfortable with fame. (pg 4, #11) By then, George argued with John and Paul regularly. It was George who absolutely wanted to stop touring with the Beatles in 1965, and definitely after their controversial Philippines and American appearances in 1966.

After spending time with musician Ravi Shankar, Harrison's spirituality began to take center stage in both his life and the songs he wrote. George was becoming more of an individual in the band. The songs he was writing were mostly not being used by the band, which was frustrating for Harrison. During the recording of the Beatles' self-titled double album, known as the *White Album*,

Harrison brought his friend and influential rock and blues guitarist Eric Clapton to the studio, and he played guitar on Harrison's song "While My Guitar Gently Weeps." When *Let It Be* was being recorded and a film crew was there every day filming the band for a documentary movie, George—out of frustration with the band—quit the Beatles and walked out of Twickenham Studios, only to be coaxed back to finish the album at Abbey Road Studios in more comfortable surroundings. It was George who refused to play to an audience at the end of the film, and that's why the band instead played the rooftop of Apple Studios to an unsuspecting crowd of Londoners.

When the Beatles broke up, Harrison went on the road with Delaney & Bonnie and Friends, which included his friend Eric Clapton. To complicate matters further, Eric had fallen in love with George's wife Pattie by 1970. Yet George and Pattie would remain together for the time being. George's first solo album was a triple album called *All Things Must Pass* and featured Eric Clapton, Ringo Starr, Klaus Voormann, Billy Preston, Jim Gordon, Bobby Keys, Gary Brooker, and a young Phil Collins. (pg 103, #11) The album shot to no. 1 on both the U.S. and U.K. charts.

Sadly, George's mother Louise passed away from a brain hemorrhage in July 1970. George was asked to help organize a benefit concert by Ravi Shankar for relief money for east Pakistani refugees displaced by wartime genocide. The Concert for Bangladesh took place on August 1, 1971, and it was headlined by many big names, including Bob Dylan, Eric Clapton, Leon Russell, Ringo Starr, Billy Preston, and a host of other acts. John Lennon, who was initially positive about performing at the event, eventually said no when Harrison told Lennon that Yoko Ono wasn't invited. Paul McCartney was also invited but chose not to perform. In total, the event raised millions of dollars in relief for the Pakistani people, and the concert was successful musically as well, with the performers displaying their A game in unison with each other. George's 1973 album *Living in the Material World* went to no. 1 in the United States and no. 2 in the United Kingdom. (pg 119, #11) George's concerts at this time were criticized for being too preachy regarding his religious beliefs, and his opening act of Ravi Shankar was criticized for playing too long. As Harrison's marriage was falling apart, he apparently slept with Ringo's first wife, Maureen, while Pattie had an affair with Ronnie Wood of Faces (and later the Rolling Stones). Pattie would end up with Eric Clapton, whom she married after her divorce from George on June 9, 1977. Clapton's marriage to Pattie didn't last long, though. After his break-up with Pattie, Harrison became an alcoholic, and by 1976 he had liver damage and hepatitis from years of drug and alcohol abuse. (pg 138, #11)

George met his future wife, Olivia Trinidad Arias, in 1974 when she was then a secretary for A&M Records. (pg 128, #11) Due to his closeness with the actors/screenwriters of the "Monty Python's Flying Circus" television show, he agreed to finance their film *Life of Brian*, thus creating the company HandMade Films, owned by Harrison. The Python film *Life of Brian* would go on to great success, even featuring a cameo appearance by Harrison. George and Olivia's son Dhani was born in August 1978. In the Sanskrit language, Dhani means "wealthy."

George wrote and published a book called *I, Me, Mine* in 1980 to great success. In it, George did not really mention John Lennon's influence on him as a musician, and Lennon was very hurt by George's book. When learning this information, Harrison did reach out to Lennon at The Dakota by phone, in an attempt to talk with him about it, but Lennon never responded. When Lennon was tragically assassinated on December 8, 1980, the situation was still unresolved between the two. Harrison was greatly shaken and upset by the death of Lennon and became more reclusive as a result. Harrison released a song called "All Those Years Ago," from his *Somewhere in England* album, as a tribute to Lennon in June 1981. George continued to struggle with cocaine and alcohol issues during this time. In 1986, Harrison released a movie on HandMade Films called *Shanghai Surprise*, which starred the newly married couple Sean Penn and Madonna and turned out to be a box office flop. In 1987, Harrison went back into the studio to make a new album called *Cloud Nine*, which was produced by Jeff Lynne. The album did very well upon its release on November 2, 1987 and made it to no. 8 on the U.S. album charts. Harrison's song, "Got My Mind Set on You" from that album went to no. 1. The next year, Harrison and Lynne formed the supergroup The Traveling Wilburys, featuring themselves along with Bob Dylan, Tom Petty, and Roy Orbison. Their self-titled album *Vol. 1* was released to great success. The group had planned to tour, but Orbison passed away in December 1988, and the tour never happened. Harrison also played on Tom Petty's 1989 album *Full Moon Fever*, which was very successful.

Beginning in 1994, the surviving Beatles reunited to do a documentary series about their career as Beatles, called *Anthology*. This included three double-disc CD sets of unreleased studio versions of their catalog, including two new songs the surviving Beatles recorded by overdubbing two of John Lennon's unreleased and unfinished songs that Yoko Ono had given them. The new Beatle songs were called "Free as a Bird," and "Real Love." The *Anthology* compilations did tremendously well and put the Beatles back into the contemporary music scene.

Meanwhile, Harrison had discovered a lump on his neck in July 1997 that turned out to be cancerous, and he had the tumor removed successfully. The cancer would return in 1998, which required further surgery. On December 30, 1999, a 33-year-old lunatic, whose name we must also never mention, broke into Harrison's heavily guarded home in England and repeatedly stabbed Harrison in front of his wife. The attacker was eventually fought into submission by George and his wife Olivia and was arrested. However, the attacker had done severe damage to Harrison, who suffered multiple stab wounds, lost an enormous amount of blood, and also suffered a right lung partial collapse. As Harrison was recovering from these wounds, the cancer resurfaced in again, and he was diagnosed with lung and brain cancer in 2001. Unlike with Lennon, who was taken away so quickly, McCartney got to visit George, and they spent hours together talking and healing from the past. Ringo Starr also spent time with Harrison during his final days. On November 29, 2001, George Harrison passed away in Los Angeles, California at a friend's house. Now (technically) three of the Beatles had passed away, with Harrison joining Stu Sutcliffe and John Lennon. Harrison was 58 years old.

Robert Nesta Marley, also known as Bob Marley, was an influential musician from the reggae/ska community. He was born on February 6, 1945 in Nine Mile, Jamaica when it was still a British colony. Marley was a singer, songwriter, musician, and performer who increased the influence of reggae music on a global scale.

Marley's father was a white Jamaican plantation overseer

named Norval Marley, while his mother, Cedella Malcolm, was a much younger black Jamaican woman. His father died when Robert was ten years old, of a heart attack. His mother remarried after Norval's death, to a man named Edward Booker, and then moved to Trenchtown in Kingston. Marley was influenced by American R & B, which successfully reached the radio stations in Jamaica that Marley had access to. His first musical group included fellow musicians Peter Tosh and Bunny Wailer and was originally called the Teenagers, then the Wailing Rudeboys, then the Wailing Wailers, and finally the Wailers. (#3) He married his wife Rita in 1966. Marley was originally raised as a Catholic but converted to Rastafarianism in the late 1960s/early 1970s, a faith that included controversial opinions, such as support for marijuana legalization and Pan-Africanism. Marley was vastly successful in fusing his music with his spirituality. Marley released two albums with the Wailers in 1973, called *Catch a Fire* and *Burnin'*, to great success. His subsequent solo albums *Natty Dread* and *Rastaman Vibration* also did very well commercially. Marley threw his heavy support behind Africans facing massive political and social oppression, including from South Africa's apartheid government. Marley signed with CBS Records in London during 1972. Eric Clapton covered Marley's hit song, "I Shot the Sheriff," to great success. In 1976, while at his home in Jamaica, Marley was shot and almost assassinated by intruders. He survived, and even performed a concert in Jamaica two days later. After this incident, however, Marley moved himself and his family to England and began a self-imposed two-year exile.

Marley released his legendary album *Exodus* in 1977. It was also in 1977 that Marley was diagnosed with acral lentiginous melanoma. He would pass away from this illness on May 11, 1981 at the age of 36. Marley's talents and abilities as a songwriter forever cement his legacy as the most influential reggae star of all time. His album *Legend*, released posthumously, became the best-selling reggae album ever. In his career, Marley sold over 75 million albums, and was inducted into the Rock and Roll Hall of Fame in 1994. (#3)

Winston Hubert McIntosh, also known as Peter Tosh, was born on October 19, 1944 in Westmoreland Parish in western Jamaica. He was a singer, songwriter, guitarist, and keyboard player who was an original member of the Wailers (1963-1974). Tosh was abandoned by his parents when he was a young boy, so he moved to Trenchtown when he was 15 years old. Tosh was a self-taught guitarist and keyboard player. He met Bob Marley and Neville O'Riley Livingston (Bunny Wailer), and the three started performing together. Tosh had thought that the Wailers were his group, because he claimed that he taught Marley how to play. Tosh got heavily into the Rastafarian faith, as did Marley. He was on the Wailers albums *Catch a Fire* and *Burnin.'* Tosh wrote the songs "Get Up, Stand Up," "No Sympathy," and "400 Years." Tosh left the Wailers after a dispute with the band in the mid-1970s, and he signed with CBS/Rolling Stones Records in 1976. He released the album *Legalize It* in 1976 to great success. Rolling Stones members Mick Jagger and Keith Richards recorded with Tosh on his album *Bush Doctor*, and Jagger sang with Tosh on the cover song "Don't Look Back," that's on the album. Tosh appeared in the Rolling Stones' video "Waiting on a Friend." He had many problems with his publishing company, EMI, over the lyrics of his material, and Tosh was never as commercially successful as Bob Marley. Tosh wrote a song against apartheid in 1977. He was beaten by police for his views on marijuana legalization in Jamaica. On September 11, 1987, Tosh's house in Jamaica was stormed by three gunmen, and Tosh was beaten and tortured for hours by his captors before finally being killed. Tosh had personally tried to help these assailants when they were released from jail, before the house attack, but was attacked by them anyway. Only one of the men was caught and eventually convicted of Tosh's murder, and the other two escaped. Tosh was 42 years old. (#3)

PART THREE: THE LEGACY

CHAPTER 27

BRIAN'S LIFE COMPARED TO TOP ORIGINAL R & B STARS

Now I will review some of the most influential rhythm & blues musicians who have passed on but heavily influenced not just the rhythm & blues scene, but also Brian Jones himself—and led to his interest in pursuing music as a career and his concept of what the Rolling Stones were supposed to be. First, there is John Len Chatman, also known by his stage name of Memphis Slim, who was born on September 3, 1915 in Memphis, Tennessee. Chatman was a singer, songwriter, and blues pianist. He made over 500 recordings in his career, starting with Okeh Records in 1940. He would settle in Chicago, Illinois, and started playing with Big Bill Broonzy. Memphis Slim was recorded by Alan Lomax, with John Lee Curtis "Sonny Boy Williamson I," playing blues music for the Library of Congress. Broonzy and Memphis Slim recorded music for Decca Records at New York City's Town Hall in 1947. Memphis Slim's body of work was heavily influential and dominant in the urban Chicago rhythm & blues scene, both in his lifetime and beyond. He was also heavily influenced by and involved with Willie Dixon's debut album *Willie's Blues*, even writing two songs that were released on the album in 1959. He moved to France in 1962, and became a successful artist there. Memphis Slim passed away on February 24, 1988 and was buried in Memphis. He was posthumously inducted into the Blues Hall of Fame in 1989. (#3)

Marion Walter Jacobs, also known as Little Walter, was born on May 1, 1930 in Marksville, Louisiana. He was a singer, songwriter, and musician who excelled at playing harmonica. He learned his harmonica skills as a child. By the age of 12, he officially quit school to obtain employment through odd jobs and hone his musical skills. Little Walter began recording with the Ora-Nelle label in Chicago in 1947. He then joined Muddy Waters' band in 1948, who were on the Chess Records label at the time. In 1952, Little Walter signed with Checker Records and had 14 top ten records with them through 1958, including two no. 1 hits. However, Little Walter was plagued by a severe addiction to alcohol, which led to him having a short temper and many legal problems resulting from drunken brawls. Little Walter passed away in February 1968 from a case of coronary thrombosis, or a blood clot in his heart. He was 37 years old. (#3)

John Lee Hooker was born on August 22, 1912 or 1917, the precise date being ambiguous, in Tutwiler, Mississippi. He was a blues singer, songwriter, and guitarist who specialized in the Delta blues. He wrote many classic Delta blues songs, including "Boogie Chillen," "Crawling King Snake," "Boom," and "One Bourbon, One Scotch, One Beer." Hooker was known for his iconic scene in the film *The Blues Brothers* in 1980, in which he performed his song "Boom" on the streets of Chicago. Hooker was inducted into the Blues Hall of Fame in 1980, and the Rock and Roll Hall of Fame in 1991. Hooker also received a Grammy Lifetime Achievement Award, and was inducted into the Mississippi Musicians Hall of Fame. Hooker died in his sleep on June 21, 2001. (#3)

William James Dixon, also known as Willie Dixon, was born on July 1, 1915 in Vicksburg, Mississippi. Dixon was a singer, songwriter, arranger, and record producer. Dixon was skilled at being able to play upright bass and guitar. In time, Dixon became one of the most influential blues artists who shaped the post–World War II sound of urban Chicago blues. Dixon wrote many songs in his career, including "I Just Want to Make Love to You," "Little Red Rooster," and "I Can't Quit You Baby." Dixon worked with Chess Records. Multiple rock & roll acts covered Willie Dixon's songs, including the Rolling Stones, Canned Heat, Steppenwolf, the Doors, Cream, and Led Zeppelin. Apart from music, Dixon was once a champion boxer in the Golden Gloves organization, even getting to spar with Joe Lewis.

Dixon found his way into Chess Records as an employee by 1951. Although Dixon was known as an R & B artist, he worked with both Chuck Berry and Bo Diddley. Dixon once said, "The blues are the roots of all American music. As long as American music survives, so will the blues." (#3) Dixon did successfully sue Led Zeppelin for not giving writing credits for his songs "Bring It on Home," and "You Need Love," the latter of which Led Zeppelin used under the title "Whole Lotta Love." An out-of-court settlement was reached between the two parties. Dixon was a diabetic, and had to have one of his legs amputated in the 1980s. Dixon died of heart failure on January 29, 1992. He was 76 years old. Dixon is a member of the Blues, Songwriters, and Rock and Roll Halls of Fame. (#3)

Robert Clifford Brown, also known as Washboard Sam, was born on July 15, 1910. He is the half-brother of Big Bill Broonzy. He moved from his home in Arkansas to Memphis, Tennessee in order to perform as a street musician. This gained him valuable experience. He would eventually relocate to Chicago to perform with fellow musicians Big Bill Broonzy, Memphis Slim, and Tampa Red for Bluebird Records. He played washboard, sang, and wrote songs. Some of Washboard Sam's hit songs include "Diggin' My Potatoes," "Mama Don't Allow," "Low Down Woman," and "Back Door Blues." He was a very popular performer, and he packed auditoriums. However, Washboard Sam's career was damaged by the establishment of the electric blues, which hurt his record sales. He left the music business to become a Chicago police officer. He passed away in Chicago on November 6, 1966 at the age of 56. (#3)

Riley B. King, also known as blues legend B.B. King, was born on September 16, 1925 in Itta Bena, Mississippi. King was a singer, songwriter, guitarist, and record producer. He grew up on the cotton plantation where he was born. His musical career began in church when he was a child, then progressed to clubs and local radio. King was a self-taught guitarist. The initials "B.B." in his name stand for Blues Boy. King was persuaded to try the electric guitar when he met T-Bone Walker. King wrote a string of R & B hits in the 1950s. He became a well-known act at both the Howard Theatre in Washington, D.C. and the Apollo Theater in New York City. He opened for the Rolling Stones during their 1969 North American tour, and was cited by guitarist Eric Clapton as having a huge influence on his career. King also performed with the band U2 on their album *Rattle and Hum*, on the song "When Love Comes to Town." King won multiple Grammy Awards, including one with Eric Clapton for Best Traditional Blues Album. He was known as being an amazing live performer throughout his career, including appearances at the Glastonbury Music Festival in England and the Bonnaroo Festival in Tennessee. He died on May 14, 2015 from vascular dementia and stroke at the age of 89. Ironically similar to Brian Jones, King reportedly fathered 15 different children with several different women, with the majority seeking paternity payments from his estate after his death. Neither of his two marriages produced any children. He was inducted into the Rock and Roll Hall of Fame in 1987. (#3)

John Smith Hurt, also known as Mississippi John Hurt, was born on March 8, 1893 in Carroll County, Mississippi. Hurt was a country blues singer and guitar player. He taught himself how to play. Hurt was a sharecropper, and he released records on the Okeh label in 1928. Hurt's musical influences covered several categories, including blues, country, folk, bluegrass, and rock & roll. Hurt recorded songs for the Library of Congress in 1964 that showcased his great skills as a blues performer. His songs have been recorded by stars such as Bob Dylan, Jerry Garcia, Beck, Taj Mahal, Josh Ritter, and Bill Morrissey, just to name a few. Hurt passed away on November 2, 1966 in Grenada, Mississippi. He was 73 years old. Hurt was posthumously inducted into the Blues Hall of Fame in 1988. (#3)

Hudson Whittaker, also known as Tampa Red, was a Chicago blues guitarist who specialized in bottleneck slide guitar, as Brian Jones himself would years later. He was born on January 8, 1903 under the name Hudson Woodbridge in Smithville, Georgia. As his parents had died when he was young, he was raised by an aunt and his grandmother, and hence adopted their surname of Whittaker. Tampa Red played with Big Bill Broonzy and Memphis Slim during their Lomax Collection recordings at the Library of Congress. Tampa was hired to accompany Ma Rainey for some performances when he moved to Chicago in 1928. Tampa Red signed with Victor Records and stayed with them until 1953. (#3) He recorded 335 records in his career. He battled alcoholism in his later years and passed away on March 18, 1981 at the age of 78 in Chicago. Tampa Red was known as the "Guitar Wizard."

Lemon Henry "Blind Lemon" Jefferson was born blind yet managed to become a great guitar player, playing alongside musician Lead Belly in the 1910s in Dallas, Texas. Jefferson was one of the most popular blues singers of the 1920s, and he was known to his legion of fans as the "Father of Texas Blues" (#3). His first recordings in Chicago were in December 1925, and almost all his recordings were with Paramount Records. He passed away on December 19, 1929 from acute myocarditis, or a heart attack. He was inducted into the Blues Hall of Fame in 1980. (#3)

Huddie William Ledbetter, also known as the artist Lead Belly, was born on January 23, 1888 in Mooringsport, Louisiana on a plantation. Lead Belly was a folk and blues singer, songwriter, and musician who was known to play a 12-string guitar. He could also play accordion. Despite marrying Aletha "Lethe" Henderson, he would leave her to become a musician and occasional laborer in Louisiana. He was arrested often from 1915 until 1939 and served several stints in prison on a wide variety of charges. In 1934, with America still in the depths of the Great Depression, Lead Belly asked John Lomax for employment as his driver while Lomax sought to find songs from the Deep South of America. Lead Belly served as the replacement for Lomax's son Alan, who was sick at the time. Lead Belly played music on the strip at Shrevesport, and was "discovered" there by both John and Alan Lomax. Lead Belly and the Lomaxes recorded for the Library of Congress in 1933 for their collections, and by July 1934 they had hundreds of songs recorded. But Lead Belly would make his money from touring, not from record sales. The Lomaxes helped keep Lead Belly out of jail in Louisiana at Angola, but they got into a dispute over contractual payments that ended their relationship. Lead Belly's hard drinking was definitely a factor in the split. Lead Belly performed independently at the Apollo Theater in Harlem in 1936, but went back to prison in 1939; 24-year-old Alan Lomax helped him with expenses.

Lead Belly was the first American country/blues musician to achieve success in Europe, and influenced folk singer Pete Seeger's style of playing the 12-string guitar. The group Nirvana played Lead Belly's song "Where Did You Sleep Last Night?" at their 1993 "MTV Unplugged" performance. Kurt Cobain credits Lead Belly for getting him interested in folk music. Lead Belly also influenced Lonnie Donegan, who in turn heavily influenced the Beatles. The hit song "The House of the Rising Sun" by the Animals was also famously covered twenty years earlier by Lead Belly. In 1939, he was diagnosed with amyotrophic lateral sclerosis, or ALS, and he passed away from its complications on December 6, 1949. He was 61 years old. He was inducted into the Rock and Roll Hall of Fame in 1988 and into the Louisiana Music Hall of Fame in 2008. (#3)

Lee Conley Bradley, also known as Big Bill Broonzy, was born on June 26, 1903 in Lake Dick, Arkansas, He was a blues singer and guitarist. He began to play country blues to mostly African American audiences in the 1920s. He wrote songs about his rural and urban experiences. He served in the First World War, and he moved to Chicago once his service to the United States was complete. His urban style of blues playing spoke directly to the working man of Chicago, and he became very influential in the development of 20th-century blues. He copyrighted over 300 of his songs. He signed with RCA Victor's subsidiary label Bluebird Records in 1934. His half-brother, as previously noted, was Washboard Sam.

Broonzy switched to electric guitar after World War II. He toured Europe in 1951, and later toured with folk artists Pete Seeger, Sonny Terry, and Brownie McGhee. Broonzy would often play in Britain, and he had a big impact on the British blues scene in jazz clubs during the 1950s. John Lennon cited Broonzy as a big musical influence on him. He was also a big musical influence on both Eric Clapton and Jerry Garcia. He died of cancer on August 14, 1958. He was 55 years old. (#3)

Aaron Thibeaux "T-Bone" Walker was born on May 28, 1910 in Linden, Texas. He was a blues singer, songwriter, guitarist, and multi-instrumentalist who is credited with pioneering the jump and electric blues sound. Walker was of African American and Cherokee descent. Both of his parents were musicians and taught him how to play multiple instruments, including piano. He left school by the age of 10, and by the time he was 15, Walker was a professional performer on the blues circuits. Walker first recorded for Columbia Records in 1929 and had a memorable performance at the American Folk Blues Festival, where he performed with Memphis Slim and Willie Dixon.

Walker was the influence behind Jimi Hendrix's theatrics on stage, such as playing the guitar behind his head or with his teeth, which Hendrix replicated from Walker's act. Walker also influenced Chuck Berry and Stevie Ray Vaughan. Walker won a Grammy Award for the Best Ethnic or Traditional Folk Recording in 1971. Walker suffered a stroke in 1974, and passed away in March 1975 from bronchial pneumonia. He was 64 years old. Walker was inducted into the Blues Hall of Fame in 1980 and the Rock and Roll Hall of Fame in 1987. (#3)

There were two Sonny Boy Williamsons in 20th-century

American music. The first, John Lee Curtis, was born on March 30, 1914, in Madison County, Tennessee. He was a singer, songwriter, and harmonica player. In fact, he was known for being a pioneer by using blues harp as a solo and lead instrument. Williamson I signed with Bluebird Records in Chicago, where he had moved in 1934. He influenced the harmonica style of Muddy Waters, Jimmy Rogers, and Brian Jones. His final recording session was in December 1947 in Chicago, accompanying Big Joe Williams. On June 1, 1948, Williamson I was stabbed and killed in a robbery on Chicago's South Side while he was leaving a club after a performance. He was one block away from his home. He was 34 years old.

Alex or Aleck Miller or Ford (Ford was his mother's maiden name) was also known as Sonny Boy Williamson, and is often referred to as Sonny Boy Williamson II. He was born on December 5, 1912 in Tutwiler, Mississippi. He, too, was a blues harmonica player, as well as a singer and songwriter. He was a very influential harmonica player in the 1950s and 1960s, and once called himself Little Boy Blue. He recorded with Elmore James on his song "Dust My Broom." Williamson recorded with English rock musicians such as the Yardbirds, the Animals, and Jimmy Page. He was influenced by Elmore James, Robert Johnson, and Big Joe Williams. His sister was married to Chester Burnett, also known as Howlin' Wolf, who taught him how to play harmonica. He signed with Trumpet Records, which was then bought by Chess Records in Chicago. He recorded about 70 songs on his own for Chess's subsidiary company Checker Records. Williamson II passed away on May 25, 1965 in Helena, Arkansas of a heart attack. He was 52 years old. Williamson II was a big influence on the Yardbirds, the Animals, and Led Zeppelin.

Mathis James Reed, also known to the music world as Jimmy Reed, was born on September 6, 1925 in Dunleith, Mississippi. Reed was a singer, songwriter, and musician who excelled at both harmonica and guitar. He played the electric blues and became a very popular Delta blues musician. Songs that Reed composed include "Bright Lights, Big City," "Big Boss Man," "Honest I Do," "Baby What You Want Me to Do," and "Little by Little." Reed was a World War II veteran, and he married his girlfriend Mary after the war. His friend Eddie Taylor taught him how to play harmonica. Reed had attempted to get a contract with Chess Records in Chicago but ultimately failed. Instead, Reed signed with Vee-Jay Records. He reunited with his friend and musician Eddie Taylor in the studio, and they recorded together. Reed had many successful records for the Vee-Jay label, and made a big impact on blues music. Sadly, Reed was a severe alcoholic and suffered from epilepsy. When Vee-Jay shut down operations in the late 1960s, Reed never had another hit song again. Reed perished on August 29, 1976 in Oakland, California. He was 50 years old. Reed was inducted into both the Rock and Roll and Blues Halls of Fame. (#3).Reed was a huge influence on both Brian Jones and Keith Richards, and was instrumental to the Rolling Stones as they developed their early style.

Eddie "Son" House was born on March 21, 1902 in Lyon, Mississippi. He was a Delta blues singer, preacher/pastor, and guitar player. House was known for his singing and slide guitar playing. He was a pastor/preacher before he began performing in front of audiences. Once he did start performing, he got the attention of Charley Patton. Patton was a well-known blues artist from the Mississippi Delta region who invited House to record with him for Paramount Records, which he did. House married a young lady named Carrie Martin when he was 19. However, after working on her father's farm and feeling used, he became heavily disillusioned by the experience and soon left her for good. House began to play bottleneck slide guitar in 1927 at the age of 25. Shortly thereafter, House shot and killed a man who came into a restaurant House was in and started shooting indiscriminately. House was sentenced to 15 years in jail for this. However, House would only serve two years. A white planter spoke on his behalf in court, which helped greatly in granting House early release. House recorded for the Library of Congress with Alan Lomax. He would be rediscovered in the 1960s after being found in Rochester, New York, and played Carnegie Hall in in 1965. He developed both Alzheimer's and Parkinson's diseases in the 1970s, which ended his career. House was inducted into the Blues Hall of Fame in 1980. House passed away on October 19, 1988 in Detroit, Michigan. He was 86 years old. (#3)

Charley Patton was born in April 1891 in Hinds County, Mississippi. The exact date is unknown. Patton was a blues musician and guitarist. Patton was believed to be from African

American, Mexican, and Cherokee descent. Patton played blues, white hillbilly, and country dance songs when he performed live. Patton was influenced by Howlin' Wolf, and was known as the "Father of the Delta Blues." Like Jimi Hendrix after him, Patton played the guitar behind his head, his back, or on his knees. Patton also had a distinct blues singing voice. He died on April 28, 1934 in Indianola, Mississippi. He was 43 years old. (#3)

Charlie Parker, also known as Yardbird or Bird, was born on August 29, 1920 in Kansas City, Kansas. Parker was a jazz saxophone player and composer who showcased a style of jazz called "bebop," which was a mixture of fast tempos and advanced harmonies. Parker was an only child. Parker was influenced by Bennie Moten and Count Basie, and would go on to influence the Beat generation. He was also a big influence on the young Brian Jones in Cheltenham, England.

Parker was injured in a car accident in 1936, in which he broke three ribs. Because of this, Parker would become addicted to painkillers, opioids, and heroin for the rest of his life. He moved to New York to explore a career in 1939. Parker worked with artists such as Dizzy Gillespie, Max Roach, Bud Powell, and Miles Davis. His heroin habit was starting to be costly, including a stint in a California mental hospital and some missed live performances. Parker also had his struggles with alcoholism, and his three-year-old daughter died in March 1954. Parker himself passed away a year later, on March 12, 1955. He was 34 years old. (#3)

Gertrude Pridgett, also known as Ma Rainey, was one of the earliest known blues singers to record. She was known as the "Mother of the Blues." She was born in either 1882 or 1886 (there is some argument on the year of her birth) in Columbus, Georgia. She changed her name to Ma Rainey when she married Will Rainey in 1904. She formed her own group—Rainey and Rainey: Assassinators of the Blues—and recorded 100 songs in a five-year span. These songs included "Bo-Weevil Blues," "See Rider Blues," and "Moonshine Blues." In 1920, Mamie Smith became the first African American woman in history to be recorded singing. Rainey was discovered in 1923 by Paramount Records. She became very popular, especially in the South. She made recordings with Louie Armstrong, to great success. After her career was over, Rainey retired and moved to Georgia. Rainey passed away from a heart attack on December 22, 1939. She was believed to be 53 years old. (#3)

Mose Allison was a blues pianist, singer, and songwriter who was born on November 11, 1927 in Tippo, Mississippi. Allison began playing piano at the age of five and had successfully written his first song by the age of 13. (#3) After serving in the U.S. Army, Allison graduated from Louisiana State University in 1952. He then moved to New York City to launch his jazz career and become a musician. Allison was known as a social critic and a music satirist. (#3) Allison's music influenced such groups as the Rolling Stones, the Yardbirds, John Mayall, Jimi Hendrix, J.J. Cale, and the Who. In fact, the Who covered Allison's song "Young Man Blues," which became a main part of their live stage show. Artists Van Morrison, Elvis Costello, and the Clash covered his songs as well. (#23) Allison was inspired by Louie Armstrong, Nat King Cole, and Fats Waller.

Allison was considered to be a Delta blues performer and wrote about 150 songs. He was compared to Bob Dylan and music satirist Randy Newman. The Pixies wrote a song about him called "Allison." On January 14, 2013, he was named Jazz Master by the National Endowment for the Arts, which is the highest honor bestowed in jazz. As a white blues performer, he helped publicize the Delta blues and all the legends that preceded him. He performed this music, along with other white musicians, to pay tribute to the music so others could be exposed to its treasures. Allison died on November 15, 2016, four days after his 89th birthday, in Hilton Head, South Carolina. (#3)

Finally, blues legend Elmore James, one of Brian Jones' biggest influences, was born on January 27, 1918 in Richland, Mississippi. James was a singer, songwriter, guitarist, and band leader. He was known in the music world as "King of the Slide Guitar." His mother, Leola Brooks, was 15 years old at the time of his birth, and his father's name was Joe Willie "Frost" James, so he eventually took his father's last name. James was heavily influenced by Robert Johnson and Tampa Red. James released his song "Dust My Broom" in August 1952 to tremendous success. James served in the U.S. Navy during World War II. James worked as a side musician for Sonny Boy Williamson II, and he recorded with Chess Records successfully during the 1950s. James was a big influence on those who played the bottleneck slide guitar, and was covered by many admirers, including Stevie Ray Vaughan. James was a huge influence on Brian Jones as well. In fact, Mick Jagger and Keith Richards both met Brian Jones the night he played "Dust My Broom" in Ealing in 1962. Elmore James's music sounds very similar to the Rolling Stones' very early recordings, when the band was firmly under the control of its creator, Brian Jones. James passed away from a heart attack on May 24, 1963. He was 45 years old. James was inducted into the Blues Hall of Fame in 1980 and the Rock and Roll Hall of Fame in 1992. (#3)

PART THREE: THE LEGACY

CHAPTER 28

WHAT HAVE WE LEARNED IN THESE COMPARISONS? WHAT IS RHYTHM & BLUES ANYWAY?

So what have we discovered in reviewing this long list of iconic rock and blues stars whose flames often burned out too quickly and who perished at an early age? Is it the business itself that extinguished the light of these stars, with its well-known reputation for exploiting talent at a young age and then abandoning them when their commercial marketability fades? Is it a lack of control or discipline in balancing their on- stage identities with their often different private personalities? Is the business a gateway to alcohol and drug abuse and constant self-destruction? Is rock & roll or R & B a pathway to an early grave, like the one Brian Jones followed? Of all the aforementioned deceased music stars, there are many examples of those who binged heavily on drugs and alcohol, just as Brian did when he was in the same scenario. There were many heroin overdoses or heroin abuse that indirectly led to death, including Hillel Slovak, Jim Morrison, Pamela Courson, Janis Joplin, Jerry Garcia, Mama Cass, and Charlie Parker. There were prescription drug overdoses, including Keith Moon, Elvis Presley, Michael Jackson, Prince, and Jimi Hendrix. There was a suicide (Kurt Cobain), and several alcohol overdoses, including Amy Winehouse, and John Bonham, Pigpen. There are plane or helicopter crash victims like Ronnie Van Zant, Randy Rhoads, Buddy Holly, Stevie Ray Vaughan, and Aaliyah. Finally, there were stars who were murdered, as Brian might have been, including Sam Cooke, Selena, Dimebag Darrell, Tupac Shakur, the Notorious B.I.G., John Lennon, Peter Tosh, and Sonny Boy Williamson I. Perhaps the music business is more perilous to those musicians involved in a quest for stardom and obscene riches. In Howard Sounes' book, *27: A History of the 27 Club*, he says, "In the first place, rock stars tend to die younger than the general population." (pg 15, #1) As we have seen, many other musicians had similar struggles with the music industry as those Brian dealt with, including the adjustment from poverty and near starvation in the early days to the lavish excesses of wealth. There is no roadmap to guide young musicians when wealth and success come their way, and no proven advice on how to avoid the many pitfalls that come with them. Any mistake or overindulgence of drugs and alcohol in this world can have fatal consequences. Was Brian's early death partly due to alcoholism/drug addiction/deep depression, or did he accept his destiny as an acceptable price in order to make the music he loved mainstream? Was Brian not the exception but the norm in this chaotic world of pop stardom?

In review, we can see that many other music stars had internal struggles while within a band. Some of them successfully got out of those situations and created better circumstances for themselves, either on their own or with new bands. Yet, some were unable to conquer their individual situations and met their fate at an earlier age than what should have been. Like Jones, Joplin, Hendrix, Gibb, Moon, Bonham, Winehouse, Johnson, Scott, etc., come to mind as having the ability to have carried on far beyond what their abbreviated lifetimes gave them. If, in fact, Brian Jones was murdered on that warm July night in 1969, he would join that exclusive category of stars robbed of their lives by others, including Tosh, Lennon, Selena, Marvin Gaye, Jr., Dimebag Darrell, and Sonny Boy Williamson I. Were Brian's surviving Stones bandmates—Jagger, Richards, Wyman, and Watts—the exceptions to the rule by surviving and thriving into the 21st century? In 2020, the Rolling Stones are still one of the most successful touring acts in the world, still building on Brian Jones' idea to start a rhythm & blues band in 1962. Though it could be argued that the Rolling Stones mostly abandoned their original concept of a pure R & B band, they have made conscious returns, periodically, to their R & B roots. This includes their 2016 *Blue & Lonesome* album, which was widely acclaimed in the music community. When you divide the Rolling Stones' music down to its square root, to use the algebraic term, what do you have? When you peel back all of the layers down to its true nucleus, the band was created by Brian out of his personal love for American urban and Delta rhythm & blues, and his desire to play it to different audiences around the world. After all, it was the music of Elmore James that led Brian to the world of slide guitar, and the music of Muddy Waters, Howlin' Wolf, Bo

Diddley, and Jimmy Reed that Brian used when creating the Rolling Stones. The music that Brian idolized was based deeply in the roots of Americana, from its controversial and morally unjust oppression of African Americans during slavery and since Emancipation, in its long and sordid history, and their will to fight on in such turbulent times. The blues music has a healing quality to it, through expressing pain and anguish, but it can also be described as a sort of revenge. It is easy to see how this could appeal to a young, rebellious Brian Jones in search of his own voice to create a mantra against the authoritative figures who were in his life at the time. But what was it about the blues that gave it its unique character in the world of music?

I went to the Library of Congress in Washington, D.C. to explore for myself the Lomax Collection that is housed there, containing truly one-of-a-kind recordings of blues artists performing their songs and telling their stories, which were often horrific. The blues originated not in the North but in the South, from those who were wrongly enslaved because of their skin color and from their stories of oppression by white men. Blues music was a healing form of expression that has spiritual and gospel influences. As Bill Wyman said, "Inspired by suffering and despair, the blues are rooted in courage and the will to survive." (pg 10, #12) I heard for myself the very recordings made by Alan Lomax in 1947, featuring Big Bill Broonzy, Memphis Slim, and Sonny Boy Williamson. The record was titled, *Blues in the Mississippi Night*, which had a surprisingly high sound quality on vinyl. It spoke of the oppression that African Americans lived through at the time and the way of finding equality by performing music that appealed to all audiences. However, blues music was also used as a way to fight back against oppression. According to Folklife Specialist Todd Harvey at the Library of Congress, "Music is never static, and it continues to evolve today." (#13) Indeed, it seems that blues artists can literally speak through time to different people in different countries from different generations. Part of blues music's value is the message that it remains important to try to be happy, regardless of personal troubles. This was the music that literally touched Brian Jones' soul. Whether it was Delta, urban, Red River, walking train, or Santa Field blues, it speaks a universal language to all people fighting oppression and searching for equal rights and justice in a world that still lacks both. Blues songs can transcend someone's daily routine as a way to self-medicate against any confrontations with one's boss or other office problems. It should also be noted that women were often the source of blues songwriting, by giving men the blues on a wide variety of subjects. These songs speak of triumph over adversarial issues and form a unifying theme of togetherness.

Early blues recordings were acoustic, including the songs "Mississippi Blues," and "Country Farm Blues." Many of the songs that I heard in the unique Lomax Collection focused on farm work and being broke, cold, tired, and hungry. I discovered, in listening to these blues artists' recordings, that many blues artists were ripped off by white artists who simply did their own version— without properly crediting the African American blues artist from whom the song originally came. This happened to many blues artists at the time, including Muddy Waters, Hollis "Fat Head" Washington, and Willie Dixon, to name a few. Yet the songs in the Lomax Collection echo the will to survive and endure, no matter the circumstances, which seems to be at the very heart of the essence of human existence. The quality of these old recordings makes the messages all the more compelling and relevant to the times that we live in today. Moreover, this was the very music that made its way across the Atlantic Ocean, from a racially segregated America before the landmark 1964 Civil Rights legislation, to the ears of Brian Jones, whose passion for music changed the course of music history forever. This was the inspiration for Brian to pursue his idea of forming a rhythm & blues band (that became the Rolling Stones) in order to pay homage to this music that had inspired him and others in England.

In the 1818 novel *Frankenstein*, written by Mary Shelley, the main character, Victor Frankenstein, an alchemist, creates a being in his laboratory that is stronger, quicker, more elusive, more evil, and more powerful than anyone on Earth, including its creator. The monster that Victor created was an independent thinker and was Dr. Frankenstein's equal intellectually, and became his greatest nemesis. In other words, the creature was at war with its creator, whom he blamed for his misery and isolation. As a result, the monster that Frankenstein had created murdered members of Victor's inner circle. The monster had asked Victor to create a bride for him of equal composition, in exchange for him stopping his vicious, murderous streak. After initially beginning the process of creating the monster a bride, however, Victor abruptly stopped and refused to create one. The monster vowed his revenge upon Victor, and ended up killing Victor's beloved wife Elizabeth on their wedding night. Because the monster was created to be superior to man, he escaped justice every time for his crimes by simply running away.

This classic novel, published in 1818, had some strong similarities to Brian's short life over a century later, in that the beast that he created (the Rolling Stones) became more powerful, more influential, and more important than the creator (Brian Jones). The exchanges between Victor and the monster have eerie similarities to the arguments that Jones must have had with his bandmates; Victor said he "had created a fiend whose unparalleled barbarity had desolated my heart and filled it forever with the bitterest revenge." (pg 159, #14) Like the dichotomy that existed between Victor Frankenstein and the monster he created, Brian's creation of the Rolling Stones grew more powerful than Brian Jones himself. This forced Jones to just be an extra in the band, with no say in the band's direction or progression, despite him having created the band in the first place. After Brian had formally lost control of his creation, the band went on to become one of the most successful acts in history. Brian's struggle to accept that he had lost control of his creation was similar to Victor Frankenstein's battle with his monster, and led Jones to self-destructive habits that hurt him both professionally and personally.

I believe that there is a valid argument to be made that Brian's best move would have been for him to leave the Rolling Stones at or around 1965, when the song "(I Can't Get No) Satisfaction" went to no. 1 on the charts. I think that Jones could have easily started a new band that hewed closer to his musical vision and recruited more qualified musicians than the less experienced musicians (at the time) in the Rolling Stones. I say this because he did successfully write the film score for the movie *A Degree of Murder*, the performance of which included Kenney Jones and Jimmy Page. This, to me, proves that had Brian been allowed to write music and contribute more, he could have successfully written music for another band in another setting. I also believe that Brian could have created another band that could have competed with the Stones throughout the 1970s and beyond.

The Stones could have just been an afterthought to the successes of any future bands that Brian could have led. Whether it was strictly the Delta and urban R & B that he loved or the Master Musicians of Jajouka, Brian demonstrated his great ability for musical growth by experimenting with different and unique music from around the world, and I believe he would have greatly expanded on this venture had he been given the opportunity for a longer life. His passions for music that was considered outside the box of his Cheltenham upbringing led to his achieving the very heights of success, and I believe that Brian could have easily achieved this again had he been given the chance. But history failed to give Brian that opportunity, with Jones' death occurring less than one month after his departure from the Rolling Stones. This is why I felt that I had to write this book about Brian Jones, a.k.a. Elmo Lewis, in order to re-examine his life, death, and legacy into the 21st century and beyond. Was Brian given a fair judgment by history as to his importance in music and culture, or was he conveniently wiped out of existence based on his shortcomings, his struggles with drugs and alcohol, and his inability to conquer his inner demons?

I feel that, based on all of Brian's accomplishments and contributions to the music business during his lifetime, he should be re-examined by those now living and by future generations. These achievements include his commitment to American rhythm & blues, his ability to play a wide variety of musical instruments, and his discovery and promotion of the Master Musicians of Jajouka, with whom Brian produced an album called *Brian Jones Presents the Pipes of Pan at Jajouka*, recorded in 1968 in Morocco. In the 21st century, Jones' influence continues, with websites dedicated to him, such as the Brian Jones Fan Club. On that site, it says, "Brian's musicianship is certainly his legacy, but his contributions to the world of fashion and experimentalism with ethnic music [are] legend." (#15) The club was formed in partnership with Pat Andrews, Brian's former girlfriend and mother to his son Mark, as a tribute to Brian and to portray him in a more favorable light. There are also three Brian Jones Facebook pages. One is a group called the Brian Jones Preservation Society, and another is called Ruby Tuesday: Brian Jones Remembered, both of which you must submit a request to join. Additionally, there is a Facebook page that anyone can like called the Brian Jones Friends and Fans page. There, regularly updated pictures and postings about Brian are uploaded on a daily basis. An American band called the Brian Jonestown Massacre was formed in San Francisco, California and has released 18 albums since their formation in 1990. (#3) It seems clear that Brian's influence on music has sustained itself for more than 50 years after his death. Questions surface as to whether or not Brian Jones should be nominated for the Blues Hall of Fame or the R & B Hall of Fame as an individual artist, based on his success playing American R & B and delivering it to a brand-new audience. Does the fact that Brian was the first electric slide guitar player in England hold add more weight to his case for these inductions? Should Brian also be remembered and honored by the jazz community, which influenced his musical concepts and ideology from a young age and throughout his career? What about any trademark protection Brian could have had for not only forming the band but also naming them? According to an anonymous source from the Copyright Office located inside the Library of Congress, when asked about Brian's legal options in regard to the previous question, the source said, "Names are not copyrightable. The law reads something like, 'words and short phrases, such as names, titles, slogans,' are not protected by copyright. His proper path is trademark. Trademarks are used to connect a name with a particular category of goods or services, so that consumers are not confused about the source or origin. So if you wish to protect your brand or band name, trademark is your path."

It has been said that jazz "has always been about community because of a revolutionary idea; the song is shared by every member of the band." (pg. xi, #16). Jones himself was heavily influenced by Charlie Parker when he was forming his musical tastes as a young man, and he excelled at playing saxophone like his idol. In fact, as already noted in Part 1, Brian Jones was the only member of the Rolling Stones to ever play an instrument on a recorded Beatles track, playing saxophone on the song "You Know My Name (Look up the Number)."

Brian's unique musical ability should be a part of his legacy: his ability to play so many different musical instruments added such great quality to the Rolling Stones' overall sound. It is easy to imagine Brian going on to create new bands, after he left the Rolling Stones, that could have competed with the best artists in music, with songs of his own composition dominating the charts for decades. But sadly, it was never meant to be. As far as the Rolling Stones themselves, they would go on to phenomenal success (both albums and touring) after Brian's departure from the band. When Brian's replacement left the band in 1974 after recording some of the very best albums in the Stones' career, the addition of Ronnie Wood in 1975, from Faces, may have been as important a moment to the Rolling Stones as when Brian formed the band in 1962. This is because Wood is the glue that holds the Rolling Stones together. He does not seek to control the band, as Brian once did, but to be the perfect teammate to the musicians on stage or in the studio while playing lead guitar. His role in the band since Mick Taylor's and Brian's departures proved to be the stability and foundation the band needed to achieve staggering success.

When Bill Wyman retired from the band in 1990, after the *Steel Wheels* tour, the addition of bassist Darryl Jones was crucial for the Stones' continuation as a touring and recording band, starting in 1994 with the Voodoo Lounge tour and all the way up to the present. Darryl Jones has filled an important role in the continuing nucleus of the Rolling Stones as a modern rock & roll act. However, it is controversial that Jones has not been made an official member of the band, despite all his contributions, but merely treated as a hired musician. Some fans believe that Darryl Jones should be made an official member of the band, considering—besides his great musical skills—he would be the first African American member of the Stones. Isn't it ironic that two members of the Rolling Stones, from past and present, were relegated to session musicians within the group, and they both had the last name of Jones?

The importance of finding both Mick Taylor and Ronnie Wood to fill the spot that was vacated by Brian, which ultimately led to phenomenal success in the touring and merchandising industry, should be noted. Despite Ronnie Wood experiencing his own heroin and alcohol-related issues, he became a stable force that gave the Rolling Stones the longevity and success they have achieved. There is no doubt about the Stones' enormous impact on both American music and culture. According to Dr. Timothy Desmond, Ph.D, a professor of philosophy in the Washington, D.C. area, the Stones "helped to spread American soul music. They mix country music with rhythm & blues music. It seemed to capture the American spirit and its history. I grew up listening to country and bluegrass, and that music was the same frequency of what I was experiencing then." When asked if he preferred the Stones to the Beatles, Dr. Desmond said, "I like them both for different reasons. The Beatles chanted Hare Krishna, to which I am also a member, but I like the Stones because they are grittier and appeal to American tastes." The Rolling Stones' music has crossed generational lines from Brian's creation of the band until now, speaking to different people from different areas. Longtime Rolling Stones fan Alev Sezer-Jacobs responded when asked about when she first experienced the Rolling Stones live: "I went to the 1989 *Steel Wheels* concert at RFK Stadium and the 1994 *Voodoo Lounge* concert at the same venue." When asked about what she thought about these shows and why, Sezer-Jacobs replied, "I thought it was powerful, sexy, and inspiring. Definitely Mick was the most appealing to me, and I felt that Mick was singing directly to me. We'd had good seats for that show, we were on the floor, and he had the audience in his hands." However, when asked about Brian's treatment by the members of the Rolling Stones, Sezer-Jacobs said, "To the outside public, it was Mick and Keith who were the stars of the band. But it was a whole different story with Brian. While Mick was getting the attention, it was Brian who should have gotten the recognition he deserves for starting the band." Setor Awunyo- Akaba, a skilled bass guitar player from the Bay Area of Northern California and a huge Rolling Stones fan, when asked if Brian Jones was a true blues man and if he had any influence on pop music today, said, "He was for sure a true blues man, but I think overall his influence was minimal on pop music today." When Awunyo-Akaba was asked if Jones was as talented as his friend Jimi Hendrix, he said, "I would compare him more to John Paul Jones due to his multi-instrumental skills. Hendrix was innovative. [Brian] Jones was very talented but not as innovative." When asked about Brian's greatest contribution to the Rolling Stones and music in general, Awunyo-Akaba replied, "Despite his shortcomings, I think that how he played with Keith [Richards] in the early days and his ability to play other instruments were his biggest contribution."

Below is an interview that I had with musician Jim Ground, who has published many music reviews in *Elmore Magazine*, about Brian's legacy and impact on music.

QUESTION: What was Brian's legacy on both the Rolling Stones and pop music in general more than 50 years after his death?
ANSWER: To me, Brian Jones' legacy is inextricably tied to the Rolling Stones. They began as his band, and of course they are still seen as one of the most important bands in all of classic rock.

Q: Do you believe that Brian Jones was murdered on July 3, 1969?
A: No.

Q: Do you believe that Brian Jones would have formed a new band as big as or bigger than the Rolling Stones had he lived?
A: Because he died so soon after being dismissed by the Rolling Stones, it is hard to say what he would have gone on to accomplish. The musician I compare him to is Peter Green, who founded Fleetwood Mac but left before they became a big commercial success. Both Brian Jones and Peter Green loved the blues, as did many of the British Invasion guitarists like Eric Clapton, Jimmy Page, and Jeff Beck. But Clapton, Page, and Beck all found initial success as sidemen, while I think of Jones and Green [as] being musicians who led early British blues bands. Green pursued blues when he left Fleetwood Mac; he remained true to that. Jones wanted the Stones to remain a blues band, but their management basically worked with Mick Jagger and Keith Richards to pursue more commercial success writing original songs. In hindsight, the Stones' management made a wise business decision. A blues cover band would not have had the commercial success the Stones went on to achieve. Jagger and Richards became a hugely successful songwriting duo.

Q: Would Brian have become involved with large music events, like Live Aid, Woodstock, or Lollapalooza, based on his involvement with the Monterey Pop Festival in

1967?

A: Brian Jones was well connected in the music scene, both in the U.K. and the U.S. It was his friendship with Hendrix and other musicians that led to his involvement with the Monterey Pop Festival in '67. I think he certainly could have collaborated with his connections to remain involved in the music scene, whether as a musician, promoter, producer, you name it. It's a shame that he died without being able to follow that path. Sadly, Hendrix and a number of others from that scene died too young, too.

Q: Do you think that Brian Jones has an argument to be inducted into the Rock and Roll Hall of Fame as an individual artist? What about the Blues Hall of Fame?

A: No. Without the Rolling Stones, I don't see Brian as a member of the Rock and Roll Hall of Fame. But that's okay. He absolutely deserves a place there because of his role in creating the Stones and contributing so much to the records he played on. Similarly, though Jones was a huge proponent of the blues, and his love of blues music introduced it to a lot of new fans, I don't see him as a blues originator, which to me is what it should take to make the cut. I know that Eric Clapton and John Mayall were later inductees into the Blues Hall of Fame, but to me it really should be more about Robert Johnson, John Lee Hooker, Howlin' Wolf, Bessie Smith, and other early inductees who made the blues what it is.

Q: Do you think that the Rolling Stones were a better band with Brian Jones, or do you prefer Brian's replacements, Mick Taylor or Ronnie Wood, more?

A: The Stones with and without Brian Jones could be considered two different bands, both because of the contributions Jones brought to the band, especially as a multi-instrumentalist, and because of the way the band matured over the years. The Stones probably would have evolved whether he left the band or not, but free of any creative differences between Jones and the rest of the band, they definitely took a different direction. While the music evolved over time, there are great songs and great records across their line-up changes. Jones' playing meshed really well with Keith Richards' playing, but so did Mick Taylor's and, later, Ronnie Wood's. Each of them brought some of their own thing to the gig, but I believe after Jones, Taylor and Wood both knew that it was Mick and Keith calling the shots.

Q: Do you think the Stones could ever have been as successful as they became if they had remained strictly a rhythm & blues band, as Brian had wanted them to be when he created the band?
A: No. If you consider Peter Green's pursuit of the blues compared to Fleetwood Mac's pop records after he left, I think there's a clear comparison to be made. Peter Green is an amazing guitar player, and his blues style has been respected and emulated by lots of guitarists, but he's never had the commercial success that Fleetwood Mac did after he left and they followed the more commercial route they took.

Q: Could Brian have established himself as a solo act as successful as Michael Jackson when he left the Jackson 5?
A: Of course not. Michael Jackson is an almost impossible comparison. The "King of Pop" enjoyed far more success as a solo artist than the Jackson 5 ever did, even though the Jackson 5 were very successful. Michael Jackson's *Thriller* was released nearly 40 years ago, and remains the best-selling single album of all time. Brian Jones was a great talent, but I don't think he'd have pulled off that kind of success. Could Brian Jones have become a successful solo artist? Yes, I think he could have, but not on the level of Michael Jackson.

Q: Did Brian have a direct role in helping people discover American R & B stars such as Muddy Waters, Howlin' Wolf, Jimmy Reed, Little Walter, Robert Johnson, etc.?
A: Yes, but he was certainly not alone in that. American audiences in the 1950s and '60s were so racially divided. White shoppers had to go to black music stores to find "race records," and the whole music business was set up along these stratified marketing lines, like a number of other businesses at the time. Part of the reason the British Invasion was so successful was white musicians there getting strongly influenced by black musicians from here, and the British artists were able to get audiences and sell records that black blues musicians sadly were not able to reach when their music was

first released. White artists here, like Pat Boone, were covering black artists, too, but their covers were so whitewashed that the soul of the original recordings [was] lost. The British blues bands got it right—they put the feeling in the music, and their performances had an energy and authenticity that the square U.S. pop records lacked. Of course, those were times of big change, with everything from Motown to the Civil Rights movement, and progressive white audiences who wanted to hear good music no matter what color the musicians were. Amid all of that, Brian Jones and the Rolling Stones were there with the Beatles, John Mayall and the Bluesbreakers, and a number of other British bands that helped to introduce Muddy Waters, B.B. King, Robert Johnson, and other great blues artists to a wider (and whiter) audience.

Q: When he wasn't heavily under the influence of drugs and alcohol, was Brian the best musician in the Rolling Stones, despite not being credited for writing any of their songs?
A: Brian Jones could play a lot of different instruments well, so I will say yes, he was probably the Stones' best musician, at least initially. Keith Richards gradually developed his own style on the guitar, particularly when he started playing his Telecaster with only five strings tuned in an open G. Lots of blues players use open tunings, especially to play slide guitar, but Keith developed his own style of doing things, and I believe it helped him creatively as a songwriter. Being able to play an instrument (or multiple instruments) well and being a great songwriter are two different skills. I'm not sure Brian Jones ever really wanted to be a great songwriter, but he had an unquestionable talent, and his playing and the way he arranged his parts were a key part of the Stones' sound on the records he played on.

Q: How should Brian Jones be remembered in the 21st century and beyond?
A: I think of Brian Jones as a tragic figure. He had great talent, but struggled with the creative differences that grew as the band he founded evolved and decided to go in a direction different from the one he envisioned. Having enjoyed great initial success, I'm sure it would be devastating to anyone to be forced out the way he was.

PART THREE: THE LEGACY

Given time, I'd like to think he could have resurfaced and made more great music with other people, and it's a shame we didn't get to hear it. Like Jimi Hendrix, Janis Joplin, Ron "Pigpen" McKernan, Jim Morrison, and even Kurt Cobain, Brian Jones died at 27years of age. Nick Drake died at only 26. All of them wrestled with their own demons, and perhaps that is also why they made the music they did. We can remember the time they had, and the music they left us with.

In an interview that I had with the music director and morning host of WNCW in North Carolina, and my good friend from childhood, Martin Anderson, I asked him some of the same questions I asked Mr. Ground in reference to Brian's legacy.

QUESTION: What was Brian's legacy on both the Rolling Stones and pop music in general more than 50 years after his death?
ANSWER: Brian's legacy has been pretty well cemented as the Stones' original "bad boy." Sure, Keith and Mick have done a pretty good job assuming that mantle, and for 50 years longer. But the '60s were the formative years of the band—they'll never be remembered as a band that wasn't rooted in the revolutionary angst and rebellion of that decade. And Brian set the stage for that trajectory with the band. He was older than Mick and Keith, and more reckless, and his early death, sadly, only immortalizes him as someone so reckless that he couldn't maintain his lifestyle, or his life. But his legacy is *also* that of being one of the more versatile, talented, and musically adventurous bad boys of rock and pop. Not only did he root the band in their blues background, it was Brian who stretched them out with instruments like the sitar ("Paint It Black"), the dulcimer ("Lady Jane"), the marimba ("Under My Thumb"), and the recorder ("Ruby Tuesday").

Q: Do you believe that Brian Jones was murdered on July 3, 1969?
A: No. The evidence I've read makes it pretty clear to me that his death was either accidental, suicide, or that gray area often in between.

Q: Do you believe that Brian Jones would have formed a new band as big as or bigger than the Rolling Stones had he lived?
A: I doubt that he would've, unless he'd been able to make some serious changes in his lifestyle. His band would've still needed someone else as the voice, and maybe that would've happened.... But it seems to be that more likely it would've been a cool band that would've faded before too long.

Q: Do you think that Brian Jones has a legitimate argument to be nominated and inducted into the Blues Hall of Fame?
A: I'm no expert on their nomination and induction process, but I wouldn't think he should be considered outside that of the Stones as a band. He should be duly credited for their blues foundation, but considering he did not have a solo career in the blues outside the band, no.

Q: Do you think that the Rolling Stones were a better band with Brian Jones, or do you prefer Brian's replacements, Mick Taylor or Ronnie Wood, more?
A: Personally, I really dig Brian's contributions to the band more than what Taylor and Wood brought later. They're all stellar, and the band seemed to really hit a great stride with the 3 or 4 years that immediately followed Brian's departure, culminating with *Exile on Main St*. But while their distillation as more of a straight rock band was great, I kind of miss their deeper blues start, and the more adventurous, psychedelic touches Brian brought.

Q: Do you think the Stones could ever have been as successful as they became if they had remained strictly a rhythm & blues band, as Brian had wanted them to be when he created the band?
A: Well, as much as I may prefer their blues background, no, I bet they wouldn't have been as long lasting and wildly successful had they not adapted and evolved as they did, particularly after Brian's departure. An act can only last for so long with commercial success and longevity without adapting and evolving. One need only look at comparable acts like the Beatles, Bob Dylan, Neil Young, and U2 to

see that. Countless others, too—Joni Mitchell, Yes, Chicago, Fleetwood Mac, John Prine.... The ones that reinvented themselves from time to time are the ones that have had the incredible staying power in popular music.

Q: Could Brian have established himself as a solo act as successful as Michael Jackson when he left the Jackson 5?
A: Hell no, considering his life trajectory. That is, unless he had been able to alter his lifestyle significantly. And, without the vocal prowess of a lead singer, that would've been damn near impossible.

Q: Did Brian have a direct role in helping people discover American R & B stars such as Muddy Waters, Howlin' Wolf, Jimmy Reed, Little Walter, Robert Johnson, etc.?
A: As far as I know, the Stones in general did, for sure! And he was one of their main proponents for their blues background. But I don't know to what extent Brian was the one making direct connections with those American blues greats.

Q: When he wasn't heavily under the influence of drugs and alcohol, was Brian the best musician in the Rolling Stones, despite not being credited for writing any of their songs?
A: Quite possibly, considering the variety of instruments he played, and I believe he's credited for teaching Mick harmonica, for what that's worth. Songwriting credits are often unfairly handed out, but they also aren't necessarily reflective of who was the better instrumentalist or musician.

I also interviewed music enthusiast and Rolling Stones fan Jim Desmond, who had these responses.

QUESTION: What was Brian's legacy on both the Rolling Stones and pop music in general more than 50 years after his death?
ANSWER: Brian Jones has a living legacy in that the Rolling Stones are still recording and touring and still relevant to this day. If not for him forming the band, the greatest rock band in history would never have been, and countless rock bands that were heavily

influenced by them would never have been. Also, his love of American blues, along with his other British contemporaries, brought the blues to white Americans [who] generally didn't know of it or would not listen to it due to it being "race music."

Q: Do you believe that Brian Jones was murdered on July 3, 1969?
A: I do not believe that he was murdered. I think he was probably piss drunk and in very bad health and died from a combination of drowning [and] cardio trauma.

Q: Do you believe that Brian Jones would have formed a new band as big as or bigger than the Rolling Stones had he lived?
A: I do think that he would have formed a new band that would have been very good, but I don't know if he would have lived past the early '70s anyway. The incarnation of the Stones immediately after he was kicked out was, in my opinion, by far the best and would have cast a large shadow over anything that Jones would have done. That's not to say he could not have done it; I have read accounts that he was trying to get together with John Lennon and other greats for a new project. Imagine what that would have been like!

Q: Would Brian have become involved with large music events, like Live Aid, Woodstock, or Lollapalooza, based on his involvement with the Monterey Pop Festival in 1967?
A: Music festivals seemed to be right up Jones' alley. Had he lived and stayed with music, I think he would have been right there, just like at Monterey.

Q: Do you think that Brian Jones has an argument to be inducted into the Rock and Roll Hall of Fame as an individual artist? What about the Blues Hall of Fame?
A: Jones was instrumental in exposing the blues to a wider audience than would have been possible at that time of horrible race relations. If not for Jones and other British blues rock musicians, someone like me probably would never have known

about the likes of John Lee Hooker, Howlin' Wolf, and the like. So I do think he has a legit claim to the Blues Hall of Fame.

Q: Do you think that the Rolling Stones were a better band with Brian Jones, or do you prefer Brian's replacements, Mick Taylor or Ronnie Wood, more?
A: It's funny that as I am typing this, "It's All Over Now'" is playing on my stereo and I had to stop to pay attention to the playing and try to pick out Jones' 12-string playing, and it is great! When he had his shit together, his interactions with Keith were very special, not like rhythm and lead guitar but intertwined leads. That is much like the Stones with Ronnie Wood. But my favorite lineup was with Mick Taylor; *Exile* is one of my very favorite albums of all time.

Q: Do you think the Stones could ever have been as successful as they became if they had remained strictly a rhythm & blues band, as Brian had wanted them to be when he created the band?
A: The Stones needed to evolve to include more than the R & B band that Jones started to become the icons that they are now.

Q: Could Brian have established himself as a solo act as successful as Michael Jackson when he left the Jackson 5?
A: Jones as a solo act would have been cool, but I don't think he could have been a Michael Jackson–level Icon. He didn't have the frontman persona that Jackson or Mick Jagger has. I think he would have been more a virtuoso-style player like Jeff Beck, admired by musicians and hardcore fans but not [on] the mainstream level that Michael Jackson achieved.

Q: Did Brian have a direct role in helping people discover American R & B stars such as Muddy Waters, Howlin' Wolf, Jimmy Reed, Little Walter, Robert Johnson, etc.?
A: Ha! See my responses in questions 5 and 1. I didn't see this until now, so yeah, I think that white Americans would not have caught on to the blues if not for Jones and other British rockers.

Q: When he wasn't heavily under the influence of drugs and alcohol, was Brian the best musician in the Rolling

Stones, despite not being credited for writing any of their songs?
A: That is a tough one. He was definitely the most versatile player they ever had; he could play so many instruments so well. The Stones would have been so much less without him in the early days. You could make the case that Mick Taylor was the best guitar player they ever had, but he was so short lived in the band! You could also make the case that Charlie Watts has the most mastery of his instrument in the band and is the best drummer they could ever have. I guess this is a cop-out, but I can't pick out the best musician in the band!

Q: How should Brian Jones be remembered in the 21st century and beyond?
A: Brian Jones should be remembered as the founder of the greatest rock & roll band ever!

PART THREE: THE LEGACY

CHAPTER 29

BRIAN'S ARCHETYPAL ASTROLOGICAL SIGN, AND HIS SIX ARCHETYPE STAGE COMPARISONS FROM INNOCENT TO MAGICIAN

What about Brian Jones' archetypal astrological sign? How does this analysis co relate to his life and legacy? Brian was born on February 28, which meant he was a Pisces. According to James Moran, archetypal astrologer and expert on this subject, "Brian Jones, founding member of the Rolling Stones, was born with the sun in a significant alignment with Jupiter. The sun is associated with our central sense of identity. Jupiter is associated with growth, abundance, and breadth of culture. Jones was known as a multi-instrumentalist. He played guitar, sitar, harmonica, dulcimer, piano, marimbas, recorder, saxophone, and other instruments. Having this much breadth of musical skill and culture associated with one's identity is commonplace for those born with the sun and Jupiter in alignment." Moran further states, "Brian Jones was born when both Saturn and Uranus were conjoined in the sky. Saturn is associated with the burdens of life, conservative attitudes, and judgment. Uranus is associated with rebellion and disruption. Saturn is by nature associated with a tendency towards humility, while Uranus can be associated with an air of excitement. We can see both of these archetypes displaying themselves in the following quote by Jones' bandmate Bill Wyman: 'There were at least two sides to Brian's personality. One was introverted, shy, sensitive, and deep thinking. The other was a preening peacock; gregarious, artistic, desperately needing assurance from his peers.' Those born with Saturn and Uranus conjoined can face possible brushes with insanity, due to the intense differences in energies between these two archetypes. Saturn is constructive and Uranus is liberating. The two together can create enough tension to threaten one's mental health." Most ironic of all, Moran says of Brian's fate, "The Saturn return is a time in our lives when Saturn returns to the degree in the sky it was when we were born. This takes approximately 27 to 28 years to occur. Saturn is associated with maturity. The function of the Saturn return is to see if we have matured enough to move on to the next phase of adulthood. Brian Jones did not live past his Saturn return. This is not uncommon for rock stars. In fact, in the two years since Jones' death, several other 27-year-old rock stars would follow: Jimi Hendrix, Janis Joplin, Jim Morrison, just to name a few." Was Jones's fate predetermined by his astrological sign?

There are some uncanny parallels to Brian's ultimate conclusion. But his influence can still be felt by both musicians and fans more than 50 years after his death. Brian's legacy is profound, despite the cards that history dealt him, which is why I felt compelled to write this book about him.

Dr. Allan Hunter, professor of English literature at Curry College and a counselor in Massachusetts, has written many books, including *Life Passages*, *The Sanity Manual*, and *Spiritual Hunger: Integrating Myth and Ritual Into Daily Life*. In another book Hunter wrote that was published in 2008, *The Six Archetypes of Love: From Innocent to Magician*, he analyzes the six stages of spiritual development and what they represent in one's spiritual growth and full comprehension of absolute love. These archetypes are: the Innocent, Orphan Love, Pilgrim Love, the Warrior-Lover, the Monarch Pair, and finally the Magician. The Innocent stage represents infancy or the toddler stage, focused on the bonding between the parent and child. The Orphan stage refers to kids who are looking for safety by attracting others and seeking adoption from those they deem safe. The Pilgrim stage is leaving behind conventional comforts to search for a sense of meaning and greater purpose. The Warrior-Lover stage represents when a relationship begins and commitment is given to both partners, but the occasional argument or fight may occur when learning about the other person. The Monarch stage is when complete trust is given to the other spouse. Finally, there is the Magician stage, which represents the customs and rites of what is holy, upholding laws and agreements, and acting in a similar manner to a priest, minister, or rabbi. I interviewed Dr. Hunter about his opinions of Brian Jones and how Brian did in regards to achieving the six archetypes of love during his lifetime.

QUESTION: What are the effects for small children who do not receive the proper love and attention from their parents or acceptance from them during the Innocent and Orphan stages?

ANSWER: In general terms, we can say this: children who do not receive love or attention from their parents tend to suffer a number of distressing symptoms, depending on the level of neglect. At its most extreme, a neglected child will tend to split off parts of him/herself to deny the "bad" part. So the child who breaks something in a rage will simply say, "It wasn't me" because it's so difficult to reconcile the destructive self with the self that he or she wishes to believe is the real self. This can continue into the creation of multiple subpersonalities. Children who don't get love and attention also tend to crave it and to seek to get it from other sources, such as from public performances. If that's too difficult to achieve, then public notoriety will be the next option. In the case of Brian Jones, he was a "bad boy" who walked away from various girlfriends and their pregnancies, denying that he was in any way to blame. He also famously appeared at a party wearing a Nazi uniform with an SS armband. This was a strange thing to do in England, only a couple of decades after World War II. It reeked of bad boy antics, attention grabbing, and a deep sense that he was, in fact, at his core, somehow dangerous, which was part of what the Rolling Stones did so well. In a sense, they went against the more wholesome image the Beatles and others had cultivated. The Stones created such tracks as "Sympathy for the Devil," in part to titillate the taste of an audience that wanted rebels and figures of that sort. It was an image that they cultivated for a long time. The point is: did the image create the reality or did the reality give rise to the images? Clearly, one fed into the other. And in case we forget, the title of the song tells us it's all about accepting the mad, destructive parts that exist within all of us. Brian was very much a part of this image, but for him, it was too close to the core of who he was.

Q: In your book on the six archetypes, you say, "the unloved child will tend to be frightened, and where there is fear, there can be no real confidence, and without confidence, there can be no learning or growth" (pg 36, #17). Could this be the reason that someone like Brian

Jones self-destructed so quickly in his short life?
A: Brian Jones self-destructed because he found the world of heavy drugs to be even more attractive than the seductive life of music. He had, as it were, an alternative reality, the world of music and the fame that came with it. But that didn't seem to be enough for him, and so the drugs won him over. He self-medicated, one could say, in order to erase (temporarily) the difficulties presented by an uncertain world.

Q: Can you explain the level of misogyny one must have in order to impregnate five different young women, and not help take care of his children or stay around at all with any of them relationship wise? Was Brian permanently stuck in the Orphan phase?
A: The question sort of dovetails with the other two. In the theory of the six archetypes, there exist six stages of growth. What we need to realize is that we all live in at least three areas of life: our professional, our personal, and our life within the community. The idea is to live at the highest level we can in all those areas of life. The Magician lawyer who can't go home and talk to his kids is, at home at least, an Orphan, so his life is badly imbalanced. Brian Jones was an absolute Magician at musical creation, but his problem was that he was an Orphan in his personal sense of himself. Within his community (musicians) he was a bit of a fighter, so perhaps we could call him a Warrior-Lover at his healthiest. Ultimately, he lost that fight. From being a vital member of the Stones, he became less important to them, largely because of drug use. The Orphan Brian Jones needed the acceptance provided by the band, and he needed the drug use to feel good. But as the drug use increased, he became less and less a part of the band, losing his community, and less and less able to play well. Now, when we talk about misogyny, I think that we have to recognize that for Brian, it was vital to feel important, even superior, so he could banish his sense of self-loathing, if only temporarily. One way to do that is to treat female fans with scorn.

Q: Could Brian Jones' archetype have been considered to be at the Monarch or Magician stage when he created the sounds of Elmore James on stage, or when he created the

Rolling Stones themselves?

A: So, yes, when Brian Jones created the Rolling Stones, he was really becoming a Monarch. We must remember that the Stones started out as a cover band, copying the Delta blues (Muddy Waters especially) and presenting that astonishing sound to a surprised British public, who knew nothing at all about the blues. That takes the courage of a Pilgrim who develops into a Warrior-Lover, and then becomes the core around which the band developed, a Monarch. Ultimately, Jones wasn't able to control the forces he'd gathered around him, or control himself. While the music was pure production of Magicians, he was, in the rest of his life, sliding back into Orphanhood.

Q: Could Brian Jones have truly loved another person, including his friends, lovers, and children, if he never really loved himself? Is this more evidence of Brian's stay in the Orphan phase?

A: Could Brian have loved another? Difficult to answer. He had a powerful need to be loved and he had plenty of demons, but I do, in fact, believe he was always looking for love. The key is to start loving yourself first, as you say, and I'm not really sure he ever really did that. When drugs (or any addictions) enter the scene, the person's primary relationship is with the substance, not with anyone else. People don't matter when the drugs have hold. Now this can change, but Brian didn't have enough time for that.

Q: Could someone as decadent and self-destructive as Brian Jones was in his short life have ever achieved the Magician status?

A: Jones was a Magician, but only in terms of his music. In the rest of his life, he was an orphan.

Q: When Brian was interacting in orgies with groupies and prostitutes, what was Brian's role in the Orphan archetype?

A: The interactions with groupies and prostitutes were pure Orphan status. The Orphan wants to belong, wants to feel accepted, wants to be able to feel special, but the unhealthy aspect of this (which is where the Orphan can go so sadly wrong) is to wish not to be attached to the messiness of human interaction. Using others is the logical continuation of that mindset.

Q: Was Brian Jones, shortly before his death and after his departure from the Rolling Stones, becoming a Pilgrim at his home at Cotchford Farm while he was planning for a new child with girlfriend Anna Wohlin (his last girlfriend) in their nursery and planning for his life after the Rolling Stones?
A: Love, support, and a home can be powerful persuaders towards change, and Jones had that at the end of his life. He "had it all," one might say, and he had no responsibilities to any band. It could be that he was at a turning point of his life, ready to find that he, too, could be happy. But the verdict on his death was that he drowned while under the influence, so he hadn't given up substance abuse. I'm reminded of another social misfit, Eric Clapton, who did kick his drug habit and found his way back to music, but never seemed able to keep a personal relationship together for very long. He found an identity anew in something he was already expert in. But for a while there, he was lost.

These six archetypes of love that Dr. Hunter describes in his book can also apply to the life of Brian Jones. There were times in Brian's life where he could be any of the six archetypes, but as history shows, he perpetually clung to the Orphan stage. This was based on the immature and self-destructive behavior that he amply displayed at various points in his life. Yet Brian certainly had his moments in the Monarch and Magician stages as well, which exemplified his brilliant musical talent and his acute ability to spot other talent. However, as Dr. Hunter points out, Jones' unfortunate traits of self-centeredness and physically violent relations with women left him in a constant Orphan stage, all the way until his death.

CHAPTER 30

THE CONCLUSION

In summary, I wrote this book as a way to honor Brian Jones, despite his checkered history, because I believe that Brian Jones was a truly unique and gifted musician whose influence can still be felt in the world of music more than 50 years after his death. Part of Jones' legacy is, of course, the band he created, which still tours the world as kings of their profession. This book is not meant to criticize the other members of the Rolling Stones, whom I believe were right in kicking Jones out of the band when they did. This was because they had to go back on the road in America to reclaim their power as a touring act, which Brian could not do because of his legal troubles. The Rolling Stones were right to go on without him. But Jones should be remembered as the true musical genius that he was, and I feel that history should treat him better, based on his many accomplishments. It is possible that Brian could have started a new life as a musician without the Stones, and gone on to the heights of success with another band or as a solo artist. Perhaps Brian could have had a successful solo career, like Anna Mae Bullock, also known as Tina Turner, who, after 14 years of enduring horrific mental and physical abuse from her husband Ike, finally decided to leave him after a wicked fight between the two after Ike had been abusing cocaine for days beforehand. (pg 99, #18) She waited until he passed out in the hotel room and left him—with hardly anything in her pocket—for good. It was then she began her new life, and succeeded in recruiting Australian Roger Davies to be her manager, to great success. Tina had incredible success as a solo star, selling millions of copies of her solo album *Private Dancer* and establishing herself as a diva on her own. Tina's *Private Dancer* tour encompassed 180 shows in 10 months and 2 million fans. (pg 143, #18) She also had a legendary performance with Mick Jagger at Live Aid in Philadelphia in July 1985.

Or maybe Brian could have had a life similar to that of Eric Clapton, who suffered terribly from his own heroin addiction and the tragic death of his son Conor on March 20, 1991, after he fell out of a window of a high-rise building. Clapton rose to musical stardom over his long and illustrious career. Clapton is the only member of the Rock and Roll Hall of Fame to be inducted three times, and became a true legend and icon in the music business after starting as a blues guitarist. (#3)

Or maybe Jones could have ended up like Brian Wilson of the Beach Boys, who, like Brian, founded an iconic band (with his brothers Dennis and Carl, along with Mike Love and Al Jardine), in 1961. Like Jones, Wilson felt control of his band slipping away from him, which caused him severe depression. (pg 15, #19) Unlike Jones, Wilson could write songs, which he successfully did many times for the Beach Boys, including the entire *Pet Sounds* album in 1966. But Wilson, like Jones, had problems of his own, including mental breakdowns and drug problems. Wilson is also almost completely deaf in his right ear. (pg 6, #19) Wilson would eventually conquer these demons, but his relationship with the Beach Boys, like Jones' with the Rolling Stones, is often contentious and dogmatic. Despite this, Wilson toured successfully as a solo act.

Brian Jones never got this opportunity, but his legacy shall always live on for those who appreciate rhythm & blues, rock & roll, and world music that meant so much to him in his life. We can continue Brian's legacy and memory indefinitely and follow the dream that Brian Jones once had when he was a boy in Cheltenham, England. In the Bob Dylan song "Ballad of a Thin Man," a song believed to be written specifically about Brian, Dylan sings, "You walk into a room with your pencil in your hand. You see somebody naked and you say, 'Who is that man?' You try so hard but you don't understand just what you will say when you get home. Because something is happening here but you don't know what it is, do you, Mr. Jones?." (#20) So, when you think about the Rolling Stones' music, rhythm & blues, rock & roll, top 40, or any strange or ethnic- sounding music, also think of Brian Jones, a.k.a. Elmo Lewis, whose influence on music and culture will continue on from the 20th century into the 21st century and beyond, into the eternal folklore that will always be his legacy.

BIBLIOGRAPHY

1. *27: A History of the 27 Club Through the Lives of Brian Jones, Jimi Hendrix, Janis Joplin, Jim Morrison, Kurt Cobain and Amy Winehouse,* by Howard Sounes. Boston, MA: De Capo Press, 2013.

2. *Here We Are Now: The Lasting Impact of Kurt Cobain,* by Charles R. Cross. New York, NY: HarperCollins, 2014.

3. Basic facts from each artist were obtained from his or her respective Wikipedia page.

4. *Thanks a Lot Mr. Kibblewhite: My Story,* by Roger Daltrey. New York, NY: Henry Holt, 2018.

5. *Sound Man: A Life Recording Hits with the Rolling Stones, The Who, Led Zeppelin, The Eagles, Eric Clapton, the Faces ...,* by Glyn Johns. New York, NY: Blue Rider Press, 2014.

6. *Led Zeppelin,* by Led Zeppelin. London, UK: Reel Art Press, 2018.

7. *No Quarter: The Three Lives of Jimmy Page,* by Martin Power. New York, NY: Overlook Omnibus Books, 2016.

8. *Michael Jackson: The Magic, the Madness, the Whole Story, 1958-2009,* by J. Randy Taraborrelli. New York, NY: Grand Central Publishing, 2009.

9. *Aretha: From These Roots,* By Aretha Franklin and David Ritz. New York, NY: Villard Books, 1999.

10. *John,* by Cynthia Lennon. New York, NY: Crown Publishing, 2005.

11. *Behind Sad Eyes: The Life of George Harrison,* by Marc Shapiro. New York, NY: St. Martin's Griffin, 2002.

12. *Bill Wyman's Blues Odyssey: A Journey to Music's Heart and Soul*, by Bill Wyman (with Rich Havers). New York, NY: DK Publishing, 2001.

13. Interview with Todd Harvey of the American Folklife Center at the Library of Congress.

14. *Frankenstein*, by Mary Shelley. New York, NY: Bantam Books, 1981 edition.

15. The Brian Jones Fan Club website. https://www.brianjonesfanclub.com/

16. *DC Jazz: Stories of Jazz Music in Washington, DC*, edited by Maurice Jackson and Blair A. Ruble. Washington, D.C.: Georgetown University Press, 2018.

17. *The Six Archetypes of Love: From Innocent to Magician*, by Allan G. Hunter. Findhorn, UK: Findhorn Press, 2008.

18. *My Love Story*, by Tina Turner with Deborah Davis and Dominik Wichmann. New York, NY: Atria Books, 2018.

19. *I Am Brian Wilson: A Memoir*, by Brian Wilson with Ben Greenman. Boston, MA: Da Capo Press, 2016.

20. "Ballad of a Thin Man," by Bob Dylan. *Highway 61 Revisited.* New York, NY: Columbia, 1965.

21. "Music: Lady Soul Singing It Like It Is." *Time.* June 28, 1968. http://content.time.com/time/subscriber/article/0,33009,841340-4,00.html

22. *John Lennon*, by Phillip Norman. New York, NY: HarperCollins, 2008.

23. "Mose Allison, Iconic Blues and Jazz Pianist, Dead at 89, " by Jon Blistein. *Rolling Stone.* November 15, 2016. https://www.rollingstone.com/music/music- news/mose-allison-iconic-blues-and-jazz-pianist-dead-at-89-120268/

ABOUT THE AUTHOR

Thomas P. Athridge was born and raised in the Washington D.C. metropolitan area. He is a federal employee working in Washington D.C for the last 22 years, after graduating from Curry College in Milton, Massachusetts in 1997 with a degree in communications and minoring in political science. Mr. Athridge is a lifelong and enthusiastic fan of the Rolling Stones, and is honored to find a specific aspect of their long and legendary career to write a book about of his own, especially about Brian Jones. Mr. Athridge's first book, American Presidents at War, was published in 2017 by aois21 media. Mr. Athridge currently resides in Bethesda, Maryland.

www.ingramcontent.com/pod-product-compliance
Lightning Source LLC
Chambersburg PA
CBHW031948080426
42735CB00007B/307